Story Tech

Story Tech

Power, Storytelling, and Social Change Advocacy

Filippo Trevisan, Michael Vaughan, and Ariadne Vromen

University of Michigan Press
Ann Arbor

For questions or permissions, please contact um.press.perms@umich.edu

Published in the United States of America by the
University of Michigan Press
First published February 2025

A CIP catalog record for this book is available from the British Library.

Library of Congress Cataloging-in-Publication data has been applied for.

ISBN: 978-0-472-07725-0 (hardcover : alk. paper)
ISBN: 978-0-472-05725-2 (paper : alk. paper)
ISBN: 978-0-472-22207-0 (ebook)

DOI: https://doi.org/10.3998/mpub.12067961

Acknowledgments

Writing a book is often a story of ongoing engagement with many people and ideas, as well as a lot of drafting and redrafting. We started this research project in 2018, and in many ways our commitment to this book about storytelling has been a "labor of love" as we only had small pockets of research funding that we could bring to this project and many other responsibilities that made time limited. During the life of this project, all of us also moved jobs, or positions, or countries at least once and have been juggling competing commitments and expectations. The Covid-19 pandemic and closed borders meant that the last time the three of us could all be together in person was early 2019. Ultimately, this—like many of the stories we discuss in the book—has been a story of perseverance and concludes with a promise: that we will all meet for a book launch somewhere soon!

Most of the chapters in this book have been presented at international conferences and invited talks, and we thank everyone who has interacted with our ideas for their questions and encouragement. We first presented our ideas on technological change and storytelling at a fabulous workshop in Portsmouth in the United Kingdom organized by James Dennis and Nina Hall. Our discussant of the paper we presented there exclaimed, "there are at least three papers in here, this should be a book"—thank you Max Halupka for the idea and encouragement! We have received helpful feedback from a generous network of scholars, including Lance Bennett, Hahrie Han, Scott Wright, Francesco Bailo, Anika Gauja, Ulrike Klinger, John Downey, Cristian Vaccari, Ana Langer, Ken Rogerson, Caty Borum, Leena Jayaswal, Rhonda Zaharna, Laura Davy, Lisa Conway, and Gabby Lawrence. We are also grateful to our editors at University of Michigan Press, Elizabeth Demers and Madison Allums, who responded enthusiastically to our idea and championed this project, and to our editorial assistants Haley Winkle and Delilah McCrea.

We also acknowledge research assistance from Bryan Bello, Asvatha (Ash) Babu, and Jing Cai at American University, as well as Serrin Rutledge-Prior and Isi Unikowski at the Australian National University (ANU). We would also like to thank all the storytellers, organizers, and technology specialists who generously gave their time to be interviewed for this project: their insights and contributions fundamentally enriched this book. This project was supported by small grants from American University's School of Communication, the University of Sydney, and ANU.

A final thank you goes out to all those people in our lives who supported us at home and helped us keep everything into perspective. In particular, Filippo would like to thank Lotta for fuelling the writing process with her Finnish home bakes (a tradition that started with his previous book) and Emilia and Luca—who were born shortly after we launched this project and just as this book went to print, respectively—for making him smile every day.

Contents

Digital materials related to this title can be found on the Fulcrum platform via the following citable URL: https://doi.org/10.3998/mpub.12067961

Tables

Figures

Introduction

It seems appropriate that a book that examines transformations in political storytelling begins with a short story. Here, it is useful to consider one from the 2020 United States presidential election. During that election cycle, Democratic Senator Elizabeth Warren put her own personal story at the center of her presidential campaign. For example, in a post on her Facebook page in October 2019 Warren spoke openly about her own experience with pregnancy discrimination at work. For a candidate, to speak about their personal story constitutes a textbook campaign approach, especially in a highly personalized campaign environment such as the United States. However, in the same post Warren went one step further and also invited her followers to share their own experiences, saying that "we can fight back [against injustices] by telling our stories." In the space of a few hours, nearly 1,500 people responded by sharing their own stories—often intimate and emotional—in comments to her post. This signals a new approach to storytelling in digital politics. In recent years, many political organizations have started to ask ordinary people to share their stories with them as a form of participation and support, beyond typical requests to donate money or sign digital petitions. As the example from the Warren campaign shows, large numbers of people seem eager to respond to these invitations to share their experiences. Crowdsourced personal stories have thus joined the repertoire of digital grassroots advocacy.

In his history of human communication, Fisher (1987) defines our species as "homo narrans" with an innate inclination for storytelling. The act of telling persuasive stories has roots back in preliterate oral traditions, and its basic relationship with human psychology has fundamentally remained the same for thousands of years. Here, stories provide "not only meaning, but also a way of being in the world with others . . . an understanding of the larger social context beyond our immediate perception" (Zaharna 2022, 135). From an organizing standpoint, storytelling has been honed over time by predigital organizing traditions like workers' unions and social movements (Davis 2002; Fernandes 2017; Polletta et al. 2021). In this tradition, stories marshal the power and authenticity of lived experiences, using the empowering personal action of "telling your story" to persuade others to take action.

In various forms and through different media, storytelling has long contributed to public discourse, as well as societal and policy change. For example, individual cases and personal stories contributed to addressing social issues through court cases and testimony before legislative bodies. The U.S. civil rights (Sullivan 2009) and disability rights (Bagenstos 2009; Vaughn-Switzer 2003) movements are good examples for use of this strategy. More broadly, from a media and popular culture perspective, documentary storytelling has played an increasingly central role in social and political change in recent decades (Borum Chattoo 2020). Since the mid-2000s, politicians have also shared more of their personal stories as a way to enhance their mediated and perceived authenticity (Dencik 2021). Building on these trends, advocacy organizations invested significantly in storytelling in recent years, moving from professionally produced content to large crowdsourcing operations that collect personal narratives directly from supporters and integrate them in their campaigns (Vromen, Halpin, and Vaughan 2022). Thus the digital age brought a radical expansion in the places and ways in which stories are shared, but digitalization has also transformed the approach of advocacy organizations with a growing data-driven focus on scalability, quantification, and optimization (Karpf 2016).

In this context, digital technologies have crept into every stage of advocacy storytelling, from collection to curation, and from dissemination to evaluation. This goes beyond the tools used to capture stories such as digital camera phones and other recording equipment, and encompasses the digital systems (e.g., databases, story submission portals, algorithms, artificial intelligence (AI) tools, and so on) that organizations use to acquire, organize, select, and disseminate stories at scale, including so-called story banks. These technologies, which collectively we call "story tech," are not usually visible to the public or even to individual storytellers themselves. Yet they play very influential roles in storytelling advocacy. These trends in narrative political persuasion have produced significant innovations, as well as moments of tension and renegotiation. Our book examines this tangled and dynamic relationship with a particular focus on the "datafication" of storytelling. That is, when stories are treated as data that can be quantified, searched, queried, or even automatically "mined" according to a logic that narrative content drawn from large datasets will generate *more* persuasive campaigns than established ways of identifying personal stories.

As outlined above, collecting large numbers of personal stories has become an important and standard strategic practice to many advocacy organizations. Requests to "share your story" via email, websites, digital forms, or social media platforms often accompany calls to action such as donating money, signing petitions, and contacting elected representatives in digital action campaigns. Their prevalence led us to ask:

- What is the significance of storytelling initiatives for advocacy organizations, communities, and politics?
- What are the changing roles for technology in storytelling initiatives? As advocacy storytelling becomes increasingly layered with digital technologies, what happens to the empowerment of storytellers and grassroots organizations?
- How are groups, communities, and their grievances represented? And how are these processes shaping the redistribution of who has the power to speak up and, crucially, be heard in political spaces?

As this book answers these questions, much of it has been researched and written in a context of crisis and significant political upheaval, in the United States and Australia. Apart from contextualizing our observations about innovation, we introduce these markers of time and place to give a sense of the challenges faced by advocacy organizations that campaign for social change inspired by progressive values, which form the main subject matter of this book. While we recognize that "progressive" has slightly different connotations in each country, it provides the best option to consistently identify the work of membership-powered organizations that oppose socially and economically conservative stances in both the United States and Australia.

Conservative organizations have used storytelling, too, often quite successfully, and have invested in technology to deliver their story-centered messages more effectively. However, there are specific reasons that make focusing on progressive organizations especially interesting and important. Most notably, their work seeks to disrupt the status quo and, by definition, is usually at odds with dominant societal and cultural narratives, which presents progressive organizations with specific challenges. Relatedly, the political left has long been affected by a "storytelling gap" compared to conservatives, as is discussed in detail in chapter 1, which makes developments in story tech particularly urgent and potentially useful for organizations that support progressive social change and wish to benefit more consistently from storytelling.

The year 2020 began with devastating bushfires in Australia causing the deaths of more than one billion animals, before becoming dominated by the global Covid-19 pandemic, which led to a staggering loss of life while also exposing and magnifying inequalities around the world. Yet, in both crises, traditional political and media institutions struggled to respond effectively: Australian politics lagged far behind the science in "debating" the role of climate change in natural disaster events, while the U.S. response to the pandemic was hamstrung by the dysfunction surrounding the Trump presidency and the increasing polarization of U.S. politics. These cases are dramatic expressions of two broader patterns experienced in the preceding years by progressive advocacy organizations in both the United States and Australia. First, these organizations face increasingly urgent problems with increasingly complex solutions, such as climate change, systemic discrimination, and rising inequality. Second, there is a perceived decrease in the efficacy of existing ways of "doing politics" based on fact-based appeals to logical reasoning, long favored by progressive organizations and traditional political institutions such as government and media.

From the outset, we argue that change in advocacy organizations is not solely produced by technological advances but in combination with these complex sociopolitical factors. Against that backdrop, we make three main arguments in this book about the proliferation of story tech, crowdsourcing, and datafication in advocacy storytelling:

- First, at the technological level: changing affordances enable experimental innovation by progressive advocacy organizations in storytelling practices. This includes the notable development of crowdsourced story banks used in collecting and curating personal stories. Technology's central role in advocacy storytelling also reveals a tendency toward more automation. We trace these innovations diffusing in a dynamic way between organizations, and between countries. In turn, this also reshapes power relationships among those involved in crafting stories and influencing public representations.
- Second, at the sociopolitical level: strategic context drives the pace and design of story tech and datafication innovations in response to the perception of new opportunities and threats within political systems. The social context also enables the empowerment and/or disempowerment of voices from different groups, issue areas, and concerns.

• Third, at the level of advocacy organizations: story tech and data-fication have significant consequences for the people organizations represent. In particular, some individuals (and issues) gain new ways to be involved and represented while others do not. Here, technological design, organizational cultures and expectations, and individual circumstances of storytellers interact in complex ways to create new "story hierarchies" based on the median that elevate some underrepresented voices while also thwarting others.

What's in a Story?

In 2012, a fifteen-year-old girl in Pakistan named Malala Yousafzai was shot in the head by the Taliban while she was on her way to school as retaliation for her activism around girls' education. Malala survived and went on to become one of the most famous advocates for education and human rights in the world, in part by sharing her story of trauma and determination. The title of her 2013 book, *I Am Malala: The Girl Who Stood Up for Education and Was Shot by the Taliban*, is a case study in both the key elements of a personal story, as well as why they hold such power in political advocacy.

A story is "an account of a sequence of events in the order in which they occurred to make a point" (Polletta et al. 2011, 111, adapted from Labov and Waletsky 1967). Stories usually involve characters, which themselves allude to similar characterizations in other stories such as heroes, victims, and villains (Polletta 2015). Storytelling in politics specifically works by transforming private individual experiences into shared public meanings (Jackson 2013). We can observe all these elements within the title of Yousafzai's book alone. We are introduced to both hero and villain, and the dramatic plot development that binds them together. The "point" of the story, in other words the public meaning that it attempts to create, is also clear, in its portrayal of the multiple injustices faced by women and girls in Pakistan and other countries.

Yousafzai's story is incredibly powerful, but its power does not lie in facts based on statistical data about girls' education or the brutality of the Taliban, which were just as true and widely available both before and after she was attacked. As this example demonstrates, the persuasive power of stories is instead allusive—readers are encouraged to empathize with some characters and not others, and in connecting characters and events together through their own interpretation they construct meaning differently than in response to fact-based argumentation. Stories are more than grievances, as they also relay a larger narrative and what is possible for social change.

For this reason, storytelling and logic have often been viewed as fundamentally different strategies for persuasion—that "a good story and a well-formed argument are different natural kinds" (Bruner 1986, 11). The two approaches to argumentation can seem so different as to be incompatible. While a good story has "the power to move others" (Ganz 2013, 2), this emotional appeal can be viewed as undermining rational thinking processes (Polletta 2006). Conversely, the introduction of statistical based arguments and generalization have been found to weaken a story's ability to mobilize due to the diminution of the "identifiable victim effect" (Small et al. 2007).

When organizations use storytelling as part of their advocacy it needs to be understood as a strategic communication choice that competes with other forms of evidence, such as quantitative and institutional level-data that are presented as generalizable and incontrovertible facts. In part, this choice reflects a strategic assessment about what "works." Lakoff's (2014) influential book *Don't Think of an Elephant* popularized the idea that the political left in the United States lost many arguments to conservatives through their inability to tell clear stories communicating values, a thread of thinking that shaped both Democratic electoral campaigning and progressive advocacy organizations in subsequent years. From this perspective, storytelling is used as a strategy to win.

In addition to the strategic imperative, there is often a normative basis for using storytelling in advocacy. From this angle, personal stories are what connect organizations and movements to the lived and "embodied" experience of the people for whom they are advocating. At least in theory, this represents a potential antidote to "the problem of speaking for others" (Alcoff 1991), which has often plagued political actors trying to best represent constituents or organization members. Arguably, a commitment to storytelling not only shapes the agenda of advocacy organizations to better serve their constituencies but transforms their membership and leadership by directly empowering individuals with a lived experience of injustice (Han et al. 2021).

Crowds, Datafication, and Story Tech

When it comes to what "works" in political communication, as well as how organizations relate to their members, there are powerful reasons to expect digitalization to tip the scales in favor of storytelling. Crucially, the increased affordability of and access to digital recording equipment and online dissemination and streaming platforms has opened opportunities for more people than ever to disseminate their stories and reach a range of different audiences. An important consequence of this trend is that the perspectives and experiences of ordinary citizens are more likely to emerge and potentially be heard. One example is the rise of citizen journalism, which has contributed in fundamental ways to exposing many important stories and adding a grassroots angle to the news agenda in recent years (Wall 2015).

In light of this, digitalization has led to an abundance of new sources of information, and the traditional role played by the news media has changed. Contemporary media systems are fragmented (Mancini 2013) and hybridized (Chadwick 2017), with declining levels of trust in traditional news and information sources (Bueno 2016). In modern political communication, success is less reliant on relationships with traditional media organizations and their gatekeeping role, and more reliant on directly mobilizing the attention and engagement of diffuse online audiences. In this new environment, the relative value in political communication between delivering verifiable information and generating individualized emotional responses is in flux.

In parallel, the digitally enabled ways people participate in politics have become increasingly personalized (Bennett and Segerberg 2013) and supported by the diffusion of participatory culture (Jenkins et al. 2016). Even though digital communications enable vast crowd-enabled mobilization, it is affect and large-scale empathy that draws these digital publics together. As Papacharissi said in her work on affective publics: "technologies network us, but it is narratives that connect us" (2015, 5). The most powerful citizen mobilizations of recent years—Occupy, #MeToo, Black Lives Matter— share an openness to individuals personalizing movement claims by digitally distributing their own stories. Contemporary political participation creates a tighter feedback loop between the advocacy agenda of movements and organizations and the lived experience of their constituent individuals and communities. The representative role of long-established advocacy organizations is subject to change as trends in participation evolve over time, and digitalization has brought the potential for a greater participatory role of individuals in advocacy campaigns through sharing their own stories.

At this point, it is important to clarify the distinction between digitalization and datafication. These technologically driven processes are related but not the same thing. Digitalization concerns the creation of media content in digital format, both textual and visual. It spans the various forms of storytelling from documentary filmmaking to citizen journalism and often includes delivery of basic training for community storytellers (Bozdağ and Kannengießer 2021). Datafication, instead, identifies a set of practices where digital story content is treated like data. In other words, datafied story content is stored electronically "in a quantified format so it can be tabulated and analyzed" (Mayer-Schönberger and Cukier 2013). Here, crowdsourced stories are not only personal narratives but also, and perhaps more importantly, "data."

Like with other forms of data, datafied stories can be queried to help identify effective narratives and, more broadly, solve complex communication problems. This process requires organizations to design and build what Murray and Flyverbom (2021) have termed "datastructures." That is, the sociotechnical systems that allow the extraction, organization, analysis, and use of digital data. In turn, this extends the influence of technologies that so far have not been considered in connection with public storytelling such as databases, algorithms, and artificial intelligence (AI). This has fundamental implications for how organizations interpret and use information (Henne et al. 2021). A crucial question asks whose priorities and values are reflected in data infrastructures, and whether the people sharing personal stories are involved in designing new datastructures or have any say in how their stories are used.

Digitalization is now ubiquitous and supports datafication via the rollout of story tech. However, the latter is not an inevitable consequence of the former. Instead, it is one possible approach that currently appears to be favored by an increasingly widespread tendency to rely on "big data" datasets to address complex social problems, associated demands to deal with large data volumes as efficiently as possible, peer-influence from other organizations that adopt data-driven approaches to storytelling, and a generalized fascination with digital metrics in society. Story tech built around crowdsourcing and datafication is at the root of the phenomena we found in undertaking research for this book and fundamentally calls into question established storytelling methods, representation trends, and campaign strategies in the hybrid media environment. We critically analyze these new dynamics and explore the culture, technologies, and participation trends that underpin them.

Investigating Storytelling Advocacy for Social Change

This book focuses on digital advocacy and storytelling in both the United States and Australia. In doing so, it responds to recent calls to better contextualize political communication research (Rojas and Valenzuela 2019) and move beyond studies of a single country. In particular, we engage with research that highlights the significance of local political, cultural, technological, and institutional factors in shaping advocacy organizations' digital strategies and related citizen responses (Hall 2022; Trevisan 2017a; Vromen 2017; Dennis 2019).

The ad hoc or episodic nature of crowdsourced storytelling requires a flexible and agile approach capable of capturing emerging trends, which may differ slightly in each country. For this reason, this book can be described as a parallel—rather than strictly comparative—investigation that helps identify and articulate differences and common threads in each country, as well as evidence of diffusion of digital storytelling strategies and the underpinning principles and theories from one country to the other. This last point is particularly important because, although the United States and Australia are politically, culturally, and institutionally quite different, previous work (Vromen 2017) found substantial evidence of diffusion of digital advocacy strategies, technologies, and theories from the former to the latter through the work of American digital advocacy specialists and other consultants in Australia. For this reason, the research in this book also provides some useful insights on how diffusion in digital politics works today.

Generating a complete picture of these phenomena required a multi-method strategy. First, we needed to illuminate the processes and technologies through which personal stories are collected, archived, organized, edited, and disseminated. As Dush (2017) noted, much of this work goes on behind the scenes, which makes it important to directly access and study storytellers and advocacy organizations. Second, we also examined story content and its integration with other elements of public-facing advocacy campaigns. We designed a mixed methods approach modeled on Thumim's (2012) pioneering study of self-representation in the digital era. The book draws on four complementary data sources, all of which were constructed and analyzed originally for this project. These include:

1. **Interviews dataset**—nearly fifty in-depth interviews with key stakeholders in digital advocacy storytelling, including:
    1.1. **Storytelling specialists** and advocacy campaign managers at major advocacy organizations, as well as advocacy-oriented communication agencies in the United States and Australia;
    1.2. **Technology specialists** from both large corporations and technology startups that sell their products to and occasionally collaborate with advocacy organizations; and

      1.3. **Storytellers and aspiring storytellers** from multiply marginalized backgrounds with recent direct experience of various stages of technology-driven storytelling for advocacy.

2. **Story banking manuals and training materials dataset**—a collection of "how to" materials focused on "story banking" and online story crowdsourcing more generally, developed by major advocacy organizations, communication consultancies, and academic institutions.

3. **Story crowdsourcing interfaces dataset**—a collection of nearly one hundred online interfaces used by over seventy "story banking" organizations to crowdsource personal stories and the associated permission and terms and conditions documents. These were analyzed both quantitatively and qualitatively to illuminate the information infrastructure, content ownership and editing policies, and any barriers to participation in these emerging story collection systems.

4. **Story content dataset**—a collection of over 1,100 social media posts from Facebook, Instagram, and YouTube focused on crowdsourced personal stories linked to disability rights, marriage equality, and workers' rights during the first two years of the Covid-19 pandemic. Given the complexity of this content, stories were coded manually focusing on representation, voice, message, narrative style, and mobilization potential.

While each of these datasets and methods is more central to some chapters than others, all chapters draw on multiple datasets that complement each other to underpin our analysis and drive the overall argument. Each chapter describes the data sources that informed it. The appendix at the end of the book provides a comprehensive detailed overview of each dataset. Below, we briefly outline the content of each chapter.

    Chapter 1 introduces the landscape in which story tech and datafication are developed by reviewing the opportunities and risks that advocacy organizations face within their nationally specific information landscapes, advocacy cultures, and political contexts. Engaging with existing research, across the scholarly disciplines of communication, political science, and journalism, we outline the changing ways in which people engage with information, become activated, and participate in grassroots advocacy. This includes research that has identified the personalization of collective action enabled by the Internet and supported by the diffusion of participatory culture; the hybrid media system and political information cycle; how attention is distributed online and the declining levels of trust in traditional information sources; how digital publics are increasingly drawn together and activated by affect; and the broader role of "mediated emotion" in how people access, understand, and act upon information.

Chapter 2 analyses the diffusion of storytelling practices within and between the United States and Australia and answers the question of "how" progressive advocacy organizations are turning to storytelling. We identify three main trends: in-house storytelling, with a long-term strategic orientation where storytelling is seen as a staple of every future advocacy effort; the more traditional model of outsourced storytelling with external consultants, which is short-term and project-based; and the emerging phenomenon of storytelling partnerships with community-rooted story brokers. In exploring these different trends, we uncover the role of influential "champion" organizations and U.S. philanthropic foundations that have awarded large grants for "story banking" projects in recent years. In addition, we identify a set of different logics that underpin and incentivize change and innovation. These include three main logics shaped by both the technological and sociopolitical context: news-making that is reactive and short-term oriented; electoral logic that is persuasion-oriented; and data science that is technology affordance-oriented.

In chapter 3, our focus is on the role of technology and datafication. This chapter discusses "story tech," i.e., the ever-expanding technological systems that now support advocacy storytelling. This includes analysis of current technologies used to acquire, archive, index, select, and disseminate personal stories. Digital story banking techniques, and the technologies that support them, have been a key innovation in advocacy storytelling. This includes the creation of both story collection forms and new digital database-driven technologies. To illustrate cutting-edge developments in this area, we conducted two in-depth case studies of influential tools: the "StoryBank" application for Salesforce and Gather Voices, a for-profit platform that provides a "one stop shop" for collecting, storing, editing, and publishing video stories. Overall, this outlines sociotechnical systems where algorithms and automation increasingly govern key junctures in advocacy storytelling processes. Personal stories—particularly in the United States—are treated as data by progressive advocacy organizations. Here, we discuss the important strategic benefits that these systems have for advocacy organizations and, at the same time, offer a critical analysis of the democratic and participatory drawbacks.

While up to this point the book has focused on the perspective of advocacy organizations as a central political actor, chapter 4 analyses community-based storytellers' perspectives on story datafication. As advocacy storytelling becomes increasingly layered with digital technologies we focus on what is happening to storytellers. Are they becoming empowered, or is their involvement merely tokenistic? How are new storytelling processes redefining who can speak up and, crucially, be heard in political spaces? Essentially, these are questions of power and "voice," both individual and collective, and whether technology and datafication are changing who can be included in advocacy campaigns. New storytelling technologies are often structured in ways that support or stifle diverse voices, including those that are at greatest risk of marginalization. We contrast the perspectives and experiences of grassroots storytellers with the perspectives of organizers, and we contextualize their experiences by reviewing both digital story collection systems and associated permission policies. We do find, however, that some advocacy organizations are now at the other end of datafication and are moving away from transactional systems and tokenistic approaches. They are attempting to mitigate the ways in which technological factors, social and political trends, and personal circumstances intersect to limit marginalized peoples' ability to be heard.

In chapters 5, 6, and 7, we analyze detailed case studies of crowdsourced storytelling in different areas of progressive advocacy. Specifically, we trace the emergence of participatory storytelling advocacy in areas where the use of personal stories has traditionally been controversial, including disability rights (chapter 5) and LGBTIQ rights (chapter 6), or restricted to dues-paying members and focused on grievances rather than individual lived experience, such as in the case of labor unions (chapter 7). Furthermore, all the story-based campaigns we analyze were successful in achieving their key policy objectives or shifting dominant frames of public discourse around emerging issues. This enables us to understand the implications and potential trade-offs involved in story crowdsourcing and datafication processes that ultimately supported strategic gains.

Chapter 5 focuses on disability rights advocacy with case studies from both the United States and Australia. Historically, disability rights advocates have been wary of incorporating personal stories in their campaigns due to the frequent distortion of disability stories in news reports, and by disability service organizations for fundraising purposes. Our analysis of the emergence of innovative story-centered disability campaigns in recent years reveals the tension between storytelling strategies capturing public attention and empathy, and impacting public decision-making, while simultaneously promoting narratives that accurately represent marginalized groups and counter widespread disempowering stereotypes. We systematically compare the story-based digital work of an organization called Little Lobbyists in the United States to that of the Every Australian Counts campaign in Australia to demonstrate similarity in the successful use of crowdsourced storytelling strategies, while the different political contexts and opportunities led to different storytelling forms. We analytically contrast the reactive, defensive campaigning of Little Lobbyists with the proactive policy agenda-setting strategy of Every Australian Counts. Both case studies show how story crowdsourcing can support the activation of stigmatized individuals but also that organizations continue to play a central role by ensuring the appropriate contextualization of crowdsourced stories so that they resonate with different target audiences.

Chapter 6 focuses on story-based advocacy campaigns to change public narratives about controversial issues to ultimately effect policy change. We examined storytelling that directly influenced public audiences, instead of in conjunction with political lobbying tactics, using the central case study of the Australian Marriage Equality Campaign. We analyze how this campaign used stories on Instagram to mobilize public opinion in response to the 2017 national vote on marriage equality. In particular, we contrast the power to influence the national political agenda, which requires winning over a broad mainstream audience, with the constraints that places on activists' inclination to articulate diverse queer subjectivities. We identify how this tension—which recalls well-established debates about radicalism and pragmatism among many activist movements—is exacerbated by processes of datafication. We label this the "double edged sword" of datafied storytelling, where the sources of additional political power (through increased scale, reach, and optimizing feedback loops in storytelling) bring with them additional representational challenges for marginalized communities.

While previous case study chapters focused on identity-based groups and grievances, chapter 7 explores the use of personal stories in conjunction with material concerns, namely workplace issues. During the Covid-19 pandemic crisis, labor unions in Australia and the United States both used social media and other digital platforms to crowdsource and disseminate essential workers' stories. They successfully changed the dominant framing of who essential frontline workers were—initially only professional healthcare workers—to also include low-paid workers, such as those employed in retail, fast food, distribution, and supply lines. In a period of time where the sociopolitical context of governments and employers were forced to fundamentally rethink how paid work was undertaken, and by whom, unions in both the United States and Australia were able to implement a storytelling approach based on their long-term campaign work to increase pay and job security for marginalized workers. This case study shows that traditional political

Table 1.1. Three case studies in storytelling, technology, and advocacy campaigns

Issue area	Disability (ch. 5)	Marriage Equality (ch. 6)	Low paid work (ch. 7)
Advocacy organizations	Every Australian Counts (Australia) Little Lobbyists (U.S.)	Australian Marriage Equality	Australian Council of Trade Unions AFL-CIO (U.S.) Other unions
Storytellers	Disabled people, families, caregivers	Equality supporters (irrespective of sexual orientation)	Low-paid workers, union representatives and elected leaders
Target audiences	National government, general public (EAC), "Persuadable" lawmakers, and their constituents (LL)	General public/voters	General public National government
Story collection pathways	Crowdsourcing through email (EAC) Crowdsourcing through social media, online forms (LL)	Crowdsourcing through email and online forms to compile original story bank	Crowdsourcing through online forms and Facebook
Story management and dissemination	Disabled people's video stories on You-Tube and Facebook (EAC) Disabled children and families' stories, multiple digital and analog formats (LL)	YouTube videos, social media posts	YouTube videos and Facebook posts with worker stories
Sociopolitical context	Low public awareness of disability issues, Labor government and successive Liberal governments (EAC) Republican-majority Congress, political/media "myths" against the Affordable Care Act (LL)	National public vote on marriage equality	Pandemic Economic downturn

advocacy organizations of labor unions, who mainly rely on political lobbying and industrial representation in acting on behalf of their members, were adaptive in successfully facilitating low-paid workers to share personal, affective stories of working during the pandemic.

Table I.1 summarizes the main contributions of the case studies to understanding the implications of processes of crowdsourcing, datafication, and story tech more broadly on story-centered advocacy campaigns. It highlights differing power dynamics between technology and strategy within advocacy campaigns, and it places cases within the broader political context through a focus on *how* storytelling is undertaken, by whom, and for which audiences. Throughout the book and especially in chapter 8, we build on Han et al.'s (2021) research on community campaigns to show that the power of storytelling-based advocacy is relational and dynamic, not static, and also occurs at multiple levels. As they argue:

> Power is not only about winning elections or passing policies; it is also about getting a seat at the decision-making table, shaping the terms of the debate, and ***impacting the underlying narratives that determine the way people interpret and understand political issues***. (*our emphasis* Han et al. 2021, 67)

Thus advocacy power is not only about resources that can be mobilized: people, money, or access to decision-makers; it is also about changing how a need for political and social change is understood. Storytelling advocacy is imbued with power through making personalized emotional appeals that persuade an audience to change dominant interpretations and narratives on an issue area. Processes of digitalization and datafication powerfully increase accessibility, reach, and type of tailored stories being disseminated.

Overall, this book argues that the past decade in progressive storytelling advocacy has been one of significant and unusual change. The processes of crowdsourcing, digitalization, datafication, and automation that enable storytelling at a larger scale have ushered in a new phase of digital advocacy in which technology more rapidly and directly influences how people and their grievances are represented in public debates. Personal digital stories will continue to be a central feature of persuasion in our advocacy systems for the foreseeable future. Understanding how organizations navigate this transitional phase of storytelling datafication, including mitigating risks to storytellers and marginalized subjects of advocacy campaigns, reveals the needs, motivations, struggles, and future trajectories of organizations in the modern communication landscape.

CHAPTER I

Storytelling in Changing Technological and Political Landscapes

This chapter reviews key trends in technology, politics, media, and culture that are relevant for the relationship between advocacy organizations and storytelling. Given the range of different factors involved in these processes, we draw from scholarship in the communication, political science, policy studies, media studies, and journalism fields of study in an interdisciplinary and complementary fashion.

We begin by reviewing the existing research on the centrality of stories to today's political landscape and public arena. Through examples from policy studies intertwined with strategic communication theory, we discuss how purposively crafted stories tend to be more persuasive than scientific evidence and facts, particularly when trying to reach and mobilize new and unexperienced publics. Then we take the analysis to a higher level, considering the relationship between individual stories and larger political, societal, and cultural narratives. Here, we discuss why actors that push for progressive social change have historically found it difficult to work with personal stories and connect them to shared, aspirational, and value-laden narratives. Countering these challenges, the next part of this chapter reviews key changes in technology and culture that have promoted a growing personalization of political action over the last decade, which advocacy organizations may seek to capitalize on. Finally, we consider how increasingly hybridized media systems and complex political information cycles may nudge advocacy organizations toward new approaches to storytelling and discuss factors likely to influence that process in the United States and Australia, respectively. This generates a mixed canvas that includes both challenges and opportunities, providing the background for the centralization, professionalization, and datafication of storytelling in advocacy organizations that we explore in the rest of this book.

1.1 Storytelling, Public Discourse, and Policymaking

Why do stories seem to matter so much for public discourse, mobilization, persuasion, and public decision-making? Stories have long been recognized as essential tools for advancing and influencing public debates and policy-making processes. Seminal work in policy analysis has described agenda setting and public decision-making as the result of a competition between alternative narratives where stories perform a fundamental role in driving debate and persuading key stakeholders. Stone (2012) first identified causal stories as important tools to guide decision-makers toward preferred policy solutions. In general, policy arguments "are stories with a beginning, a middle, and an end, involving some change or transformation. They have heroes and villains and innocent victims, and they pit the forces of evil against the forces of good" (2012, 158). Within this framework, it has also been shown that incorporating ambiguity and openness is especially important to create persuasive stories because these elements give listeners the impression that they reached conclusions independently (Polletta and Lee 2006). Here, stories are used to articulate key values at the root of proposed policy solutions indirectly and, when relevant, to "dress up" other forms of evidence (e.g., science results, statistics, and so on) in more accessible and persuasive messages (Rhodes 2018). This has clear implications for all the stakeholders involved in public debates and decision-making, including advocacy organizations.

For example, Roe (1994) suggested that public managers and policy-makers use narratives to transform policy uncertainties and complexities into manageable "chunks" of rationality, such as risk. Empirical work has shown that civil servants—the supposed "custodians" of evidence-based policy—routinely arrange information to create "policy stories" to guide decision-makers toward a preferred solution (Stevens 2011). Crucially, this has cemented the notion that "those who wish to persuade others to shift their preferences—including their preferences for specific public policies—must develop arguments that facilitate this shift" (Mintrom and O'Connor 2020, 851). This applies to social change advocates and campaigners just as much as it does to any other stakeholders. At least to an extent, they must play this "game" if they want to successfully influence public debates. For example, research on Covid-related health policy found that policy-makers and advocacy organizations share an interest in reducing complexity and addressing "wicked" problems through the construction and presentation, to the public and to elite actors, of meaningful narratives (Mintrom and O'Connor 2020).

Beyond breaking down complex issues into more manageable and accessible pieces of information, storytelling has also emerged as a vital tool for those seeking to ensure the uptake of evidence in public decision-making (Davidson 2017). To be persuasive, story-based arguments do not necessarily need to be based on "hard" or data-driven evidence and, at times, can even oppose commonly accepted facts, as is shown by some of the examples discussed later in this chapter. Instead, the reverse is true. That is, arguments underpinned by evidence enjoy much better chances of being persuasive when they are presented not through numbers or "facts" but through stories. This is because data-driven arguments alone struggle to reach people who are not already interested or invested in an issue, who miss the context that is needed to grasp their meaning and broader implications (Loeb 2015, 57). Instead, stories resonate with politically inexperienced and relatively uninterested people more easily.

The situational theory of publics—a strategic communication framework—helps explain these dynamics: whereas facts may be useful to mobilize an organization's base, which is already cued up about the issues and can be characterized as an "aware public," they are insufficient to reach and activate broader "latent publics" that may potentially be interested but lack prior knowledge about the issues (Aldoory and Grunig 2012). Thus, stories perform an important role because, through the mechanism of plot, they can make causal relationships more apparent, helping unaware audiences process complex information even when they are engaging in fast thinking and offering mental models that help frame facts for the first time (Davidson 2017).

Recent research in the policy field has focused on problem definition and individual policy stories. While on paper these may look like straightforward processes, researchers have also acknowledged that, in practice, they play out within a complex environment that is constantly changing due to changes in politics, media, and culture. This creates both opportunities and challenges that stakeholders in these processes—in our case advocacy organizations—must learn to navigate and, possibly, adapt to. For this reason, the rest of this chapter explores this environment by focusing on the following issues: the relationship between stories and higher-level narratives, political culture and mobilization dynamics, changes in digital media and participation that facilitate storytelling, and today's increasingly hybridized media system and political information cycle.

1.2 Strategic Narratives

A useful starting point to better understand the changing context for advocacy storytelling is by considering the relationship between stories and overarching cultural and narrative contexts. The terms "story" and "narrative" are sometimes used interchangeably. However, they are conceptually different. Although the boundaries are not always completely clear, story and narrative operate on different levels. This moves beyond the difference between *policy* stories, which tend to be clearly defined (Veselková 2014), and *political* stories, which often embrace ambiguity and allusion as powerful rhetorical and persuasive elements (Polletta 2006). In particular, observers of public decision-making have noted that the most persuasive stories tend to be infused with fundamental ideas, themes, and values that are commonly understood as integral and distinctive of a society or country (McDonough 2001, 210). As such, public debates informed by stories are discussions about ideas and values (Stone 2012), and effective stories simultaneously resonate with and fuel these higher-level narratives about societies and peoples. As discussed in more detail below, some have called these "alpha stories" (Ricci 2016), which is another term for broad, value-laden narratives that can be tapped into to boost the persuasiveness of individual stories.

Taking advantage of and challenging societal narratives is important but difficult. Some political actors are better equipped than others for this kind of approach from cultural, organizational, and financial perspectives. For example, governments and other state actors are especially adept at tapping into narratives as part of their communication outreach, which has stimulated a lively theoretical debate and conceptual developments in the fields of international relations and public diplomacy. An important concept that originally emerged in that research field, but is relevant to apply to all political actors, is that of "strategic narratives," which are "representations of a sequence of event and identities [. . .] through which political actors—usually elites—attempt to give determined meaning to past, present, and future in order to achieve political objectives" (Miskimmon et al. 2013, 5). Strategic narratives operate at the international level to explain how the world is structured, at the national level to "set out what the story of the state or nation is, what values and goals it has" (Roselle et al. 2014), and at the issue level to "set out why a policy is needed and (normatively) desirable, and how it will be successfully implemented or accomplished" (Roselle et al. 2014). At each of these levels, actors wishing to use a narrative strategically ought to pay attention to its reception and interpretation by intended audiences, if they want to ensure its persuasiveness.

Pamment (2016) has researched how strategic narratives work in a variable media ecology where "transmedia" storytelling is common as stories that originate on one platform are shared and edited through other channels, and into different formats. Digitalization and convergence have changed approaches to storytelling, creating multiple narratives spread across several campaign assets that may be tailored to intersect with the media repertoires of diverse audiences. Here, campaigns can use values, norms, and brand identities that resonate with people because they can be co-opted, shared, or otherwise rearticulated but at the same time also contribute to an overall campaign outcome through their association with broader narratives.

Crafting strategic narratives requires some level of control over story production and dissemination processes to ensure that individual stories effectively resonate with relevant ideas and values, supporting a specific outcome. However, not every high-level narrative that can influence contemporary public debates is centrally coordinated. Crucially, influential macro-level narratives can also emerge in organic ways from participatory digital storytelling that occurs online, especially—but not exclusively—in response to important events. Page (2018) calls these "shared stories." These, in a nutshell, are narratives that are constantly mediated and remediated as "a retelling, produced by many tellers, across iterative textual segments, which promotes shared attitudes between its tellers" (Page 2018, 18). These processes also serve to infuse online symbolic trends with meaning through participation in personalized action frameworks that generate "movements" that would not be recognizable without narrative. For example, this was the case of the #MeToo movement, which became understood as a social event and then framed as a "movement" through a process of narrativization whereby individual tweets produced by viral behavior were aggregated to form a cultural narrative that spoke to collective sensemaking (Dawson 2020).

When this occurs, organizations can move to co-opt or otherwise exploit these narratives. However, these are processes fraught with risk as steering or controlling narratives that first emerged organically online is difficult, even for typically influential voices and organizations with large followings. Irrespective of the intentions of those who seek to co-opt these narratives, this can lead to negative outcomes. #BlackoutTuesday, a hashtag that originated in music industry circles but was subsequently co-opted during the U.S. protests for racial justice in June 2020 illustrates this effectively. Here, social media influencers who acted strategically but were unaware or unconcerned about the cumulative effects of their actions, posted black squares on Instagram without references to broader narratives as a sign of allyship with racial justice activists. This, however, had the ultimate effect of drowning genuine grassroots activist voices under a sea of black squares that lacked strong symbolic meaning (Wellman 2022). The unpredictability of these mechanisms compounds difficulties that advocacy organizations already seem to have in connecting their story-based appeals to broader narratives, as is discussed in detail below. Nevertheless, linking personal stories to higher-level cultural, social, and political narratives clearly provides a strategic advantage. For these reasons, it is important to understand to what extent emerging practices in advocacy storytelling support this type of long-term strategic connections.

1.3 Progressives' "Storytelling Gap"

Progressive social movements and social change actors more broadly have long used stories to construct themselves both internally and externally as legitimate depositaries of "sacred" civil values (Alexander 2006). In particular, Marshall Ganz has written extensively on the importance of generating a coherent sequence of what he called a "story of self, a story of us, and a story of now" (2011, 1) that facilitates identification by foregrounding shared values instead of scientific evidence or policy preferences. Here, activists and organizers help storytellers develop personal stories by highlighting their links with shared group or community experiences and adding elements that urge listeners to act sooner rather than later. This process transforms personal experiences into "public narratives" that occupy and influence public discourse on key societal and political issues.

Advocates and organizers on the political left have found this technique to be effective for mobilizing supporters. For example, one organization that famously adopted this strategy was Barack Obama's Organizing for America (OFA) election campaign, which "trained its staff and volunteers to tell stories as Obama did at the [2004] DNC [Democratic National Convention] as a way of encouraging people to take action with the campaign" (McKenna and Han 2014, 111). Although some have noted that this approach and "standardized" story sequencing tend to strip away "the actual complexity of people's life histories" (Fernandes 2017, 34), it succeeded in mobilizing more than two million volunteers who were central to the Obama campaign's ground game in 2008 and 2012.

Fundraising is another area in which storytelling has traditionally performed an important role. Fundraisers for advocacy and nonprofit organizations more broadly have long sought to capitalize on the so-called "identifiable victim effect" (Small et al. 2007), which sees potential donors' propensity to give increase if they can connect their actions to an individual's story. Although sometimes this has led to the development of fundraising strategies that controversially exploit feelings of pity and perpetuate stigma, it nevertheless provides further evidence of the persuasive power of storytelling and its relevance for advocacy organizations. For these reasons, it is important to consider whether progressive advocates, in today's changing media and political landscape, can use storytelling not only to mobilize and organize their base but also to reach broader publics on key issues, establish a specific narrative in the public arena, and possibly win others over.

Introducing or significantly expanding storytelling in the communication toolbox presents social change advocates and activists with some specific dilemmas, particularly with regard to the use of personal stories. First, there is a risk that individual stories, depending on how they are framed and understood by audiences, could support the interpretation of grievances and concerns as "private issues," while in fact they are collective problems that require policy solutions. Moreover, as Polletta noted, "effecting real change may require people to identify with experiences that are very far from their own; and [. . .] told badly, stories may discourage an emotional identification rather than foster it" (2006, 167). Second, if personal stories require a substantial level of editing in order to adequately support specific policy objectives or become more persuasive, there is also a risk that individual narratives may become distorted in the process. This could lead advocacy organizations back to the days in which they were criticized for "speaking for others" (Alcoff 1991), from which they have generally sought to move away in recent years by adopting a more collaborative and representative communication style. Third, advocates and activists working to advance progressive social change tend to promote stories that are likely to challenge the status quo and therefore run contrary to extant narratives (Delgado 1989). In some ways, this puts them at a disadvantage compared to other actors—particularly conservative campaigners—who can more easily link their messages to "alpha stories" rooted in dominant cultures and traditions.

In light of this, some have argued that social change campaigners and progressive politicians—particularly in the United States—are negatively impacted from a "storytelling gap." Ricci pointed out that "conservatives tell political long-term stories while liberals do not" (2016, 1). This is because conservatives intentionally seek to connect their policy preferences to dominant narratives that "proclaim that, now and forever, from long ago and far into the future, markets are terrific, tradition is wonderful, and government, for the most part, should be small" (Ricci 2016, 2). In contrast, because they work to challenge the system, social change advocates find structural difficulties that prevent them from capitalizing on the persuasive power of existing narratives to boost the persuasive power of their stories. In the United States, this means that progressives "don't have a story identifying the general causes of America's problems" (Entman 2015, 2) that hangs together "as a coherent frame that explains the nature, cause, and remedy to problems in an emotionally compelling way" (Entman 2015, 2). This makes them more likely to "promote immediate policy proposals" (Ricci 2016, 1) that emphasize hard evidence over shared narratives, with the hope that this will be sufficient to sway audiences their way. Yet, as was mentioned above, this type of argument tends to be trumped by story-focused communication even when the latter is not supported by facts.

Notable examples of campaigns in which conservatives linked individual stories to popular narratives include the battles against the Affordable Care Act (ACA—colloquially known as "Obamacare") and antiabortion policies in the United States. In the first case, conservative groups successfully spread the rumor that the ACA would lead to the establishment of "death panels" responsible for discussing whether older patients should receive care or consider "end of life" options. Although this assertion was completely baseless, it echoed the American ideal of individual freedom, which made it extremely difficult for grassroots campaigners to contrast effectively, particularly among older people (Berinsky 2017; Meirick 2013). In the second case, antiabortion activists have used individual "abortion regret" stories to support several successful legislative campaigns and legal advocacy efforts that restricted access to abortion in several U.S. states despite the fact that the prevalence of "abortion regret" in women who decide to terminate a pregnancy has been disproved by a wide body of scientific evidence (Doan et al. 2018). This is also a transnational trend as conservative campaigners and media in other democratic countries have used stories to build sweeping generalizations that form the basis of a "politics of resentment" toward groups such as people with disabilities and people of color in which powerful anecdotes that reinforce widespread negative stereotypes consistently trump systematic evidence in the minds of most people (Hughes 2015).

Clearly, these examples confirm that stories can be persuasive without needing to be anchored in facts and evidence. Depending on how different political actors act to pursue their goals, this can be a problem because effective public decision-making can only stem from information that is "true and presented in a context that does not distort its relevance to the policy choice at hand" (McDonough 2001, 212). From a strategic standpoint, this also creates an imbalance because it puts organizations determined to align their campaigns with facts at an unfair disadvantage compared to political actors that are less concerned about acting ethically and prioritize winning an argument or scoring a political point at all costs. In the United States, this trend started before Donald Trump was elected president in 2016 but has become especially significant since then. For these reasons, it is important to consider whether technological changes, user expectations, and motivation can provide progressive organizations with opportunities to close this problematic "storytelling gap" in an environment that is quite challenging.

1.4 Digitalization, Personalized Action Frames, and Advocacy

Digital technologies have implications for how people mobilize and act collectively. In turn, the changing dynamics of citizen participation matter a great deal for how advocacy stories come together. Crucially, storytelling is affected by digitalization and a "convergence culture" characterized by the flow of content across multiple media platforms and audiences that generate and use it in the same ways (Jenkins 2006). Digital technologies open new avenues for cocreating persuasive stories and activating publics. However, technology alone is not enough for this to occur. There is a long line of research showing that digital participation depends, in addition to access and accessibility factors, on motivation, aspirations, and previous patterns of political socialization and activity (Bimber et al. 2012). In other words, digital media are relevant but insufficient for mobilization because "impact is not determined by the technology but rather by the historically singular interplay of the various sociocultural, economic, and political conditions at work" (Papacharissi 2015, 8).

An important element that can boost motivation and facilitate participation through online media is what Bennett and Segerberg (2013) have called "personal action frames," a concept that plays a central role in their "connective action" theory of mobilization. These participatory frames are highly personalizable but at the same time also sufficiently broad to define a collective. These can be strategically orchestrated by organizations or emerge organically on online platforms, in which case organizations can seek to coopt them. They allow individuals, free from organizational ties and detached from strongly defined ideological claims, to connect and disconnect more fluidly, contributing to the emergence of activism by inserting their own personal narrative in a broader framework that supports collective action. In defining personal action frames, Bennett and Segerberg (2013) examined the anti-G20 and #Occupy protests of the early 2010s, but there is a large body of evidence that shows the relevance of this concept well beyond those movements. For example, one area in which these dynamics have played a prominent role in recent years is that of health and patient advocacy where crowdsourced communication processes on social media have been more central to activist networks than any other sites (Vicari and Cappai 2016). It is significant to see these dynamics stand out in an area that, as we will see later in this book, has performed a fundamental role in developing crowd-sourced and "datafied" approaches to storytelling.

In sum, participatory culture, convergence, and personalized action frames make people more willing and able to share, which creates multiple opportunities for organizations. There are opportunities to use personal stories for both mobilization and for persuasion. Integrating personal stories into advocacy campaigns has been shown to fuel positive impact at the micro- (individual) meso- (community) and macro- (national or international policy) levels. For example, Matthews and Sunderland's (2017) analysis of "listening" to personal stories in a healthcare policy setting shows that a groundswell of public or service provider response to digital stories can lead to policy-makers taking direct and indirect action. At the same time, however, they also note that there tends to be a "black box" effect of what happens to personal stories from the moment organizations collect them to when they are published. This highlights the tension that emerges between organizations seeking to take advantage of people's willingness to share and the availability of stories online, on one side, and participatory culture and user expectations, on the other: to what extent, if at all, is it fair (and possible) for organizers to curate narratives that emerge organically online to support organizational and community goals?

Michie et al. (2018) discussed this in the context of abortion rights advocacy, exploring whether organizers could effectively curate abortion narratives to promote public awareness and support engagement with pro-choice advocacy in Ireland. In particular, they contrasted the "top down" approach to story curation that was popular among professional organizers with digital grassroots narratives created by marginalized communities. This led them to highlight open questions about both strategy and voice in story-based approaches to political advocacy that this book—particularly chapter 4—also engages with. In addition, another important factor that intersects with these processes is today's media and information environment. Although grassroots advocacy has tended to become more participatory over the last few years, it could be argued that curation and the strategic positioning of stories have become even more important in the current information landscape, which heightens the urgency of public-facing communication for mobilizing one's base, persuading others, and controlling the public narrative around an issue agenda.

Storytelling is a powerful tool in these processes, and the intuitive primacy of digitally organic narratives over organizationally curated stories should not be taken for granted but, instead, questioned and examined carefully. This is not only for strategic reasons. Rather, it is also because research has shown that the openness to interpretation and ambiguity that usually characterize curated advocacy stories can benefit traditionally marginalized voices, as they encourage both storytellers and listeners to collaborate in drawing lessons from personal experiences, making it possible to suggest compromise or third positions without antagonizing fellow deliberators (Polletta and Lee 2006). This makes it important to better understand the relationship between advocacy storytelling and today's broader news and information landscape.

1.5 Advocacy Stories in the Hybrid Media System

Today, political organizations operate in a hybrid media environment "built upon interactions among older and newer media logics" that "blend, overlap, intermesh, and coevolve" (Chadwick 2017, 4). Since this concept first emerged in the early 2010s, it has served as a foundation for a vast amount of research. Providing a comprehensive review of this corpus would go beyond the scope of this book. Instead, it is useful to focus briefly on the implications that these changes have for advocacy organizations as they seek to achieve one of their main goals: influencing the public agenda and shaping the public perception of certain issues, groups, or events.

Crucially, the increasing hybridization of media systems has supported a shift from "news cycles" as they were traditionally intended—that is, controlled by few elite actors (politicians, communication staff, journalists and media executives, and so on)—toward broader "political information cycles" that have "complex temporal structures" and "include many nonelite participants, most of whom now interact exclusively online in order to contest specific news frames or even entire stories" (Chadwick 2011a, 8). In the early studies that developed this conceptual framework, Chadwick (2011a, 2011b) took a deep dive into the new dynamics that regulate strategic information sharing and determine news agendas. Today, newer actors (e.g., bloggers, citizen-journalists, fringe politicians) exploit the logic of digital media—particularly social media platforms—to challenge more established actors (parties, incumbent politicians, journalists), who in turn seek to claw back their influence by adapting to and adopting new logics.

Much work in this area has focused on how politicians, parties, and election campaigns have responded to the exponential growth in the number, types, and interdependence of media outlets and, oftentimes, the resulting unpredictability of information flows. For many of these actors, this has translated into an increased focus on and investment in analytic tools and data-driven campaigning. While this trend may not be as radically innovative or impactful as the journalistic hype that has surrounded it has suggested (Baldwin-Philippi 2019), it has certainly affected party and campaign structures, creating a more porous relationship between political operatives and technology companies and consultants, which hold a significant amount of influence on the shape of today's political campaigns (Dommett et al. 2021). So far, there has been less work that focused directly on advocacy organizations compared to other types of political organizations, even though these changes in the media and information landscape clearly affect them too and may push them to reconsider their approaches. That said, some important insights have emerged that are useful to review here.

Through in-depth case studies of transgender rights issues, Billard (2021) has examined how the hybrid media system's new dynamics—particularly stories that erupt unexpectedly on social media platforms and diffuse to more traditional media outlets—have challenged established advocacy organizations to rethink their approach to communication. Looking at PR "crises" faced by a major U.S. trans-rights organization in the wake of controversies that first emerged on Twitter, this research highlights the growing "urgency to respond substantively" to emerging and unexpected news with a framing that "needed to reflect truth *and* be compelling, that it needed to speak to the press *and* to the community on social media" (Billard 2021, 351). This can be hard for progressive organizations to do because most of them have traditionally favored evidence-based communication over narratives centered around direct experiences. This, however, is at odds with today's publics and news systems that increasingly reward affective and emotionally charged communication over truthful but "plain" or technical facts (Papacharissi 2015). These challenges are also compounded by the fact that, in the current media environment, advocacy campaigns compete for attention with an unprecedented amount of content. This is especially important for those "latent publics" mentioned earlier in this chapter, which are potentially interested in issues that matter to an organization but have not yet "tuned into" those and whose attention is directed by increasingly subjective mechanisms (Thayne 2012).

Ultimately, these information dynamics present advocacy organizations with a four-fold challenge. First, they must consider whether and, if so, how best to align their communications with direct experience and emotional content, highlighting "embodied knowledge" (Belenky et al. 1986) over other arguments. Second, they ought to assess how this personal communication resonates with larger, possibly collective, narratives. That is, both "stories of us" (Ganz 2011) and broader, value-laden "alpha stories" (Ricci, 2016). Third, they need to balance these innovations with their traditional focus on evidence-based arguments. Fourth, it raises the urgency to constantly gather "narrative ammunition" to try to be always ready to respond to events and news that pop up unexpectedly and quickly capture the political information cycle. Irrespective of an organization's specific strategy, responding to these challenges involves costly changes, in terms of resources, and cultural adaptation that takes time. In this context, storytelling is undoubtedly a valuable tool for advocates and organizers, but it is important to ask how it is reshaped amid these tensions.

1.6 Exploring Story Tech in the United States and Australia

Given this mixed landscape of opportunities and challenges, we begin in the next chapter by investigating the motivations that drive or discourage progressive grassroots organizations in the current information environment to incorporate personal stories in their advocacy initiatives. Within this framework, it is important to consider whether contextual elements such as culture, politics, local media and information environments, and specific catalyzing events influence these processes in different countries. Looking simultaneously at both the United States and Australia is a particularly effective way of doing that for several reasons.

Crucially, U.S. organizations have been at the forefront of much innovation in digital advocacy and campaigning in the last two decades (Gibson et al. 2014) and have operated in a challenging political and information context in recent years. In addition, Australian advocacy organizations have a history of learning from the tactics employed by their counterparts in the United States via both direct links through shared personnel and indirect links driven by academic books, networks, and conferences, particularly the work of Ganz on stories of "self, us, and now" mentioned above (Vromen 2015; 2017). There are differences between the U.S. and Australian contexts that mean some innovations diffuse more successfully than others. For example, the historical development of Australian interest and advocacy groups more closely parallels the United Kingdom in emergence of strong national organizations holding close relationships with governments dominated by strong and formalized political parties (Marsh 1995; Warhurst 2007). Furthermore, the U.S. and Australia media systems are different, with the former commercialized and highly polarized and the latter including a strong public broadcasting sector. Since media polarization has been shown to reinforce the persuasive power of campaign stories (Polletta and Callahan 2017), this difference potentially influences the value of storytelling in the eyes of advocacy organizations.

Furthermore, during the period examined in this book, U.S. advocacy organizations were affected by significant external challenges, particularly during the years of the Trump presidency and in the first two years of the Covid-19 pandemic. In Australia, political circumstances were not as extreme despite advocacy organizations being cast in an "opposition" role during successive Liberal-National Coalition conservative governments between 2013 and 2022. This provides a useful test case to examine the relevance of traditional patterns of innovation in digital advocacy where smaller, younger organizations are usually more open to new technological innovation than larger, more established and institutionalized organizations (Schmitz et al. 2020) in different political climates.

For these reasons, our investigation can be characterized more accurately as a "parallel" rather than strictly "comparative" study. Macro-trends were mapped at country level and in-depth insights were drawn from particularly significant or representative cases in each country. This enabled us to focus on innovative examples in each country, better contextualize the data, and offer a richer analysis than if we had focused on only one country. In sum, this project builds on two insights from existing research: first, that the United States is highly likely to be a source of innovation and experimentation diffusing to Australia; and, second, that the successful diffusion of those innovations will be subject to differences around the characteristics of advocacy organizations, as well as the local political and media environment.

The Covid-19 pandemic was a third contextual factor that emerged shortly after we began this research. Despite differences in national responses to this emergency, there is evidence that the pandemic—like other crises—acted as a powerful accelerator of digital innovation in advocacy strategy because it challenged established organizations to move their entire operations online and engage with supporters remotely until vaccines became widely available in both countries. This affected all types of political organizations at all levels, from grassroots groups to election campaigns, sparking several questions, considerations, and experimentations with innovative solutions for digital inclusion (Trevisan 2022). The pandemic's implications for advocacy storytelling provide important context throughout the book and are addressed directly in chapter 7, which examines labor unions' use of stories about essential workers between 2020 and 2022.

With this complex landscape in mind, the next chapter analyzes the main organizational changes linked to the intersection of technology and advocacy storytelling. In particular, it explores the logics and motivations behind technological innovations in this area, and charts their diffusion across different types of organizations and between countries.

CHAPTER 2

Logics of Digital Storytelling and Their Diffusion

As highlighted in chapter 1, changing media and political environments, as well as shifting patterns of access to, consumption, and evaluation of information, generate challenges and opportunities for advocacy organizations that seek to reach, persuade, and mobilize broad publics. In this chapter, we begin to explore why and how progressive advocacy organizations in the United States and Australia have responded to these challenges by increasingly turning to personal storytelling in recent years. In particular, this chapter details the different standpoints being developed on innovation and diffusion of digital storytelling tactics, as well as the challenges to more traditional forms of advocacy based on direct lobbying and research.

In addition to mapping current advocacy storytelling practices in the two countries, we consider critical moments in the evolution of these techniques over the past decade. This sheds light on the different rationales, logics, and incentives at the root of recent changes in progressive advocacy storytelling. These are, of course, associated and conditioned by ongoing changes in digital technologies, which are discussed in detail in the next chapter. This initial landscape was mapped through thirty in-depth interviews with advocacy campaign managers and other executives at major national progressive advocacy organizations, as well as communication agencies specializing in advocacy and community work in the United States and Australia. In general, interviewees were recruited directly from organizations that have supported storytelling programs in recent years. These include prominent advocacy organizations, as well as specialized media consultants and public relations agencies that worked on storytelling projects with a range of advocacy clients in a variety of policy areas in each country.

Although the purposive nature of this interview recruitment constitutes a limitation of this study, it also enabled us to focus specifically on prominent actors and pioneers in this area. For example, some of the largest and most significant organizations for which our interviewees worked included AARP (formerly called the American Association of Retired People), the Center for American Progress, Families USA, and Everytown for Gun Safety in the United States, as well as Australian Progress, the Brotherhood of St. Laurence, and the Cancer Council in Australia. A complete list of organizations and consultancies and more information about the interviewees are available in the appendix. Interviews focused primarily on three topics: (1) the perceived value of personal storytelling in the context of the broader information environment and vis-à-vis existing advocacy strategies; (2) story collection, selection, development, and dissemination techniques; and (3) the roles of technology, organizations, and individual storytellers in these processes.

Important macro-trends emerged with regard to how digital storytelling work is approached and integrated within existing advocacy structures and strategies. Most notably, the growing use of personal stories and the increasingly influential roles played by a range of digital technologies in these processes have been fueled by three complementary logics drawn from newsmaking, election campaigns, and big data science, respectively. Each one of these is identified and described in detail in this chapter. While there is evidence of general diffusion of storytelling practices and their foundational logics from the United States to Australia, since 2017 significant changes in politics, the media, and culture have incentivized American organizations to invest in, centralize, and institutionalize storytelling functions especially rapidly. This has generated innovative and experimental approaches to advocacy storytelling, as is discussed both here and in the next chapter.

2.1 Brief Taxonomy of Advocacy Storytelling Practices

Like any innovation, advocacy storytelling does not happen in a vacuum. For this reason, we asked progressive advocacy organizations how they were integrating persuasive storytelling and personal stories in their existing workflow and structures. Considering who has responsibility for this work and what kind of resources are allocated to it provides a first sense for the logics that underpin and inform the evolution of this persuasive strategy. Through our interviews, we identified three main types of story brokering, development, and dissemination practices. These are differentiated by three fundamental criteria, including (1) whether storytelling is planned, developed, and implemented inside or outside the advocacy organization; (2) who is responsible for them (namely, in-house specialists versus paid consultants); and (3) whether they constitute "one-off" special projects or long-term ongoing operations. These three processes can be described as:

a. **In-house storytelling**, where the entire process takes place within the advocacy organization itself, which has permanent staff members tasked with focusing solely or primarily on storytelling. This approach is characterized by long-term investment in storytelling and has become increasingly popular among large progressive organizations. Notable examples of organizations that have operated this model include the Center for American Progress, Everytown for Gun Safety, Public Citizen, and Families USA in the United States, and Australian Marriage Equality in Australia.

b. **Outsourced storytelling**, where story brokering and development are contracted out to external consultants, typically a public relations agency or other professionals that often specialize in nonprofit communication. In this case, storytelling work is connected mainly to special projects and time-limited campaigns. Traditionally, this was the most popular advocacy storytelling model, but it has become less common as advocacy organizations invest to develop their own dedicated story teams. In response, PR agencies active in this space are reinventing themselves to provide training and specialized production services that may not be sustainable for an organization to host in-house. Examples of this include Resource Media and First Person Politics in the United States, and Essential Media and Principle Co. in Australia.

c. **Storytelling partnership with community-rooted story brokers**, with two slightly different options. In one, advocacy organizations carry out story brokering and development in partnership with a specialized media agency that employs individuals who are skilled in production and editing, and at the same time are also members of the communities represented in advocacy stories. In the other, organizations train members of the communities they serve and represent to become digital storytellers themselves and then disseminate the content they produced through institutional platforms. Both of these are still relatively niche and experimental approaches but are making inroads into certain communities with specific needs and stories to tell, such as the disability community, patient healthcare advocacy groups, and refugees. Examples of the first model include Rooted in Rights and Ramp Your Voice. Examples of the second model include Rooted in Right's storytelling fellowship for people with disabilities and the World Food Program's "Storytellers Program" for refugees.

Although personal storytelling can follow any of these paths, all those interviewed agreed that in-house storytelling is rapidly becoming the preferred model, particularly among U.S. social change advocacy organizations. This was corroborated by interviewees from PR consultants who used to be employed for special storytelling projects but said that now advocacy organizations display:

> an increasing understanding [that storytelling matters], it's something that we provide workshops and training on a lot, and we get asked for those trainings a lot some time we'll find that the in-house communications staff have been trying to make that case that the organization needs to focus more of their attention on gathering stories but they need an 'outside expert' to come in and make the case more firmly. (Interviewee, Resource Media, July 2018)

Three main reasons were mentioned to explain the growing popularity of in-house storytelling. First, changes in digital media technologies have enabled organizations to more easily acquire, store, develop, and disseminate personal stories, facilitating the move of these functions inside advocacy organizations. Second, maintaining an in-house story archive was seen as increasingly important to be able to intervene rapidly and effectively in today's political information cycle as was described in the previous chapter. Third and final, interviewees also mentioned the desire to establish a direct relationship with individual storytellers due to the sensitive nature of the issues contained in their stories and to take care of them from the start to the end of this process. This relates to the broader emotional and psychological aspects of advocacy storytelling for both storytellers and communication practitioners, as well as the risk of backlash from Internet trolls and other actors that individual storytellers become exposed to when their personal narratives are highly publicized. Chapter 4 returns to this last set of issues and discusses them in detail.

The organizations that are pursuing in-house storytelling have generally sought to centralize this function within a specific individual or team that acts as a story resource for the rest of the organization. As this practice is still evolving, storytelling functions have been located under different umbrellas depending on the priorities, existing structure, ethos, and size of each organization. For example, when we carried out our fieldwork, Public Citizen had one communication staff member that looked after its story bank as part of a broader portfolio. In contrast, storytelling functions for Everytown for Gun Safety fell under the responsibilities of its gun violence survivors' network team. Furthermore, the Center for American Progress had established a dedicated "story bank" team with three staff members. This mirrored the setup at healthcare advocacy organization Families USA, which pioneered storytelling advocacy and story banking. Indeed, "story banking" (sometimes also styled "storybanking"), which can be described as the ongoing collection, digital archiving, and cataloguing of large volumes—sometimes tens or even hundreds of thousands—of personal stories for incorporation in present and future advocacy campaigns, constitutes a popular approach, particularly among U.S. organizations. Advanced by a handful of innovators at various points from the late 2000s onward, this technique appears to have "gone mainstream" since about 2017 as part of the effort to bring storytelling in-house and institutionalize it. The next chapter comes back to story banking in detail as part of the discussion on changing technologies and the growing datafication of advocacy storytelling, to which this technique and the principles behind it are central.

Returning to our three categories of story brokering outlined above, there was substantial evidence in Australia of both in-house storytelling and outsourced storytelling with external consultants. Increases in these two forms of story brokering were explained partly in terms of the rise of digital communications technologies, which facilitated both crowdsourcing a wide range of contributions and disseminating the resulting stories through social media in particular. Regarding the third type of story brokering (partnership with community story brokers), we did not find an example of a community-rooted organization in Australia. For example, even the "Every Australian Counts" campaign for disability services reform, which was run by a coalition of sector organizations and focused heavily on the personal stories of people with disabilities—a community that in the United States has been experimenting with community-brokered storytelling—engaged an external communication agency to help run the digital storytelling component of the campaign, as is discussed in detail in chapter 5.

In contrast with the United States, story banking was not widely recognized as a term in Australia. Instead, interviewees in this country used a variety of labels including "catalogue," "database," and "warehouse" to describe crowdsourced collections of personal stories. Moreover, the systematic accumulation of story content was usually addressed to a specific campaign in an ad hoc way rather than being an ongoing resource maintained indefinitely for the organization's future needs. There are three points of contrast with the U.S. case, including (1) the ongoing strength of external consultants alongside in-house solutions; (2) the lack of community-rooted story broker organizations; and (3) the lack of widespread story banking institutionalization.

Australian interviewees largely explained these differences in terms of the scale of their advocacy campaigns. Smaller organizations, working with smaller supporter databases, pitching to a more concentrated media market, often suit a targeted media case study approach. This was indirectly confirmed by U.S. interviewees, too, who said that, to work effectively, digital story banks need very large pools of potential storytellers, as is discussed in detail in the next chapter. Yet large established advocacy organizations with the most resources to overcome these scale constraints tend to also be the least open from a strategic perspective to investing in new or experimental digital techniques, including storytelling (Schmitz et al. 2020), given their institutionalization is often accompanied by a more conservative insider "theory of change." Typically, they innovate in response to external challenges and other stimuli, which in Australia, unlike in the United States, seemed to be lacking. Therefore, the organizational layer of storytelling in Australia seems less developed than in the United States due to a combination of scale and political context, and is better described as a collection of story brokers working in-house and as external consultants on ad hoc advocacy campaigns.

That does not mean, however, that Australian advocacy organizations have stopped seeing their U.S. counterparts as sources of inspiration for many tactics, including storytelling. In their conversations with us, Australian interviewees pointed out recent training sessions with U.S.-based storytelling experts and work with U.S. consultancies, as is described in detail below. Thus there was evidence of diffusion, but at the same time these interviews also revealed that Australian and American progressive advocacy organizations have been following somewhat distinct paths in developing their current approaches to storytelling. On one hand, recent events and the broader political climate in the United States marked a profound shift toward the long-term institutionalization of personal storytelling in progressive advocacy. On the other hand, Australian organizations continue to prefer an issue-based approach and favor a more incremental path to innovation. To better understand the drivers behind these two paths, it is useful to review in more depth the recent history of changing approaches to storytelling and identify the various logics that supported these changes in both countries.

2.2 Crisis and the Changing Value of Storytelling in the United States

U.S. interviewees offered some important background that helps explain their shifting attitude and approach toward the use of personal stories in organized advocacy settings. This identified a definite trend to make personal stories an organic component of every and any progressive advocacy initiative, highlighting the fact that many organizations had made significant investments toward centralizing and institutionalizing storytelling functions. This approach reflected the need to respond to different political and media contexts, which interviewees framed in part as a need to respond more effectively to the election of Donald Trump as U.S. president in 2016. Beyond events and the urgency brought on by a rapidly shifting political climate, these changes were also spurred by the need to respond to a changing information environment dominated by the hybridization between traditional and digital forms of media discussed in the previous chapter and the growing amount and efficacy of misinformation. In doing this, U.S. advocacy organizations blended logics and expertise imported from other fields and organizations, including the news media, election campaigns, and big data science.

2.2.1 Toward Institutionalized Storytelling

Historically, two main incentives have promoted the diffusion of storytelling among U.S. progressive advocacy organizations. First, interviewees noted that particularly controversial policy battles tend to act as catalysts for the collection, development, and dissemination of personal stories. Second, many of these efforts have been supported through grantmaking from U.S. philanthropic organizations that are invested in the promotion of social change and regard storytelling as an effective strategy to achieve their goals. Event-oriented and philanthropy-funded advocacy storytelling initiatives— many of which have overlapped—have typically been project-based and time-limited, preparing the ground for a broader strategic shift toward the institutionalization of advocacy storytelling that started in 2016–2017.

One policy debate that interviewees from organizations that pioneered crowdsourced and datafied storytelling systems before others—namely Families USA and AARP—identified as a watershed moment was the one over the Affordable Care Act (ACA) in 2009–2010. In conjunction with this legislative push, both these organizations created very large digital archives of story "kernels" or ideas from supporters with potential to be developed into fully fledged healthcare advocacy stories. Together with a handful of other large advocacy organizations—most notably the Service Employees International Union (SEIU)—this characterized Families USA and AARP as precursors in the creation of "story banks" that have become popular among progressive advocacy organizations in the United States in more recent years. Interestingly, these interviewees specifically mentioned the need to contrast Obamacare "death panels" rumors promoted by conservative politicians, activists, and media, which were mentioned in the previous chapter as examples of effective but unfounded conservative storytelling, as a key reason for boosting the use of personal stories in their own campaigns. This resonates with work that showed that other advocacy based on facts and hard evidence such as numbers and statistics was largely ineffective in debunking those very same rumors (Berinsky 2017).

These prototype story-centered campaigns contributed to turning public and policymakers' opinion in favor of the ACA, which eventually became law in 2010. This policy success cemented the belief in those responsible for these story programs that this strategy could play a much bigger and more permanent role in social change advocacy campaigns as it compared favorably to previous attempts to innovate advocacy storytelling that had backfired, such as hiring bloggers to produce "authentic" content (Cooper 2015). In the wake of this experience and backed by digital metrics about the reach and engagement generated by story content, story program managers proposed to organization leaders that the digital crowdsourcing, archiving, development, and dissemination of personal stories become institutionalized practices worthy of long-term investments from core budgets. For example, a former outreach specialist with AARP's "Stories Program" said:

> in 2011 we started to spend a lot of time developing and tracking metrics just to show the impact and we were able to give very clear numbers [to support the stories program]. (Interviewee, AARP, July 2018)

However, despite this evidence, organization leaders were not necessarily convinced about the need to secure the long-term future of storytelling programs after the ACA was approved. The AARP program in particular lost steam and was not afforded the investment that was needed to grow it into a centralized resource that could benefit the entire organization. Instead,

> after the ACA was passed we wanted to try to institutionalize the stories program or maybe more operationalize it for at least the mid-term future and then we started to get this chilly reception [from the leadership]. (Interviewee, AARP, July 2018)

This is almost ironic given the centrality that digital metrics have gained in advocacy strategy planning since then (Karpf 2016) and suggests that early experiments with crowdsourced storytelling were underpinned by the urgency created by a particularly controversial policy debate, but, once that was over, organizations' leaders tended to retreat into an "advocacy as usual" mode in which the centralization and growth of storytelling functions were not seen as a strategic investment. Despite the positive experience with ACA stories, the choice of leaders is explained by the broader context, which did not incentivize more permanent innovation. With Obama—a Democrat—in the White House, a vital political driver of digital innovation such as the need to find ways to respond effectively to a hostile administration (Trevisan 2017a) was missing. Thus, for the time being, personal storytelling continued to be approached more as an ad hoc tactic in support of specific issues than an ongoing activity fully integrated with advocacy campaign management.

Interestingly, U.S. philanthropic organizations picked up on the success of ACA story programs and invested considerable amounts of money to support the creation of story banks as a way to help protect the new healthcare legislation from the attacks of its opponents even after it was passed. Data from the Foundation Directory Online—the largest database of grantmaking organizations in the United States—shows that both the Robert Wood Johnson Foundation (RWJF) and the Kresge Foundation gave money to support this type of initiative in 2012. Notable grantees included Families USA—the progenitor of advocacy story banking—which received over one million U.S. dollars from RWJF to support the collection of "Obamacare success" stories, and Community Catalyst, a Boston-based organization that focuses on promoting affordable care for all, which received more than two million U.S. dollars for a healthcare stories story bank from the Kresge Foundation. Other major funders of story banks in this initial stage included the New York-based Surdna Foundation, which funded more localized initiatives in its focus on improving the health of cities in 2013, and the Hewlett Foundation, which gave $250,000 to the Center for American Progress for the production of an energy and climate change story bank in 2017. These initiatives ensured continued interest and engagement in digitally crowdsourced storytelling in the progressive advocacy space, but it is important also to remember that they were all special projects tied to external funding. Together, they showed the potential of this type of work in the context of ad hoc initiatives. These experiences, while time-limited, had a fundamental role in preparing the ground for more strategic and long-term approaches based on deep internal commitments—both financial and organizational—to storytelling in more recent years.

Building on these foundations, interest in personal stories among progressive advocacy organizations in the United States skyrocketed from 2016 onwards. This rapid acceleration was supported by what our interviewees described as a "mind shift" in favor of this tactic as an ongoing practice that should be integrated in every campaign. Significant investments toward the institutionalization and centralization of digitally crowdsourced storytelling in U.S. social change advocacy have been informed by a combination of three complementary logics, including (1) a news-making logic, (2) an election campaigns logic, and (3) a big data logic. Each organization is likely to blend these three logics in slightly different ways. However, all together they have contributed to the diffusion of advocacy storytelling processes that are large-scale, crowdsourced, technology-centered, increasingly institutionalized, and funded from internal budgets rather than more sporadically through external grants. Some large and influential organizations have also acted as "champions" of this model, boosting its diffusion among other progressive groups in the Washington, D.C., advocacy sector, as is discussed in more detail in the next chapter. Interviewees who had worked as both in-house communication staff for multiple advocacy organizations and as storytelling consultants for a range of external clients confirmed that this went beyond individual groups and organizations and was a field-wide trend among progressive advocates in the United States.

2.2.2 News-Making Logic

A fundamental driver behind this change was political isolation. During the Obama presidency, progressive organizations could count on a Democratic administration and partially Democratic U.S. Congress. This enabled progressive advocates to operate effectively through traditional channels and tactics, except for highly contentious issues such as the ACA, which led some to experiment with innovative strategies as was discussed above. This situation changed radically after the 2016 election with Republicans firmly in control of both the White House and Congress. Interviewees argued that this created a sense of urgency in their field for which it had become particularly important to tell stories because the Democrats were no longer in power.

Reflecting on long-term trends that separate progressives from conservatives in the United States, another interviewee added that integrating personal stories and emotion effectively in advocacy work

> is something that the Right figured out decades ago, every time Republicans come back in power you see a growing awareness on the Democratic side about the shortcomings of a strictly rational approach to persuading and influencing people and so because you have Trump in power and Republicans in control right now and as every time that Democrats lose en masse they start looking for alternative solutions, so I think right now we are in a moment when there is more openness to non-rational approaches to communication and organizing and persuasion. (Interviewee, Public Citizen, July 2018)

This suggests that being relegated to an opposition role acted as an important driver of innovation for progressive advocacy organizations in the United States, with personal storytelling occupying a central place in this process. As Tilly and Tarrow (2007) noted, changes in activist repertoires are often linked to external events that act as catalysts.

Many of those we interviewed said that the attempt by the Republican-majority Congress and Trump administration to repeal the ACA in 2017 was behind the expansion of progressive storytelling campaigns. This issue created conditions that incentivized major innovation because it was both a policy crisis, given the controversial and regressive nature of the issue, and a political crisis, given that progressive actors were locked out of government (Trevisan 2017a). However, the reasons behind the recent turn toward personal storytelling in U.S. progressive advocacy have much deeper roots than this important set of circumstances. This is because, in contrast with social movement repertoire changes brought on solely by specific events that tend to be temporary and short-lived (Tilly and Tarrow 2007), this new trend is supported also by long-term changes in the information environment that are systemic, transcend a given political season, and have contributed to ushering in a logic of advocacy storytelling akin to that of news-making.

Several interviewees explained that their efforts to institutionalize storytelling were tied to the current decline in trust in traditional information sources, which made people even less likely than usual to listen to other types of evidence, irrespective of the authoritativeness of the sources. One interviewee explained:

> The reason why [storytelling] is feeling more resonant in maybe the last year or two years is this fake news concept that is really unprecedented in American society that people just believe and I think the kind of way you can combat that if people aren't going to trust politicians telling them something, they might trust their neighbor [instead]. (Interviewee A, Center for American Progress, July 2018)

Awareness of these new information consumption and evaluation trends has created a sense of urgency among U.S. progressive advocacy organizations, which feel that seeking to influence news coverage is no longer sufficient. Instead, interviewees argued, organizations should implement strategies that enable them to reach target publics directly, including through a range of alternative digital platforms and other media that are popular within certain parts of the population.

To reach this goal, storytelling organizations have taken on a newsmaking logic that sees them constantly collecting and archiving new story ideas, monitoring the news for anything they should respond to immediately, and trying to be always ready to deploy the most effective personal narrative at virtually no notice. Most notably, this is the case for organizations that have implemented story banks, which are discussed in detail in the next chapter. For these, story collection is not confined to specific issues or particularly acute moments in policy debates. Instead, stories are captured on an ongoing basis on any issue that is relevant to the organization through a variety of online channels, and dedicated teams have been established to review submissions and follow up on those that should be developed further with considerable investment on the part of the organization. Given that these innovations are designed to respond to long-term systemic changes in the information environment, they constitute a strategic shift that is not strictly dependent on certain political circumstances and, as such, are likely to outlast them. During our research for this book, this was confirmed by the continued popularity and high levels of investment in digitally crowdsourced personal storytelling systems following the 2020 U.S. elections. Although the Democrats took back not only the White House but also both chambers of Congress, progressive U.S. advocacy organizations continued to recruit high-profile story bank staff and include story collection interfaces on their websites and social media accounts through 2022, as is described in more detail in chapters 3 and 4, respectively. Here, crisis acted as a catalyst that precipitated change, but innovations were designed to address systemic issues and continued to expand even when the emergency had passed. Digitally crowdsourced stories were not just a "fad" of the Trump years, and it could be argued that they have now entered the main repertoire of U.S. grassroots advocacy.

2.2.3 Election Campaign Logic

A second logic that has supported the institutionalization of large-scale storytelling within U.S. progressive advocacy organizations in recent years is that of election campaigning. Links between Democratic election campaigns and organizations that pioneered story banking go back to at least the early 2010s. Most notably, Barack Obama's Organizing for America campaign transferred its archive of more than 25,000 ACA stories to Families USA after the 2012 election. These connections were strengthened in the wake of the disappointing results of the 2016 election for the Democrats, with several storytelling specialists with election campaign experience joining progressive advocacy organizations. For example, in 2017 the Center for American Progress hired the former "inbound correspondence manager" for the 2016 Hillary Clinton campaign to be the director of its newly created story bank, where she was able to implement the lessons learned on the digital campaign trail. While until recently these transfers of both personnel and content from Democratic campaigns to advocacy organizations happened under special circumstances, now they are part of a broader trend for which storytelling is becoming institutionalized and part of the routine of progressive advocacy.

These storytelling professionals with election campaign experience brought with them the logic by which technology and personal stories can be constantly leveraged not only to mobilize one's base but also to win over independents, undecided people, or even those who are usually on the other side. This has influenced the very ways in which storytelling initiatives are structured and their location within advocacy organizations. For example, the story bank of the Center for American Progress is part of its Action Fund's "war room." As the name suggests, this operates in a similar way to an election campaign "war room," monitoring the news for reports and events that require an immediate response or provide opportunities to influence the news cycle and public agenda (Debenedetti 2016). In this context— interviewees explained—story banking staff constantly keep abreast of breaking news and query story databases for personal narratives to include in immediate responses and other communications from the organization.

This association with "war rooms," which are central to the "permanent campaigns" style of U.S. electioneering that was exported to many other countries over the last two decades (Dulio and Towner 2010; Scammell 1998), corroborates the impression that current initiatives contribute to the institutionalization of storytelling as an ongoing and increasingly ubiquitous strategy in U.S. progressive advocacy. Moreover, this setup represents an attempt to learn from election campaigns to find a way to systematically respond to the challenges and opportunities present in today's increasingly hybridized and very fast-paced U.S. political information cycle, which many advocacy organizations have been struggling to adapt to in recent years (Billard 2021). This makes digitally crowdsourced story collections, including but not limited to story banks, especially valuable assets in highly hybridized media environments. This, in turn, also raises the issue of whether organizations in other countries will import this model in the future. In any case, the U.S. experience makes changes in the structure of the information and media environment crucial factors to observe in order to understand the trajectory of advocacy storytelling in the long term.

2.2.4 Big Data Logic

As U.S. advocacy organizations seek to adapt to a new information environment and take inspiration from election campaigns, digital technologies occupy a central place in these processes. This, in turn, has introduced a third logic that supports this shift toward "permanent" storytelling: that of big data science. Some of the organizations involved in this study and others in the U.S. social change advocacy space have amassed story ideas databases that number in the tens or even hundreds of thousands and are constantly growing through the crowdsourcing of new material. Personal stories are collected, organized, and archived using sophisticated case management database software from companies such as Salesforce, Countable, and Base-Camp. These packages enable organizations to store a range of content (text, photos, video) and attach metadata such as thematic labels, demographic information, location, and electoral district. Organized in this way, story databases can then be queried through keyword searches that shortlist the "best" stories to respond to a particular piece of breaking news or target a specific public with a persuasive argument in accordance with the news-making logic that was outlined above. In short, this is where digital story content becomes "datafied" as these systems enable advocacy organizations to treat it as data, as is discussed in detail in the next chapter.

Database software is essential to build and manage massive story collections effectively, which raises some important questions about the intersection of technology, voice, representation, and power. However, before focusing on the technological piece and its implications, it is useful to consider why U.S. progressive advocacy organizations increasingly see added value in very large story archives, which constitute a strategic choice rather than an inevitability. In particular, interviewees explained that organizations feel that extremely large crowdsourced collections governed through algorithmic sorting afford them better chances to find the "best" stories that are out there compared to more traditional scouting strategies that focus on limited pools of stories shared by a few constituents or volunteers. This approach aligns with a general orientation toward quantitative science and a growing faith in big data approaches among organizations and society more generally to provide effective solutions for complex problems of which the "battle" among competing narratives in the political information cycle is a good example.

Crucially, this "big data logic" raises two potential problems that are not yet fully understood. First, there is the issue of whether this approach truly produces more effective story-based campaigns. Second, the impact of algorithmic sorting on story selection and its implications for how groups and issues are represented in advocacy campaigns and broader public debates through personal storytelling is also potentially problematic. This big data approach may seem like a good way to address the problem of convenience bias that is typical of more traditional story scouting methods. At the same time, however, it is important to understand how its algorithmic mechanisms risk introducing other forms of bias in these processes and what could help organizations mitigate them. Chapter 3 dives deeply into these questions by focusing on the technological infrastructure from the perspective of organizations. Chapter 4 takes an in-depth look at these issues in the context of voice, power, and representation by focusing on the perspectives and experiences of storytellers and aspiring storytellers from marginalized groups and backgrounds.

2.3 Storytelling in Australian Advocacy: Normative Diffusion and Incremental Change

There is evidence of a different pace of storytelling innovation in Australia. Although increasing in prevalence within advocacy organizations over the past decade, there is no equivalent clear systemic spike in interest in the past couple of years, or "crisis" moment that catalyzed widespread changes in organizational strategy, as with Trump's election and the ACA repeal debate in the United States in 2017. Instead, Australian interviewees often talked about storytelling as in competition with the more traditional advocacy approach that pairs an insider focus on directly influencing institutional elites with a media and advertising communications strategy. The purpose of storytelling compared with this traditional approach can be separated into its instrumental and inherent value.

The instrumental value of storytelling includes the following factors: making the individual advocacy efforts of supporters more effective, such as incorporating personal stories into emails to Members of Parliament; increasing the investment and future engagement of those supporters in their advocacy (and by association the advocacy organization); and generating leads for high quality content for either social or legacy media. The inherent value of storytelling, on the other hand, is that it expresses an organizational commitment to advocacy being authentically directed and enacted by its supporters, especially where that advocacy can be informed by lived experience. As one interviewee summarized:

> there's really a factional, ideological dispute around, do you distribute or consolidate authority? I think that that debate, which affects every single thing an advocacy organization does, sits above [storytelling], and that the way that these tools are applied or not, reflects where that debate sits on everything that the organization does. (Interviewee, Principle Co., August 2018)

This debate echoes the need for today's grassroots organizations to carefully balance centralization with independence for their constituents in order to project their voice effectively and lend legitimacy and power to their leaders (Han et al. 2021). Here, crowdsourced stories can make a significant contribution toward more participatory structures and distributed authority. Whereas the increase in storytelling in the United States appears driven by systemic shifts in the political and media context, no Australian interviewee talked about the particular significance of post-2016, the election of Trump and growth of right-wing populism, the rise of (online) misinformation, or the outcomes of any specific Australian elections. Instead, the rise of storytelling in Australian advocacy was explained primarily through the diffusion of information and norms. One interviewee commented:

There was a sense [in 2012] that groups didn't actually have the language to communicate complex ideas. They didn't have a way to communicate that was effective. They used facts rather than stories. (Interviewee, Australian Progress, February 2019)

Out of this sense of the deficit in Australian storytelling capacity, organizations deliberately looked for international models, and in particular to the United States. Three interviewees, unprompted, referenced the public narrative work of Marshall Ganz and his framework of the "story of self, the story of us and the story of now" (Ganz 2011) as being significant in shaping their understanding of storytelling. This corroborates the findings of previous work that has documented the significance of Ganz to the storytelling advocacy of GetUp!—a prominent digital focused progressive activist organization—and the large network of organizations in Australia with which they exchange information, norms, and staff (Vromen 2015, 2017).

Australian Progress—an influential capacity-building organization that serves progressive movements and causes—also repeatedly brought renowned messaging expert Anat Shenker-Osorio from the United States to speak at conferences and work directly with Australian campaigners on the importance of effective framing rather than overreliance on facts, going so far as to say "we have popularized her work in Australia" (Interviewee, Australian Progress, February 2019). In 2017, Australian Progress also hosted two international "guests in residence," Nicole Aro and Michael Whitney, who had worked on the 2016 Bernie Sanders campaign in the United States and were tasked with working intensively with partner organizations on their digital strategies. These examples illustrate how innovation in Australian advocacy, including storytelling, is heavily shaped by established mechanisms of transnational diffusion, most notably from the United States.

However, since they started, Australian Progress has also quickly built themselves into a distinctive and significant actor in Australian civil society, primarily through capacity-building via hosting sector-wide conferences and running training programs. They have prioritized this role of networking and diffusing the ideas behind storytelling-driven advocacy, rather than being a recognizable public advocate themselves.

Three different types of conferences have been convened by Progress Australia since 2013:

- Progress: This has become the flagship two-day conference for the Australian civil society sector, and has run every two years since 2013. It hosts more than one thousand delegates, runs panels and workshops, and is premised on a cross-pollination of ideas, lessons, and skills, and by fostering new relationships and networks.

- Leadership: In 2016 and 2019, Australian Progress brought together more than two hundred of Australia's nonprofit CEOs, union secretaries, and other community leaders at Old Parliament House to focus on networking and cross-sector collaboration.
- FWD Digital Organizing: has run at least four times since 2013 and focuses on digital campaigning and community organizing, connecting advocates to cutting-edge technologists and organizing approaches from Australia and internationally, especially. They have brought digital technology and campaigning experts from movements (such as Black Lives Matter) and organizations (such as from the Bernie Sanders campaign) from the United States and also the United Kingdom and New Zealand.

Participant observation of the Progress conference in 2013 and 2015 made it evident that organizations with a story-led approach were dominant in keynote addresses and panel organizing. While more traditional Australian advocacy organizations, such as charities, service providers, and unions, were present at the conferences, they were rarely headlining the event and were instead there to be trained on new approaches to campaigning and organizing (Vromen 2017). In the early years there was more active criticism of this approach from those who favored traditional lobbying and direct political contacts based on research, as well as from far-left social movement activists. Yet, as the conservative national government continued in Australia, significant alliance and cross-sectoral organizing emerged that diluted criticism and mainstreamed the importance of storytelling to successful advocacy. Similar to its focus on conferences, Australian Progress also runs regular fee-paying masterclasses and training programs. For example, it runs ad hoc training on social media campaigning techniques and role-playing for effective political lobbying.

The other major area of Australian Progress's remit is a regular fellowship program and an incubator program that has focused on start-ups for born-digital campaigning organizations. Storytelling training again takes center stage in this program. The fee-paying Progress Fellowship takes individual campaigners and trains them over a six-month period in organizing and leadership, based on a story-based approach to advocacy and change. Nearly eight hundred individuals have now completed the Progress Fellowship creating a very powerful network of like-minded people within the Australian advocacy sector. The incubator program has run at least four times and included twenty-two organizations; for the last three times the program has been promoted as Progress Labs. It directly mentors new, small organizations, often providing shared office space as well as direct input into organizational strategy and individual leader development. Many of these organizations are now successful and distinct leaders of story-focused campaigning and advocacy in Australia. These include, for example, Fair Agenda, which promotes fairness and equality for women; The Parenthood, promoting lobbying to create policy change for parents and caregivers; and Democracy in Colour, which is trying to change the institutions and systems that cause racial and economic injustice.

We also found examples of particularly intense storytelling in Australian advocacy beyond the influential network of like-minded organizers supported by Australian Progress. These, however, were usually related to issue-specific factors. Among recent examples of Australian issues and debates that incentivized story-centered campaigns based on massive databases, the most high profile is the marriage equality for LGBTIQ couples, which was finally decided by a nationwide postal survey in 2017.[1] The Australian Marriage Equality campaign embarked on a focused storytelling campaign that is examined in detail in chapter 6, crowdsourcing around 15,000 stories from their supporters that formed the basis for almost all the campaign's advocacy material. Three key reasons for this campaign's adoption of storytelling do not generalize easily to other issues and organizations. First, marriage as an issue involves high personal emotional stakes suited to expression through personal narrative, high credibility in terms of the public's reference points within their own lived experience, and many familiar narrative structures around marriage that place high cultural value in romantic relationships. Second, the organizational structure of Australian Marriage Equality as a standalone campaign meant that the usual incentive for legacy interest groups to centralize authority within organizational leadership did not apply, facilitating the distribution of authorship to a wide base of supporters. Finally, the strategic imperative of the national public vote that required mass persuasion of the electorate rather than influencing elite decision-makers steered efforts toward outsider tactics that could simultaneously emphasize the campaign's breadth of representation and appeal.

These three factors, which were significant in shaping the marriage equality campaign's adoption of storytelling, do not necessarily apply in other Australian advocacy campaigns. So, in contrast to the United States, it is the incremental factors driving storytelling (like norm diffusion and the creation of a storytelling "culture" through training programs) that operate systemically in Australia, whereas the more transformative factors (like strategic necessity) play out in a more uneven, campaign-specific way. This leads to an overall pattern where storytelling has steadily been increasing in prevalence, with episodic peaks. This also signals that the big data logic outlined above is somewhat independent of the other two logics described in this chapter (news-making logic and election campaign logic) because it informs advocacy storytelling strategies not only in conjunction with systemic changes in media and politics—like in the United States—but also when more specific issue-based circumstances suggest it may be a valuable option.

2.4 Conclusion

Storytelling strategies in progressive advocacy organizations in the United States and Australia are experiencing considerable expansion and innovation. One underlying shared driver of this trend is the perceived failure of traditional strategies. Advocates for progressive social change have found themselves in an opposition role following elections that returned conservative governments in Australia between 2013 and 2022, and in the United States between 2016 and 2020. This has acted as an incentive to change their tactics, which is in line with previous work that showed political isolation to be a fundamental driver of innovation in progressive digital advocacy in democratic countries (Trevisan 2017a) and has spurred substantial investments in story-based campaigns. These initiatives have contributed to some significant policy successes in recent years, including marriage equality legislation in Australia and protecting the Affordable Care Act in the United States. Despite this underlying commonality, however, the diffusion of storytelling in progressive advocacy has occurred at a different scale and pace, and is supported by different rationales in each country.

Building on the success of ad hoc story-centered campaigns and capitalizing on the lessons learned from grant-funded storytelling work, U.S. progressive organizations have moved rapidly from 2017 onwards to institutionalize digital storytelling work, centralize its functions in dedicated teams, and make long-term investments in this area. Although Trump's election dramatically accelerated these developments, they also represent a response to broader long-term changes in how people access and engage with information. This is confirmed by the fact that significant investments in building massive story archives through crowdsourcing continued after the Biden administration took over in 2021. These shifts in the information landscape have sparked sustained efforts that promise to make personal stories an integral part of any progressive advocacy initiative and are shaped simultaneously by three complementary logics.

These include (1) a news-making logic for which new advocacy stories are constantly being prepared alongside the constant monitoring of established and emergent news media outlets for breaking stories that require rapid responses; (2) an election campaign logic that sees personal stories as fundamental not only to mobilize one's base but also to win others over; and (3) a big data logic that puts faith in large databases and new technologies to provide effective solutions to complex problems. Together, these logics chart a new path for advocacy storytelling that rests increasingly on crowdsourced content and datafication to permanently mobilize personal narratives to influence public discourse, activate key publics, and secure policy goals. Importantly, this change has involved not only smaller and less-resourced organizations, which are typically associated with digital innovation, but also large and established ones, characterizing this as a sector-wide shift.

In contrast, over the past decade Australian progressives have perceived this lack of influence less systemically and urgently than their U.S. counterparts. This means that Australian innovation is currently concentrated in organizations and issues whose theory of change relies on a broad shift in public sentiment, whereas U.S. organizations are increasingly dedicating a significant part of their budgets to building storytelling systems that they see as central to their general approach to advocacy in the years to come. Indeed, there is clear evidence of the diffusion of storytelling techniques that originated in the United States to Australia through workshops, trainings, and consultancy work. Yet Australian progressive advocates have embraced personal storytelling more incrementally through normative diffusion from the work of scholar/activists such as Marshall Ganz who have argued in favor of the use of storytelling as a theory of change.

This has led to an approach to storytelling as a values-driven advocacy philosophy that applies to specific debates in which more traditional lobbying techniques and forms of evidence are unlikely to work. Personal stories have been used mainly in conjunction with campaigns dominated by emotional and ideological arguments where other forms of evidence, such as numbers and statistics, have found to be less persuasive. The Marriage Equality campaign is a good example of this trend and is discussed in detail in chapter 6 as an important case study in how progressive advocates can use digital storytelling to change public narrative and influence a vast public directly. Australian approaches to storytelling vary significantly between issues and organizations, however, with a general divide between larger and more institutionalized ones that show a tendency toward more traditional strategies (fact-based appeals directed to governmental elites through insider channels), and smaller or younger campaigns that tend to display greater openness to experimentation, such as using personal storytelling to shift a much broader public narrative. This uneven experience is also demonstrated in the chapter 7 case studies on how labor unions used storytelling in their campaign during the Covid-19 pandemic to elevate the cause of low-paid workers as essential workers. Australian unions obtained less public engagement on social media channels for the personal stories they shared then their U.S.-based counterparts, and subsequently relied heavily on charismatic leaders to propel their campaign storyline.

Taken together, these developments in advocacy storytelling raise two fundamental issues. First, there is the role that digital technologies play in these processes. Technologies are embedded in culture and far from neutral. As their centrality to how personal stories are collected, organized, curated, and deployed grows, so does their impact on how issues and groups are represented in the public arena. U.S. organizations in particular, including those with a stronger storytelling tradition, have shown considerable fascination with the big data mantra in ways that may inhibit reflexivity and a critical perspective on these practices, which is potentially problematic. Though not as frequently and systematically as in the United States, big data approaches to storytelling have emerged in recent issue-focused Australian campaigns, too, which makes investigating these issues even more important. Second, there is the issue of voice and representation. The emerging logics that drive advocacy storytelling in both countries are dominated by external inputs including, but not limited to, the need to respond to conservative governments' agendas; the need to appeal to external audiences through A/B testing and other digital engagement metrics; and the use of algorithm-based software to sort through massive collections of crowdsourced stories. This bears risks for the collective representation of lived experiences, interests, grievances, and identities, particularly for marginalized and minority groups, if editorial and curatorial practices are audience-driven rather than grassroots-driven. In this context, it is important to ask whether the advocacy stories that emerge from these processes reflect more the imagery and interests of the intended audiences or those of the groups on behalf of which advocacy organizations operate. Chapters 3 and 4 unpack each of these sets of issues and discuss them in detail.

CHAPTER 3

"Story Tech" and Datafication

> Savvy organizations are always collecting personal stories, even when issues have cooled. Many organizations create a Story Bank they can draw from later, when the issue surfaces again—and they almost always do.
>
> (Phone2Action's *Getting Started in Advocacy* guide, 2020)

This chapter shines a light onto what we call "story tech." That is, not the tools that make it possible to capture stories (e.g., cameras) but rather the ever-expanding technological systems that enable organizations to acquire, organize, select, and disseminate stories at scale, including the emergence of story banks. These technologies are almost always hidden from public view but have a deep impact on advocacy storytelling. In doing so, this chapter unpacks the evolution of the "big data" logic introduced in chapter 2 and considers its interaction with the other two logics behind the storytelling turn in digital grassroots advocacy: the news-making logic and the election campaign logic. Digital storytelling research has tended to focus more on content, representation, and identity than on the processes, technological infrastructure, and organizational cultures behind it. This chapter flips this paradigm, and in doing so it responds to a plea for "qualitative studies with organizations that are making or have made DPEN [Digital Personal Experience Narrative] collections in order to better understand practitioner aims and the social and technological obstacles to achieving those aims" (Dush 2017, 213–14).

To generate a complete picture of this phenomenon, we employed a combination of methods in line with the general approach we took in this book. First, we interviewed nearly three dozen specialists including story bank managers at national advocacy organizations, engineers and executives at major software firms, and nonprofit technology consultants (details can be found in the appendix). Second, we reviewed the story banking manuals and other training materials (Bonacini 2015; Center for American Progress 2019; Center for Social Impact Communication and Meyer Foundation 2016; Community Catalyst 2017; Girardin 2016; Spitfire Strategies n.d.; The Arc 2017) developed by organizations that pioneered and championed new techniques in this area in recent years (more information about each of these materials can be found in the appendix). Finally, we developed in-depth case studies of two cutting-edge and influential tools: the "StoryBank" application for Salesforce developed by the Center for American Progress, and Gather Voices, a for-profit platform that provides a "one stop shop" for collecting, storing, editing, and publishing video stories. Through this work, we illuminate the technological infrastructures and "datastructures" that increasingly shape fundamental aspects of contemporary advocacy storytelling. We map the technologies that are central to these processes, consider their affordances, and highlight the strategic rationale behind progressive advocacy organizations' technological choices. In doing so, we also foreground the experiences and perspectives of organizers responsible for building and maintaining massive advocacy story collections and other key stakeholders including technology companies and strategic communication consultants.

Overall, this outlines sociotechnical systems where algorithms and automation govern key junctures in advocacy storytelling processes. Personal stories—particularly in the United States—are increasingly treated as data by advocacy organizations that campaign for progressive social change. Here, we discuss the important strategic benefits that these systems have for these organizations and, at the same time, we offer a critique of their potential democratic and participatory drawbacks. While this chapter focuses closely on the organizational perspective, the next one completes this landscape by illuminating the opportunities and limitations of different technological affordances for individual storytellers and their communities, particularly those that are traditionally underrepresented and marginalized.

3.1 The Crowd Will Fix It!

As was discussed in chapter 2, advocacy organizations tend to view very large story collections as especially valuable. This trend has been particularly pronounced in the United States, but prominent examples have emerged in Australia, too, though less frequently and systematically. Big volumes of story "kernels" are often equated with bigger chances of finding more persuasive narratives by querying digital archives. Crowdsourcing stories through open calls on social media and other channels dramatically expands the range of potential storytellers compared to the traditional method of asking known members or supporters of the organization for story ideas. While the uneven volunteer nature of crowdsourced stories makes talking about a democratization or diversification of advocacy storytelling premature, this method takes advantage of personalization and individualization trends in politics.

Following the personalization of election campaigns (Langer 2011; Stanyer 2013), citizen political participation has become increasingly associated with personalized frameworks too. As was noted in chapter 1, digital media have accentuated this trend, enabling entire movements from Occupy to #MeToo to be built on what Bennett and Segerberg (2013) have called "personalized action frames" that are flexible and can easily be attached to direct experiences. This has created a path to participation that is more accessible to people who are unfamiliar with and possibly uninterested in traditional politics. Today, people are attuned to personal stories in politics. At the same time, sharing individual lived experience does not require specific political knowledge and the threshold for entry is set very low due to facilitation by interactive digital platforms. In light of this, crowdsourcing offers distinct opportunities to advocacy organizations committed to strengthening and expanding the use of personal stories in their work. Yet crowdsourcing also presents immediate challenges due to the high volume of content generated by it, and the resources required to properly review, organize, and manage mass stories effectively.

Many of the organizers we interviewed said that, ideally, they would like to be able to read each story idea submitted to them to grasp the complexity and nuances of personal narratives. This is how pioneers of story-centered advocacy with dedicated staff such as Families USA operated for quite some time. However, the growing number of potential storytellers, coupled with the heightened political climate and increased propensity to share personal information on social media, has made this practice increasingly impracticable and unrealistic. This is especially the case for volunteer-run or chronically understaffed organizations, as well as new advocacy organizations that are starting to build a strategic profile. For example, a representative from Parents Together—a U.S. youth and children's rights organization—explained that, when they first started to collect personal stories, they "had like eight or nine people on the [entire] organization" staff so, they continued, "if we put out a big call for stories, like we might get 400 [submissions] back, and going through those [. . .] could be really challenging [. . .] because we're a really small team" (Interviewee, Parents Together, February 2022).

This tension between the opportunities and challenges of crowdsourcing has acted as a strong incentive to lean on an increasingly broad range of digital technologies to facilitate these processes. Thus advocacy organizations have sought to systematize story collection, archiving, development, and dissemination. At the same time, companies that sell digital advocacy tools have helped popularize the narrative that storytelling technologies can greatly simplify these processes, saving organizations both time and money, through their marketing. For example, Speak4—a Washington, D.C.-based company that sells a suite of "easy to use" digital advocacy tools—uses "Advocacy. Done." as its main slogan. Taken together, these trends have cemented the centrality of digital technologies such as online submission forms and databases in advocacy storytelling. Collectively, this can be described as "story tech." That is, a combination of digital tools and technological practices that develop organically from within the advocacy space and in each organization, following the example of others but at the same time also adapting new techniques to their own circumstances.

A crucial trend that has emerged in this area and was first introduced in chapter 2 is the creation of so-called digital story banks, particularly among U.S. advocacy organizations. Although there is some controversy around this term, as is discussed below, it usefully summarizes an increasingly popular set of story collection, development, and dissemination practices that rests primarily on crowdsourced user-generated content. Here, a central concern is with the datafication of stories. That is, as was defined in the introduction to this book, the extent to which stories are turned into data by "putting phenomena in a quantified form so that it can be tabulated and analyzed" (Mayer-Schönberger and Cukier 2013, 77). Crucially, this squeezes communication specialists "who are trained to be conscious of the impact of their work on society" (Holtzhausen 2016, 23) out of these processes to the advantage of algorithms designed by technology companies that are often far removed from the people represented by advocacy organizations. The rest of this chapter unpacks these trends and discusses their implications.

3.2 The Rise of Digital Story Banks

"Find the perfect story" (StoryBank App's video presentation, 2014).

In a recent article, we defined digital story banking as

the systematic and ongoing large-scale collection, digital archiving, and cataloging of personal stories for future development and incorporation in advocacy initiatives. (Trevisan et al. 2020, 150)

This definition still captures the essence of this practice. If anything, crowdsourcing and digital technologies appear to have become even more central to story banking since we wrote those words. As we mentioned in the previous chapter, the term "story bank" is commonly understood and widely used in U.S. advocacy circles, while Australian organizers are generally not familiar with it. Overall, "story bank" is somewhat of a controversial term and tends to generate strong, sometime contrasting reactions among grassroots advocates.

For example, many Australian organizers reacted negatively to this term in a convening we facilitated in Melbourne in 2019 to discuss advancements in digital storytelling with leading digital organizers. Story bank, they said, seemed to cheapen story-centered advocacy work. However, others had the opposite reaction upon hearing this term for the first time. Activists at an international conference on digital storytelling where we presented preliminary insights from this book in 2021 were positively impressed by story bank. For instance, representatives from a U.K.-based patient advocacy organization commented that it aligned with a widespread discourse in advocacy circles about making an emotional "investment" in storytelling that will ultimately generate new social and political capital. At the same time, some American advocacy specialists with several years of experience in story banking have developed a more critical outlook on this terminology. As one of them explained to us in an interview, they have come to consider the term "'bank' controversial because of that transaction, monetized, just everything that comes with it. And people will say to me, 'Can I make a withdrawal?' It's like no, it's not [well-known U.S. bank] Wells Fargo" (Interviewee, Families USA, June 2018).

While the debate over terminology is ongoing, the popularity of story banking practices has grown significantly in recent years. Indeed, these are especially widespread and developed in the United States. That said, organizers in other countries too—including Australia—have incorporated key elements of this strategy in some notable recent campaigns, including those examined in this book's case study chapters, while not necessarily using the term or contributing to the institutionalization of these practices in the long term. This warrants an in-depth examination of the new and potentially disruptive roles that digital technologies take in advocacy storytelling centered on story banks.

It is important to note at this point that digital story banks—like persuasive storytelling more generally—are not exclusive to advocacy organizations that campaign for progressive social change, nor they are limited to advocacy organizations more broadly. U.S. conservative organizations such as the Heritage Foundation, the Job Creators Network, and Americans for Prosperity have long engaged in story banking, too, arguably to boost their "grassroots" credentials and counter their reputation as astroturfing bodies. Beyond advocacy organizations, U.S. businesses such as banks and pharmaceutical companies have also used story banks to improve their reputation among consumers and project a sense of community around their products. This undoubtedly expands the market for digital technologies associated with story banking. However, there is not a single community of practice in this area. Rather, organizers, consultants, programmers, and other specialists with story banking skills seem to gravitate toward either the progressive or the conservative camp. This is understandable, given the political nature of this work, but it also limits know-how sharing and influences the development of story banking.

3.2.1 Story Banks Diffusion and Foundational Elements

Given this broad landscape, we first sought to map which organizations in the U.S. progressive advocacy space use digital story banks and what, if anything, may act as a common denominator in their experience with this technique. As Dush (2017, 194) noted, much crowdsourced storytelling work goes on behind the scenes, which makes it difficult to capture this phenomenon comprehensively. While we initially encountered important story banks almost by accident and were alerted to more examples by colleagues and advocacy professionals in our networks, we also wanted a more systematic way to generate a useful overview of this phenomenon. To do this, we employed two complementary strategies.

First, we checked the websites and social media channels of America's top national progressive advocacy organizations as aggregated by nonprofit assessment organizations such as Charity Navigator and START (Study, Think, Act, Respond Together) for evidence of story banking, looking mainly for story submission opportunities. Second, to expand this map beyond a large but nevertheless not fully comprehensive set of organizations, we also searched LinkedIn—the largest professional social networking platform in the United States—for profiles that listed "story bank(ing)" or "storybank(ing)" in their recent work experience. Previous work has shown

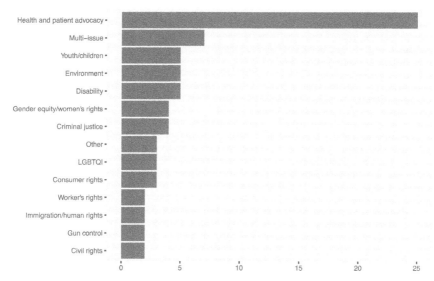

Fig. 3.1. Focus of U.S. progressive story banking organizations

that LinkedIn provides a very robust record of professionals working at the intersection of politics and technology (Campagnolo et al. 2017; Kreiss and Jasinski 2016). Therefore this search generated a useful proxy measure of the diffusion of digital story banks in the U.S. progressive advocacy space.

After filtering out results from businesses and other nonadvocacy focused organizations, we found seventy-nine major national U.S. progressive organizations that actively maintained digital story banks as of the end of 2021, with ten of these maintaining two or more banks. About a third of these story banking organizations (n=25) focused on health and patient advocacy (fig. 3.1). This was expected given the role of health-focused organizations as one of the main "cradles" of progressive story-centered advocacy in the United States, as was discussed in the previous chapter. That said, the other organizations were spread across a broad range of different areas, from environmental issues to criminal justice. This signals that digital story banking has taken roots across a diverse set of advocacy areas. In particular, it was interesting to note the presence of several very large and influential multi-issue organizations among those engaged in story banking, such as the Center for American Progress and People for the American Way (a detailed list of U.S. story banking organizations in each sector is included in the appendix).

Behind the diffusion of digital story banks—our interviewees explained— was a sense of urgency and excitement among U.S. advocacy leaders based on the perceived opportunities of story crowdsourcing, which in turn were precipitated by the "shock" result of the 2016 presidential election. In the wake of this crisis, budgets were adjusted to allocate internal resources specifically for story banks. However, these new priorities were also underpinned by challenging expectations from advocacy leaders, which often were either unrealistic or excessively vague. For example, one story bank specialist with experience at several organizations said:

> leadership often wants [. . .] the stories but they don't know what they want to do with them [. . .] people that like, "we can send the [story collection] survey to our 400 members in this one [congressional] district, but we're probably not going to get any responses." And people [in a position of leadership] will be like, "Okay, well, just send it anyways." (Interviewee, Parents Together, February 2022)

Historically, advocacy leaders have often embraced new digital techniques with overblown expectations and limited planning (Taylor and Burt 2005). Under these circumstances, many story bank specialists have worked to dispel the myth of these systems as "silver bullets" and offer more pragmatic approaches. Drawing on their experience, these organizers have sought to establish a culture that values digital story banks as important opportunities but also encourages organizations to look critically at these systems and review them periodically both for effectiveness and for their sociopolitical implications. This also means countering a simplistic narrative supported not only by a general fascination with computational techniques and the "big data" logic in advocacy circles but also by technology startups and larger digital services companies that see story banks as a business opportunity and frame crowdsourcing as an "easy fix" that facilitates the identification of "perfect stories."

Given the broad range of advocacy organizations involved in terms of focus, size, funding, and structure, there is naturally some variation in how digital story banks are implemented by each organization. That said, in previous work (Trevisan et al. 2020) we identified five key principles of story banking that serve as common denominators across the entire field. In general, digital advocacy story banks are:

1. Never "complete": stories are constantly collected to ensure the organization is always ready to step into in the political information cycle;
2. Oriented toward political persuasion goals, rather than toward fundraising or mere awareness-raising goals;

3. Crowdsourced and open to anyone who wishes to share their story, not just organization members, volunteers, or other traditional stakeholders;
4. Reliant on digital media for story collection, archiving, and selection; and
5. Primarily intended as internal resources (although a small number of organizations have also opened their digital story collections to the public for browsing, as the next chapter explains).

Considering these five common factors, it is useful to reflect closely on how the role of digital technologies in story banking has changed and expanded over time. In addition, it is also important to consider the different actors behind these processes and the broader cultural and political trends capable of influencing them.

3.2.2 From Crowdsourcing to Story Banks

Story crowdsourcing for advocacy purposes first started in the United States in the early 2000s, before interactive Internet platforms became available. Thus, the first technology that supported story collection for advocacy purposes on a large scale was the telephone. Typically, this would involve a specialized agency fielding several hundreds or thousands of phone calls to potential storytellers on behalf of a client organization, recording their first-person accounts, and collating this information in ways that facilitated story selection and further development by the client. Perhaps the most notable example of this type of operation is the "Voice Capture" service offered by the Washington, D.C.-based agency Stones Phones, which was founded in 2000 and continued to operate at the time of publication. "Voice Capture" involves calling a list of individuals likely to be affected by a certain issue and recording their stories in an audio format that may be posted on social media and integrated into websites, radio ads, podcasts, and other distribution channels.

Although this is a somewhat rudimentary "story tech" system, it presents some distinctive traits that served as important stepping stones toward the first digital story banking initiatives. First, story crowdsourcing was delegated to a specialized outside agency. This was the norm until recently, when organizations decided to invest some of their core resources and develop these skills in house, as was discussed in chapter 2. Second, it was associated with a specific issue or event, which was a function of multiple factors. In general, story crowdsourcing predicated on highly salient issues that spur a sense of urgency and encourage people to share their experiences tends to yield plentiful submissions, giving organizations more content to choose from. While interviewees in both countries talked about the natural ebb and flow of story collection, this was especially relevant in Australia, where crowdsourcing practices have not become as institutionalized as much as in the United States. Furthermore, the event- or issue-focus is also often associated with external circumstances and opportunities. This was the case for many of the first story crowdsourcing initiatives funded through the philanthropic grants mentioned in the previous chapter, and many other occasions where organizations used this technique to respond to events promoted by others. For example, the Center for American Progress's very first foray into story banking in 2014 was linked to an Obama administration's event called the White House Summit on Working Families.

Over the course of several years, story banks have emerged as an evolution of these initial story crowdsourcing practices. In addition to the circumstances outlined in chapter 2, most notably crisis and changes in information and media systems, the diffusion of story banks has been supported specifically by three sets of actors, including (1) story bank pioneers, champions, and educators; (2) other story bank staff; and (3) for-profit stakeholders including technology companies and advocacy consultancies. As some of our interviewees noted, large and influential story bank adopters such as AARP and the Center for American Progress have promoted this technique through informal advocacy networks. Many of these efforts have been directed at smaller organizations active in salient policy areas but that lack the personnel and financial resources to set up digital story bank operations from scratch. For example, one interviewee from an environmental organization said that the Center for American Progress offered to set up a story bank system on their behalf saying, "We will give you the tools. We will embed it in your website. We will help you create the platform. We will do all the work for you" (Interviewee, Defenders of Wildlife, December 2018). More recently, story banks have also entered the mainstream of U.S. sector-wide conferences. For example, the 2021 edition of Netroots Nation—North America's premier professional conference for digital organizers—included a dedicated training session on using survey platforms for story crowdsourcing. Similarly, story banks were also highlighted at the 2022 Nonprofit Technology Conference, another major gathering in this sector.

These trends have also been reinforced by personnel changes in advocacy organizations, especially after the 2017 handover between the Obama and Trump administrations. As one interviewee explained, there were "a lot of people coming out of the Obama administration and campaigns where they're being told the power of story, the power of story, the power of story" (Interviewee, Families USA, June 2018) who joined progressive advocacy organizations where they brought with them that experience. More recently, there is also evidence of story banking diffusion from progressive advocacy organizations back to government in the Biden administration. For example, the founding director of the Center for American Progress's story bank was hired by the office of the U.S. Surgeon General in December 2021 to establish a similar initiative. At the same time, the same organization also featured "Share Your Story" as a key "action" on its advocacy website, continued to hire new story bank associates, and included a dedicated "Stories" team of four staff as of early 2024, suggesting that this tactic was not just a "fad" of the Trump years.

Finally, the expansion of digital story banks has also supported the growth of commercial actors that see this trend as a business opportunity. This includes both established players in this field—for example, the global software firm Salesforce and large advocacy consultancies such as Every-Action and Capitol Canary, formerly called Phone2Action—and smaller startup organizations like Gather Voices, which is discussed in detail later in this chapter. In their sales pitches to advocacy clients, these companies highlight opportunities to use their products—primarily Constituent Relationship Management (CRM) packages—to collect and organize personal stories. In addition, some of them have also embedded specialists in some of the larger advocacy organizations who liaise directly with story bank staff.

Taken together, these trends signal considerable interest in story banking among U.S. progressive advocates, suggesting that further diffusion of this "story tech" is possible in the future. One important caveat that organizers regularly pointed out in interviews is that digital story crowdsourcing is most useful for organizations that can reach very large numbers of potential storytellers online while lacking the type of strong ground organizing that has historically facilitated story collection. This emerged in conversations with both U.S. and Australian organizers. For example, one U.S. interviewee specialized in designing story collection forms said that crowdsourcing personal narratives is "like messaging 100,000 people to get 20 strong spokespeople. So [. . .] if you have a big list that you're trying and you're trying to find those needles in the haystack, then this is like a good strategy" (Interviewee, Parents Together, February 2022). Similarly, an Australian storytelling consultant told us that "all of this is about scale. You need to really build your list up, and then kind of get them to do these [story sharing] actions, because [. . .] it is an action that requires a lot of effort" (Interviewee, Principle Co.,

2018). Overall, this aligns digital story banks with analytic activism tactics such as online petitions and A/B testing, which are best suited to organizations with very large networks and contact lists (Karpf 2016). Inevitably, these dynamics also have relevance for how organizations approach technology, which is useful to discuss in detail.

3.3.3 The "Technology Arc" of Story Crowdsourcing

"Graduating" from issue- or campaign-specific story crowdsourcing initiatives to a permanent story bank requires a qualitative shift from short- to long-term planning and investments. As one Australian organizer explained, a "story bank sort of implies something that's useful for everything, they [organizers] can draw it out in the future" (Interview, Cancer Council, 2018). Typically, this transition occurs organically, without predetermined plans and prepackaged solutions, and organizations try to deal with the new needs involved in this process as they arise. This has important implications for "story tech," which in permanent story banking ought to support an expanded set of requirements related to timing and focus (from short- to long-term use, and from single-issue campaigns to multiple initiatives on different issues), volume (from a defined collection to a constantly expanding and potentially limitless one), and personnel (from outside contractors to in-house specialized staff who change over time).

As story banks grow, these tensions manifest themselves through the need to track story submissions, identify the most useful story ideas, and contact potential storytellers over time, which become primary drivers of technological choices. For example, an organizer from Everytown for Gun Safety—one of the largest U.S. organizations advocating for gun control measures—explained that their story bank

> was born out of necessity [. . .] more people were becoming interested [in telling their stories] and our reach was growing, and so [. . .] went from like a Google Doc or something that the "survivors' team" just listed everything in, [. . . to] using an actual database. (Interviewee, Everytown for Gun Safety, July 2018)

As was mentioned before, our research showed that some elements of story banks vary across organizations depending on their exact needs and on the populations they serve. This is true for both the frontend (storyteller-facing) portion of these systems, which is discussed in detail in the next chapter, and for their backend (organization-facing), which is examined here. Nevertheless, despite these differences, it was possible to trace a typical "technology arc" that organizations generally follow in their transition toward story banking.

At one end of this arc there are inexpensive everyday tools for record-keeping such as Excel sheets (with SharePoint for collaboration) and Google Sheets. These have the advantage of being readily available to organizations and familiar to staff. However, they present obvious limitations as soon as a given collection grows beyond a few dozen stories and have the distinctive disadvantage of being unable to store visual content. At the other end of the arc, there are specialized database software packages that require specific investments but can handle very large amounts of data—including visual content—and can be integrated with other systems used by advocacy organizations such as CRM software and social media management platforms. All the story banking organizations we examined in this project started off at one end of this arc and eventually moved to the other, sometimes quite quickly. By way of example, some of these technological "journeys" are outlined in table 3.1.

Without exception, interviewees told us that purchasing new software or investing in expanded capabilities and customized tools for existing databases are always careful decisions. Given the type of resources involved relative to the average organization's budget, they require story bank staff to advocate with organization leaders. Nevertheless, every interviewee also felt that these were necessary investments to set up a functioning story bank because they enabled them not only to work more effectively but also to streamline story collection and create a centralized resource that would benefit the entire organization. AARP serves as a useful illustrative example here. As is typical for campaign- or issue-specific story crowdsourcing, AARP's first few story collection efforts used multiple submission paths that fed into separate Excel documents. Then when they launched a unified Stories Program in 2010, AARP organizers "spent time tracking down all of these various entry points [. . .] that were not being officially run and realize, oh, if you are collecting a story, you need to be coming through us" (Interviewee, AARP, June 2018). This suggests that the technological development of story crowdsourcing and its centralization proceed in lockstep and support each other.

Despite the differences that characterize each organization, those committed to story banking for the long term eventually tend to settle on a solution whereby digital content collection and archive management are as integrated as possible with their other digital systems. Some of the most resourceful organizations such as the Center for American Progress have

Table 3.1. Technological journeys of story banking organizations

Story banking organizations	Starting tech	Final tech
AARP	Excel	DDC Database
AFSCME Union	Excel/Sharepoint	Countable
Center for American Progress	Excel	Salesforce CRM
Defenders of Wildlife	Excel/Sharepoint	DAM (Digital Assets Manager)
EarthJustice	Excel	BaseCamp (database); Portfolio (visual content)
Everytown for Gun Safety	Google sheet	Salesforce CRM
Little Lobbyists	Email	Wufoo (Survey Monkey)
Parents Together	Google sheet	Survey Monkey

even been able to customize this technological infrastructure creating new dedicated database tools, as is discussed later in this chapter. In turn, this also presents a business opportunity for startup companies and others that want to develop "one-stop shop" tools that seek to integrate the various processes where technology performs essential roles including story collection, archiving, organizing, retrieval, prioritization, development, and dissemination. Given this general trend, the next useful step is to ask which are the key priorities of organizers committed to digital story banking and story crowdsourcing more broadly, and which are the technological solutions they have adopted to address them.

3.3 Story Tech Priorities

In this context, two main sets of story tech priorities emerged from interviews, which were also corroborated by the review of story banking manuals. The first set of priorities relates to information organization, retrieval, and matching. The second set relates to the types of content that are most valuable in today's information and media environment. Each of these has a significant impact on how specific stories ultimately emerge from vast digital collections and are incorporated in advocacy initiatives, as is discussed in detail below.

3.3.1 Filtering and Search

Organizing story collections in ways that make them usable was the top concern for every organization we spoke with. Advocacy organizations generally recognize this very quickly as the volume of crowdsourced stories increases and it becomes impossible to have a clear overview of the entire collection just by glancing at the different entries in a spreadsheet. This constitutes one of the primary drivers of story tech architecture across the entire advocacy sector. Organizations try to address this need through two main strategies, which are different but not necessarily alternative. The common denominator between these approaches is their reliance on digital technology to separate more "useful" personal stories from those that are less so in these burgeoning collections.

The first strategy tries to resolve this issue at the root by using highly structured submission forms that help filter out or set aside less relevant content from the outset. This in turn results in smaller story archives that organizations consider to be of "higher quality." Typically, this is operationalized using online submission forms structured as surveys with "screener" questions. If a story submitter chooses an answer deemed less relevant or important in one of these questions, these systems do not necessarily skip to the end. Rather they enable organizations to "presort" submissions according to their priorities and focus on those expected to be more useful. Among the organizations we interviewed, Parents Together and Little Lobbyists championed this strategy and used Survey Monkey-based software to design their collection forms. One of their representatives explained that "you really have to know what you're going to want your outputs to be before you write your [story collection] questions" (Interviewee, Parents Together, February 2022). "Screener" questions can focus on story content, as well as on personal and demographic information such as age, race, gender, location, and so on, as is discussed in more detail in the next chapter.

This approach is especially important for smaller, volunteer-run organizations that hesitate to invest in database technology that for them is relatively expensive and may require a steep learning curve without a guarantee of success. A conference session at Netroots Nation 2021 focused on this very approach and attracted attendees from over one hundred organizations. On the one hand, this certainly makes a story archive more manageable for smaller organizations. Another potential benefit of this approach is that it can help organizations more deliberately identify and prioritize stories from traditionally underrepresented people. On the other hand, however, there is also a legitimate question about whether a story collection system designed to automatically flag and prioritize certain kinds of content or storytellers—or both—in effect interferes with the crowdsourced nature of the resulting narratives. This clashes with the broader "big data" logic that underpins story banks and may mitigate one of the main benefits of online story collection over more traditional scouting methods.

The second strategy uses less structured submission forms, giving storytellers more freedom, and relies primarily on sorting algorithms to organize story archives after content has been collected. As organizations have invested more of their own resources in story banks, this has become a popular approach. This is corroborated by the fact that most "share your story" forms require the submission of only very limited—if any—personal information, as is discussed in detail in the next chapter. Here, tagging and search functionalities—not filters set a priori—constitute the technological linchpins of story banks. This makes these functions central to software selection and other technology decisions. Database packages that do not allow tagging are considered unfit for purpose and need to be customized or swapped for different platforms. For example, one interviewee said that any "standard off-the-shelf CRM tool is not built for story collecting purposes [. . .] to do any sort of tagging" (Interviewee, AARP, June 2018). This, they continued, led them to creating a workaround while looking for a more efficient and sustainable solution.

Tags that enable organizations to quickly identify stories according to one or more defining features are generated both deductively and inductively. Deductive tags are typically based on organizers' expectations, tend to focus on somewhat predictable and factual information such as demographics (age, gender, race, etc.), topics, location (e.g., state or congressional district), and are usually identified through keyword searches. In contrast, inductive tags are based on features that emerge organically from crowdsourced content. For example, one popular inductive tag mentioned in interviews is "story type." This, however, can mean different things depending on the organization, ranging from Marshall Ganz's (2011) "public narrative" typology (story of self, story of us, and story of now) to others based on outcomes (e.g., "success" stories). Traditionally, tagging story submissions inductively involved reading every story submission. However, this function is now performed increasingly often through automated methods such as word frequency searches and, more recently, artificial intelligence (AI) tools, as is discussed in detail below. This is considered such an efficient method that some organizations that collect primarily visual stories prioritize the creation of "searchable transcripts of the actual storylines" (Interviewee, Defenders of Wildlife, December 2018) to facilitate inductive tagging and speed up story retrieval. Taken together, we can call these search and filtering practices "algorithmic shortlisting." This technique is widespread among story banking organizations and deserves close consideration.

3.3.2 Algorithmic Shortlisting

With digital story banks, even though organizers determine deductive story tags and ultimately select the stories that will be developed and disseminated through advocacy initiatives, database algorithms are trusted to populate the shortlists that organizers inevitably choose from. A typical advocacy story bank includes several thousand entries. Yet information archiving and retrieval software fundamentally determines which of these stand a concrete chance of being included in advocacy campaigns. This is both a necessity dictated by the practical impossibility of sorting through extremely large amounts of crowdsourced content manually and a practice fully aligned with the "big data" logic discussed in the previous chapter, as well as the ethos of crowdsourcing outlined above. There is a basic assumption here that very large amounts of content drawn from a broad range of people beyond organization members and supporters, and sorted automatically, will generate "better" and more effective advocacy narratives. This has some important advantages, but it also raises potential concerns that ought to be highlighted.

One of the main advantages of algorithmic shortlisting, which was mentioned by multiple interviewees, is speed. This is essential to intervene in timely and effective ways in today's fast-paced political information cycle (Chadwick 2017), whereas "if every single time [one needs a personal story] you're going back to someone saying 'remind me again about all of this back story,' [it] just takes time" (Interviewee, Defenders of Wildlife, December 2018). A second and somewhat less obvious—but no less important—advantage of large searchable databases and algorithmic shortlisting is that they facilitate an intersectional approach to using stories in advocacy work. Given the consolidation of multiple collection streams into centralized story archives, "one person generally isn't just relegated to one topic, unless that's the only thing that they want to talk about" (Interviewee A, Center for American Progress, June 2018). For example, stories "that can come in on a women's team collection platform may end up being best used for a climate story, [. . .] you'll get different coalitions buying into something that maybe they probably wouldn't have done on their own" (Interviewee A, Center for American Progress, June 2018). This suggests a new way of seeding storytelling throughout multiple advocacy areas that is both intrinsic to and dependent on database technology. Here, intersectionality takes on not only a social but also a strategic value that supports an arguably more effective way of doing progressive advocacy.

Conversely, an important concern associated with the growing automation of information organization and story shortlisting relates to a potential overreliance on algorithms into which advocacy organizations themselves have little, if any, input and that learn from and reproduce previous searches and selections. This opens the door to the creation of story "hierarchies" informed by both known preferences (e.g., for submissions that include photographic or video content) and unconscious biases toward certain kinds of stories or storytellers. The biggest risk here is that search algorithms will tend to privilege results similar to those selected in the past and may therefore hinder the emergence of new and disruptive but also potentially attention-grabbing and persuasive stories. In addition, algorithms are also informed by digital metrics and can privilege stories that are likely to elicit more clicks, shares, and engagement because they resonate with median audience members, which can exclude traditionally marginalized voices as is discussed in the case study chapters, particularly chapter 6.

Finally, another limitation is that, by and large, our interviews evidenced story tagging and search as primarily reactive. The location of the Center for American Progress's story bank in its "war room," which was discussed in the previous chapter, is a good example of this reactive setup. One could argue that this is a function of the fact that U.S. progressive organizations were in the opposition during the Trump administration years, when many of their story banks were established. Yet this was corroborated also by a tendency to tag and search stories—as evidenced in interviews—according to demographics, issues, and other factual aspects, instead of their possible association with values or emotions, which would orient them toward more proactive and long-term uses. In particular, the lack of shared moral values as organizing principles clashes with best practices in persuasive storytelling (Matthews et al. 2017). This echoes and simultaneously reinforces a difficulty that the U.S. political left has had for some time to connect its campaigns to overarching "alpha stories" capable of supporting long-term social change (Ricci 2016), as was discussed in chapter 1.

3.3.3 Sustainable and Interoperable Story Tech

Organizations that have transitioned from one-off story initiatives to story banking have sought to design story tech that would last over time and capable of integration with the systems used by its different departments, from political campaigns to member relations. Interviewees talked extensively about their efforts to "future proof" story bank systems. This reflects the permanent nature of advocacy storytelling and involves a combination of three factors, including sustainable technology choices, institutional practices and culture change, and access to specialized expertise, when needed.

The affordability and value for money of story database software packages and storage space emerged as common concerns across the sector. Crowdsourced story content can take up very large amounts of space—especially when video is included—and for this reason tends to be housed on external servers. For a fee, most of the companies that provide story collection and management software such as Countable, Gather Voices, and Salesforce also offer to store the content on behalf of their advocacy clients. This is a convenient option, but one that requires careful financial considerations, particularly for smaller organizations. In addition, this system also exposes advocacy organizations to the risk of losing access to their story archives should they no longer wish to renew or be able to afford these subscriptions, or should a service provider run into financial problems that make it difficult for it to continue to operate. For these reasons, most organizations also maintain copies of the most important content on their own servers. However, these are usually limited backups as not everything can be saved internally and, just as important, they do not include the same functionalities in terms of search and interoperability with other packages.

More broadly, concerns with the sustainability and interoperability of story collection and storage systems were also informed by the awareness that moving the needle on some key issues can take multiple years, if not longer. Although interviewees talked about this truly long-term use of story banks quite rarely compared to the reaction-driven uses mentioned above, it reinforced the permanent nature of this tactic and hinted at the possibility of more proactive uses in the future. A typical example are campaigns on environmental issues, which can easily span several years. For example, one organizer spoke about "fracking [. . .] going to go on for decades, if not more. So [. . .] those stories and the way they inspire people, you can still resuscitate that and bring it up again in future fights" (Interviewee, Earth Justice, October 2018). Related to this is the determination to build a shared culture and shared practices to support story bank technological systems. This is especially important given that story banking staff tends to turn over quite frequently because this work can be emotionally and psychologically taxing, and those who do it typically commit to it only for a couple of years or less (Trevisan et al. 2020). The aim here is to provide "an opportunity for the next person to take over and still roll with that particular project" (Interviewee, Earth Justice, October 2018) by creating

> a system that anyone can walk in and say, "If I'm logging XYZ this is how I log it in." And everyone does it the same way [. . .] not just communications or marketing [people] but anyone [. . .] and then it

would just become second nature. (Interviewee, Defenders of Wildlife, December 2018)

Different organizations were at different stages in this process and acknowledged that its success depended not only on the implementation of clear guidelines but also on internal cultural changes that take time. Australian organizations, given their tendency to focus on campaign-specific story crowdsourcing rather than investing in ongoing story banks, were relatively unconcerned about this, while their U.S. counterparts regularly reflected on it as part of their next steps toward more prominent and better integrated advocacy storytelling. Those furthest along in this process had begun to integrate both their systems and people in a new structure simultaneously connected to the entire organization. Perhaps the best example of this is the "StoryBank" application for Salesforce developed by the Center for American Progress.

3.3.4 The "Storybank" App for Salesforce

The Center for American Progress (CAP), through its advocacy arm called the CAP Action Fund, first invested in technology to crowdsource stories in 2014. This preceded and, in many ways, facilitated the creation of the single centralized story bank that this organization established shortly after the 2016 U.S. presidential election, when it hired multiple staff specifically to manage this operation. Since 2014, the cornerstone of CAP's story tech has been an application called "StoryBank," which was built in-house as a Salesforce extension. Immediately, this represented an example of innovation and advanced system integration in this area. At least three factors contributed to this, including the determination of CAP's leadership to invest in this area, technology specialists embedded within the organization with experience in customizing and expanding CRM platforms, and external events (e.g., the 2014 White House Summit on Working Families) that generated momentum behind these opportunities. We sought to acquire a rounded perspective on this system by interviewing those who designed it, staff members who used it, other organizations to which CAP presented it, and relevant individuals at Salesforce, the technology platform on which it is based. In light of this, we offer some critical considerations on a system that has inspired the story tech choices of other organizations going forward.

CAP's "StoryBank" application provides Salesforce users with a "one-stop shop" solution for collecting, managing, and publishing crowdsourced stories.[1] More recently, advocacy consultancies such as EveryAction have developed similar tools. Yet when it was launched, CAP's application was unique because it brought together, for the first time, the frontend and backend of story-centered digital advocacy in one tool. In other words, it provided an integrated solution for building and publishing story collection interfaces, managing story collections, liaising with storytellers, and publishing stories on websites and other platforms. This enabled CAP to streamline most of these processes, which thus far were admittedly scattered "all over the place [. . .] and not all that helpful, like [. . .] asking [people] to submit their stories over email, or, you know, people being reached out to over the phone" (Interviewee B, CAP, February 2022).

The app was an internally driven project stemming from a campaigns team's request to "leverage CAP's Salesforce environment [. . .] for everything [related to personal stories] from start to finish" (Interviewee B, CAP, February 2022). The "StoryBank" app was not built to be officially endorsed by Salesforce. However, a company executive confirmed in a conversation with us that they looked favorably at this tool and believed it signaled a need for "information acquisition tools" (Interview, Salesforce executive, June 2019) that led them to pursue "market research, including considering AI [artificial intelligence] capabilities" in this area. Throughout all of this, CAP made its "StoryBank" app freely available to other Salesforce users, promoted it at tech sector events such as the company's "Dreamforce" annual conference, and presented it directly to other advocacy organizations in Washington, D.C.

The level of integration offered by CAP's "StoryBank" app and its reliance on existing technological infrastructure that is already familiar to staff has some important advantages. First, it facilitates institutional memory, which in turn makes it more resilient in case of personnel changes. Second, it is also likely to be a cheaper solution than subscribing to an entirely new service. Third, and perhaps most important, being developed by specialists embedded with the organization, it has the potential to be more sensitive to its culture and needs, and to the circumstances of the storytellers it hopes to attract compared to digital tools purchased "off the shelf."

An example of this is the importance attributed to information security in the development of CAP's tool. Given the sensitive nature of personal story submissions, "a very big part of building this [system] out was that only those that needed to know could actually see these records" (Interviewee B, CAP, February 2022). In light of this, our interviewee continued, Salesforce has a competitive advantage because, "as a platform, [it] is designed to support this kind of use where you want to have a subset of information, isolate it from a large contingent of Salesforce users" (Interviewee B, CAP, February 2022), which would be more difficult or impossible with other software like Access databases or Excel spreadsheets.

CAP's integrated story bank solution not only offers a robust keyword search function aligned with the technological priorities outlined above but also has additional analytical features including summary reports and dynamic dashboards. Reports make it relatively easy to isolate stories that fit certain criteria—for example, stories that include visual content or not. Dashboards capture key story bank trends in real time, such as showing story distribution by topic or U.S. state/city using IP address information harvested directly from storytellers. This information can then be "elevated to executive leadership at CAP, to give them a high-level overview of the [story bank's] performance and success" (Interviewee B, CAP, February 2022). These are especially clear examples of story datafication intended to inform advocacy strategy.

This system has potentially positive and negative implications for representation. On one hand, using the report function to, for example, isolate all the stories with visual content, can contribute to the creation and strengthening of the representation hierarchies described earlier in this chapter. On the other hand, this function and dashboard data could also be used to identify missing stories or demographics and support specific story collection efforts to help expand and diversify the range of storytellers represented. In practice, which of these implications are emphasized depends on the ability of a given organization or individual user to fully understand the potential ramifications of these tools and use them to steer story banks toward a specific direction.

More broadly, it is interesting to reflect on this system's automation capabilities. The technology consultants and other specialists we interviewed confirmed that there are frequent requests to automate processes like story tagging and selection. Salesforce's automation capabilities—based on an AI system called "Einstein"—are vast. Compared with just a few years ago, this means that organizations can automate some of these processes without needing to possess coding skills in-house. Yet this also clashes with some of the information security principles outlined above because it requires sharing data—including stories—with Salesforce itself. In addition, there are also doubts about the ability of AI systems to interpret "the emotion, the emotional component, you know, the way that you as a person would feel when you're reading a story" (Interviewee B, CAP, February 2022). This again points in the direction of a system where automated and human judgment cooperate in identifying stories worthy of publication, but where, crucially, user-generated submissions that do not pass basic machine-controlled filters have only a very slim or no chance of ever being considered. With story banks becoming ever larger and more reliant on automation to whittle down useful content, these are likely to become increasingly pressing issues for grassroots advocacy organizations going forward.

3.3.5 Visual Story Tech

A second set of technological priorities was driven by story format. While text functionalities are ubiquitous in online submission forms—as is discussed in detail in chapter 4—and textual entries constitute the backbone of advocacy story banks, organizations clearly identified visual content as highly valuable and particularly desirable. This is in line with the media consumption and attention economy trends outlined in chapter 1, which make images and videos more likely to cut through the "noise" created by the sheer amount of content that is available on the Internet. For these reasons, a final factor that plays a central role in story tech decisions is its ability to handle visual content. More than three quarters of U.S. interviewees explained that story submissions that include at least one photograph are more valuable than text-only ones. Similarly, Australian organizers showed a tendency to favor database tools that supported visual content. For example, one interviewee from Australian Marriage Equality described a system "where people would send in a story to [the crowdsourcing platform] NationBuilder and then we'd transfer it into [the CRM platform] ProsperWorks, [. . .] if people sent in a photograph we were able to have photographs on there" (Interviewee, Australian Marriage Equality, July 2018). In addition to photos, video content was even more highly prized, having been discussed in all but one U.S. interview, and—somewhat unexpectedly—mentioned more often than any other type of content, including text.

Interviewees also emphasized the growing importance of user-generated over professionally produced visual content for both strategic and logistical reasons. In addition to the fact that, for advocacy organizations, producing professional photos and video is very expensive and often impractical, user-generated visual content also seemed to provide an impression of authenticity that has become increasingly important in political campaigning in recent years (Dencik 2021). This echoes the current information consumption and evaluation trends outlined in chapters 1 and 2, which favor "ordinary" people and other peer sources over elite ones. As one organizer with a U.S. labor union explained, "the preference may lean towards authentic sides which are scripted and less edited. It feels less like a commercial and more like someone is talking to you on social media or through some other digital channel" (Interviewee, AFSCME Union, February 2022).

This represents a significant break with the traditional approach to creating advocacy videos—which historically has been relatively rare and almost always commissioned to specialized agencies—and is underpinned by a new common wisdom that "content trumps production value every single time" (Interviewee, Resource Media, July 2018). This opens the door to a much bigger number of video stories in advocacy campaigns, given the significantly lower cost of acquiring and maintaining user-generated content. At the same time, however, this clear preference for visual content also contributes to the creation of hierarchies within story databases whereby, as was mentioned above, submissions that include photo or video files are placed routinely above those that do not in search results. From a purely strategic perspective, this is understandable and even desirable. However, it could also have potentially controversial effects as it risks excluding storytellers for whom, for several reasons that are discussed in detail in the next chapter, it is difficult to share visual content in their initial submissions. For this very reason, one veteran story banking expert reflected that their organization, in initial story submissions, "only do[es] text, and [. . .] do[es] not ask for video or photos, [. . .] 'cause it's a barrier to submission" (Interviewee, Families USA, June 2018). Considering this, it is useful to shed some more light on the dynamics of video story crowdsourcing and the technologies that support it.

3.3.6 Video Stories

Crowdsourced videos seem to respond to a real need for time- and resource-efficient ways for advocacy organizations to acquire more engaging and persuasive story content. At the same time, they also provide useful solutions to multiple challenges posed by the traditional process of video production. Initial solutions to these problems typically included asking other organizations or individual professionals to help out with videos pro bono or making choices on what elements to "cut" from video stories in order to stay within budget. For example, an organizer from a volunteer-run disability organization told us that some of the folks who've worked for [the online news publications] *Now This* or *Amplifier Network*, you know, they've also become friends. So if we're working on something, we'll reach out to them and [. . .] they'll show up with the video cameras [. . .] We just don't have the bandwidth for it. (Interviewee, Little Lobbyists, November 2019)

DYI solutions like these make video stories possible, but they are also unsustainable in the long run and can result in suboptimal content if important elements must be omitted due to budget or other restrictions.

In theory, crowdsourcing video stories directly from supporters is a more reliable strategy and requires less compromise. However, it also involves some specific challenges. Obvious technical concerns with crowdsourced video stories focus on audio and video quality, as well as other aspects such as lighting, angle, setting, and backdrop. While it is important for video stories to appear authentic, they also need to be sufficiently clear to be credible. Even with home-made videos, organizers told us, "the goal is always to get the sort of best quality content that you can get" (Interviewee, Public Citizen, June 2018). In addition, besides meeting minimum technical standards and requirements, video stories also need to be coherent, relevant, and suited to the platform or medium through which they will be disseminated. A key trend that emerged from interviews with organizers experienced in video stories is that the rise of platforms like TikTok and auto-play features on other social media sites "are prioritizing very short videos [. . .] and you can tell a better story with a few images [. . .] and production value doesn't have to be particularly high" (Interviewee, Resource Media, July 2018).

This has contributed to story tech choices that organizations hoped would enable them to address some concerns at the root and collect as many video stories as possible with minimal or no need to be edited. One interesting aside here is that this could have positive implications for the "voices" of storytellers, which in this approach run a lower risk of being distorted, as is discussed in detail in the next chapter. This has fueled a demand for tools capable of handling the collection, storage, organization, editing, and dissemination of user-generated videos in one place. Some major campaign management software companies such as Countable have included this type of tool in their suite. In addition, startup companies were also established specifically to develop "one-stop shop" video crowdsourcing tools. An organizer with the AFCSME union, which used the Countable tool at the time of writing, explained that aspiring storytellers can record a video by being walked through steps that say "keep it under 30 seconds, keep it a respectful tone . . ." [. . .] and we see if we wanna publish it on the site or we can download it or reject it [. . .] it's a pretty useful tool. (Interviewee, AFCSME Union, February 2022)

Startup companies see this as an expanding and promising market, and have contributed some of the most interesting innovations and integration in this area. Notable startups that have built their business model around "one-stop shop" video crowdsourcing tools include Sydney-based Vloggi in Australia and Chicago-based Gather Voices in the United States. Others, such as Speak4 and the aforementioned Countable, have added video story tools to their comprehensive digital advocacy suites alongside other features such as email campaigns, petitions, and targeted call to action messaging. While some of these companies work with commercial clients, too, advocacy and community organizations represent an important market for them. To better understand what animates this trend and discuss its potential implications, it is useful to review Gather Voices's product and development plans in some detail.

3.3.7 Automated Video Crowdsourcing: Gather Voices

Gather Voices was founded at the start of 2017 by Michael Hoffman and Joel Resnik, two executives with significant prior experience in nonprofit public relations and games marketing, respectively. Its main product is a "one-stop shop" video collection tool that enables organizations to source and manage videos directly from individual users while also helping the latter prepare and submit better videos, from both technical and narrative standpoints. In contrast to other systems that require storytellers to shoot videos first and then upload them as files, here videos are captured directly from Internet browsers and stored on the company's servers. A Gather Voices interviewee described this company and its product as

data processors, and our clients are the [data] controller [. . .] we contractually are able to hold that [user-generated] video on behalf of our clients [. . .] but it's not owned by us, we can't publish it, or reuse it, or share it. (Interviewee, Gather Voices, February 2022)

On its website, Gather Voices describes its products as "turnkey" solutions for organizations interested in unlocking the potential of user-generated video content. To borrow an effective marketing analogy from a competitor platform—Vloggi—this tool is like an octopus, because it has eight arms that work together to help client organizations source, script (where necessary), share upload links, chase intellectual property (IP) rights, collate, edit, manage, and publish user-generated video content.

This approach has some important similarities with StoryCorps, a non-profit program that, for more than twenty years, has archived self-recorded audio stories at the Library of Congress through traveling recording booths and, more recently, a dedicated smartphone app and online recording software. Tools like Gather Voices—although they also collect video—resemble StoryCorps in two main ways. First, they help organizations avoid "a lot of hand holding" (Interviewee, Gather Voices, February 2022) when looking for video stories. This is because they not only walk storytellers through the process but also streamline legal rights and IP issues. Second, they capitalize on instances where the online and offline worlds interface—like StoryCorps does with libraries and other public venues—to create original opportunities for timely story collection. For example, Gather Voices worked with a major hospital in Boston in 2021 to turn Covid-vaccine waiting areas into story collection "hubs" by displaying QR codes that linked to its platform and encouraged people to record short videos describing their experience with vaccines while waiting.

Due to ever-limited resources, advocacy organizations that invest in tools like this inevitably face a cost-benefit analysis. Increasingly, however, they decide to pay for this type of service because without it "a lot of times the stuff that is recorded [by users] it's just not useful. It's too dark or they're too far away from their camera and you can't hear them or it just rambles on for too long" (Interviewee, AFSCME Union, June 2021). Designing and updating a system like this one requires competences that most advocacy organizations do not have in-house. In other words, advocacy organizations are not natural innovation leaders in this area. Instead, they seek out "turnkey" solutions to respond to the fact that, nowadays, "everybody has devices, everybody can make content; people trust the content from each other more than they than they do before; and all the organizations realize that video is a really important part of the strategy" (Interviewee, Gather Voices, February 2022).

In fulfilling an emerging need for advocacy organizations, tools like Gather Voices go beyond a program like StoryCorps not only because they collect video instead of audio content but also because they facilitate the integration of video stories with other aspects of the advocacy process in real time. This creates opportunities for the companies that develop these tools to significantly influence which stories are prioritized and disseminated by advocacy organizations, particularly when new features and other major innovations are introduced within their products. Again, algorithms and the perceived need for more automation play a key role in these processes. A conversation with a Gather Voices executive and a review of some of its internal marketing material shared with us provided a useful window into how their thinking may influence the next iterations of advocacy storytelling.

Overall, there seems to be an underlying assumption that

> if you create a culture that says, your story matters, you matter [. . .]—it's really [. . .] Marshall Ganz and his storytelling framework—[. . .] If I feel like I'm listened to that I'm important, even if you don't use the video [. . .] we [will] get tremendous amount of engagement from the community. (Interviewee, Gather Voices, February 2022)

In turn, this leads to the assumption that crowdsourced story "volume will grow, and [. . .] we want to be ready for a really different type of volume" (Interviewee, Gather Voices, February 2022) where manual review, tagging, and sorting become unsustainable. According to a startup like Gather Voices, the most effective response to this challenge is seeking to automate these processes using AI. This can be integrated into systems that, like this one, already operate as story bank databases and enable not only tagging and advanced search but also automatic transcription in several different languages. For example, at the time of writing Gather Voices was experimenting with AI-powered tagging and automated story suggestions that, in a first stage, would be based on transcripts and, after more piloting, would also account for video elements and visual cues such as quality, lighting, head position, emotions, and so on. This is considered a valid option to "not only sort [video stories] and create some taxonomies, but actually deliver up to different people the videos that are going to be the most resonant with them" (Interviewee, Gather Voices, February 2022). This feature is planned to be used both internally when stories are selected for dissemination and externally with public-facing story collections.

This presents new opportunities for using massive story collections in more proactive and effective ways. However, there are also risks that should caution against representing AI-powered story sorting uncritically in marketing pitches and encourage advocacy organizations to reflect carefully before adopting this kind of solution. On the one hand, AI-powered sorting enables organizations to use much larger story collections and discover "hidden" trends that would not be apparent to manual reviewers. On the other hand, there is a real possibility that AI-driven sorting may reinforce existing biases and strengthen echo chambers and narrow perspectives. This is especially likely when this system is applied to public-facing video story archives where

> the more a person clicks on things, the more the AI learns about what they're interested in and [. . .] should be able to, you know, match [. . .] somebody who lives my experience [. . .] that could be much more persuasive to me than somebody that is so far from my own reality. (Interviewee, Gather Voices, February 2022)

Software companies—including Gather Voices—claim that organizations will be able to override some of these features. However, it remains unclear what exactly this will mean in practice. For now, these are important open questions that weigh on future developments in this area and outline the need to carefully balance opportunities to deliver tailored and therefore more persuasive stories with the possibility of elevating more diverse and traditionally underrepresented stories.

3.4 Algorithmic Storytelling Futures

In closing, advocacy story tech sits at the nexus of strategic communication objectives, technological advancements, and organizational cultures. In this complex environment, the growing popularity of "big data" logic, widespread support for crowdsourcing approaches, and effective marketing from technology companies that seek to facilitate these processes have steadily encouraged advocacy organizations to treat personal stories as data. With burgeoning story collections, some of which include hundreds of thousands of stories, automated content handling becomes both a practical need and a self-fulfilling prophecy.

This has led to the rise of algorithms as broadly influential tools in contemporary story-centered advocacy. Algorithms intervene at key junctures in crowdsourced advocacy storytelling, including:

1. Story sorting and tagging, both deductively and inductively, through search database functions and, increasingly, AI systems that automate these processes, at least partly;
2. Story shortlisting, which is dominated by database search algorithms; and
3. Analytic reports on story submissions, collection trends, story

use, and effectiveness, which inform key strategic decisions and future planning.

In addition to these functions performed by algorithms that are internal to story databases, other "external" algorithms also influence these processes indirectly. For example, there are the algorithms of the social media platforms used to publicize calls for story submissions, which determine which users see these requests and can respond, and which do not.[2] Another example mentioned by interviewees are the algorithms of legal databases such as LexisNexis, which some organizations use to "vet" potential storytellers checking whether they were ever involved in controversial legal proceedings.

Search and sorting algorithms have especially deep and dual implications for advocacy storytelling. On the one hand, they facilitate the very grassroots nature of massive, crowdsourced story advocacy campaigns that, without them, would simply be impossible to manage. On the other hand, however, they can also open the door to several biases, whether strategic or more implicit in nature, in story selection and evaluation. Story tagging and algorithmic shortlisting can help build successful campaigns responsible for major policy wins. Yet they are also underpinned by a logic that prioritizes "what works" with a general audience over more nuanced but also more authentic or representative narratives. This can generate representations that address immediate policy issues, but at the same time may have controversial implications for certain groups in the long term, as in the case of the campaign on the Australian postal survey on marriage equality that we discuss in detail in chapter 6. More broadly, this makes content hierarchies inherent in crowdsourced storytelling for advocacy and shows that they are tied to a combination of collection form and database affordances, rules, and database uses. Here, organizers and story tech interact in ways that run the risk of reproducing existing representation trends and their limitations instead of renovating them by bringing them in line with the current needs and aspirations of the communities they serve.

A central question going forward, particularly considering that many U.S. progressive advocacy organizations have signaled story tech to be a long-term investment, is what may help lessen these risks. One important issue is certainly who is responsible for designing story tech systems, particularly sorting algorithms. Given that most advocacy organizations tend to purchase database solutions from external firms rather than develop their own, "the primary forms of expertise recognized in technology companies (e.g., software engineers, 'data scientists') and their underlying value systems (commercial and cognitive) become more central" (Murray and Flyverbom 2021, 633) to these processes. In contrast, as Holtzhausen (2016) pointed out, the input of communication and mobilization experts who have a clear understanding and appreciation for the impact of their work on society is essential to avoid some of the potential pitfalls of datafied storytelling as outlined in this chapter. Even better, making space in these technological design processes for the very people and communities whose instances are represented in advocacy campaigns is an effective way of balancing the potential benefits and risks of algorithms for crowdsourced story advocacy.

How this is accomplished is, of course, tied to organizational structures, culture, and resources. In recent years, participatory technology design models have emerged (Costanza-Chock 2020) that can provide useful inspiration for future advancements in datafied advocacy storytelling. These work by flipping the usual "human-centered design" paradigm and ensuring that professional designers serve community actors, rather than the opposite. Similarly, the partnership between in-house technology specialists and organizers pioneered by CAP is another innovative model in this area. Nevertheless, the extent to which "off the shelf" tools—which catalyze substantial economic interests and continue to be the default choice for many advocacy organizations—can be adjusted to mitigate these risks remains an open question.

CHAPTER 4

Whose Voice?

The Role of Storytellers and Representation

In 2010, Save the Children UK was looking for new ways to capture the news cycle and raise awareness about its initiatives around the U.N.'s Millennium Development Goals. One of its strategies was to "parachute" three British "mummy bloggers" into Bangladesh to write about its projects from a perspective and in a style increasingly popular among its supporters and that would also be attractive to media organizations. This "undoubtedly captured the media's attention," inspiring other nonprofits to follow in Save the Children's footsteps and set up similar initiatives, "but it [also] risked the marginalized fading into the background again" (Cooper 2015, 38). This is because, while the intention of these organizations to bring their supporters "at home" and the communities they serve "on the ground" closer together was laudable, the way in which they pursued this objective was marred by a longstanding problem in advocacy and nonprofit communication. That is, the issue of "speaking for others" (Alcoff 1991) by prioritizing external and typically privileged perspectives and analysis at the expense of the voices of those who have firsthand experience and a direct stake in the issues at hand. Frequent examples of this include doctors speaking for people with disabilities, social workers and psychologists speaking for young people, Westerners speaking for people in developing countries, and so on.

Little over a decade after these attempts to spotlight "alternative" voices, we are at another inflection point in the relationship between grassroots communities and the advocacy groups and campaigns that represent them in political spaces. In the early 2010s, some advocacy leaders raised concerns about crude but pioneering experiments in which organizations let their constituents "take over" their social media channels for a day (Cooper

2015, 30). Today, there are opportunities for more nuanced and multilay-ered forms of engagement with grassroots storytellers as both technology and organizational cultures have evolved. While this book has examined primarily the perspective of organizers, it is also imperative to focus on the changing relationship between organizations and grassroots storytellers to illuminate both the potential for individual empowerment and any barriers to change. Given the growing popularity of digital story banks filled with crowdsourced narratives, this chapter focuses on what this technological, cultural, and organizational shift in the advocacy sector means for grassroots storytellers themselves.

In essence, this is a question about "voice" that encompasses both its individual and collective dimensions. While it is critical to understand what happens to individual stories, it is also essential to take a step back and cap-ture the significance of these technology-powered storytelling processes for communities. Are crowdsourced storytelling systems set up to support com-munication that is genuinely centered around, and representative of, com-munity concerns, or do they orient narratives toward organization-driven agendas? Given that approaches to storytelling vary between organizations and practices in this area remain in flux, there are multiple answers to this question. Digital media platforms offer new opportunities for the emergence of authentic and underrepresented community voices (Jackson et al. 2020). However, they also lend themselves to appropriation and silencing of voice, too, sometimes inadvertently as the example of "Blackout Tuesday"—the Instagram viral phenomenon briefly reviewed in chapter 2—clearly demon-strated (Blair 2021). For these reasons, this chapter focuses on what is hap-pening to storytellers as advocacy storytelling becomes increasingly layered with digital technologies: how are these processes redefining who can speak up and, crucially, be heard in political spaces? Are storytellers empowered, or is their involvement now tokenistic?

To address these questions, this chapter turns to the perspectives and experiences of grassroots storytellers with technology-driven crowdsourced campaigns. These are contrasted and compared with the perspectives of organizers and contextualized through a review of both digital story col-lection systems and associated permission policies. Innovations and trends across story submission, development, dissemination, and evaluation are examined. We identify the type and significance of the input, if any, afforded to grassroots storytellers in these evolving processes. Crucially, we analyze how structures support or stifle diverse storytellers, including those that are at greatest risk of marginalization due to broader cultural, social, and politi-cal trends. The picture that emerges is one in which advocacy organizations are increasingly moving away from transactional systems and tokenistic approaches. That said, only a few pioneering advocacy organizations have started to revise their processes in ways that account for the unique ways in which story tech, social and political trends, and personal circumstances intersect with each other and affect marginalized individuals' ability to participate. As these practices remain in flux, these exemplars are useful for deeper reflection on how social change advocacy organizations can build more diverse, richer, and more effective digital story collections for inclusive advocacy.

4.1 The Limits of Publishing Stories "in Bulk"

One initial consideration about voice and representation is whether organizations publish all the personal stories that people share with them, or they choose, develop, curate, and disseminate a select group of the story submissions they receive. While these two practices are not mutually exclusive and, in practice, organizations that engage in the former have also invested in the latter, publishing every story received through online crowdsourcing undoubtedly opens up space for a larger and potentially more diverse set of voices. This follows the work of pioneering participatory campaigns from the early 2010s, which used collaborative story-based blogs to push back against dominant media and cultural narratives on disability, welfare, and social security (Trevisan 2017b). Typically, unedited story submissions are published on public-facing websites that employ sophisticated visual design elements and advanced user features—e.g., story maps and searchable topic clusters—that are populated with entries drawn directly from story collection forms. This system projects a great number of voices—often numbering in the thousands—to which considerable freedom is afforded in how they structure their accounts. Examples of this approach include Everytown for Gun Safety's "Moments that Survive" journal-style memorial to gun violence victims (fig. 4.1), the G Word Campaign's thematic display of stories related to gender identity, and Patients for Affordable Drugs' story map of the United States (fig. 4.2).

Another aspect of these story-based websites is that they enable users to create their own path through the content according to their interests through features such as keyword search, tagging, and geolocation, instead of following a predetermined narrative laid out by the organization.

The practice of publishing crowdsourced stories "in bulk" needs to be placed within the broader dynamics of contemporary digital advocacy. If all

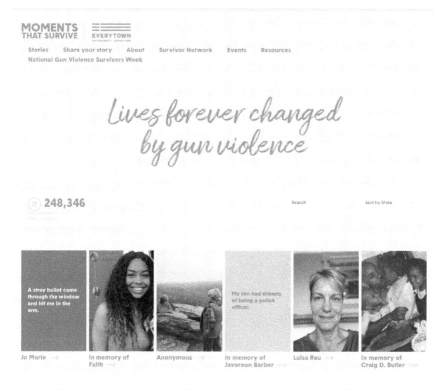

Fig. 4.1. Everytown for Gun Safety's "Moments that Survive" story collection

story content is uploaded to a web page with only minimal or no editing, it risks undermining the more strategic elements of story-based advocacy. Furthermore, regardless of how slick or sophisticated the hosting platforms look, user-generated story submissions have lower production values both in text and video formats. While this gives stories an "authentic" feel, it can also harm their ability to compete for attention with professional-looking content and, ultimately, could even put the credibility of organizations that overutilize this approach at stake. Finally, individual story submissions tend to vary substantially in length, narrative style, and focus. This generates a diffused lack of coherence in the resulting story repositories, as was found previously in crowdsourced protest websites (Trevisan 2018). These very large collections can also lead to content overload between users and, due to their open nature and limited editorial control, could potentially be "hijacked"— deliberately or inadvertently—by the wrong voices or disinformation.

Taken together, these downsides emphasize attention economy princi-

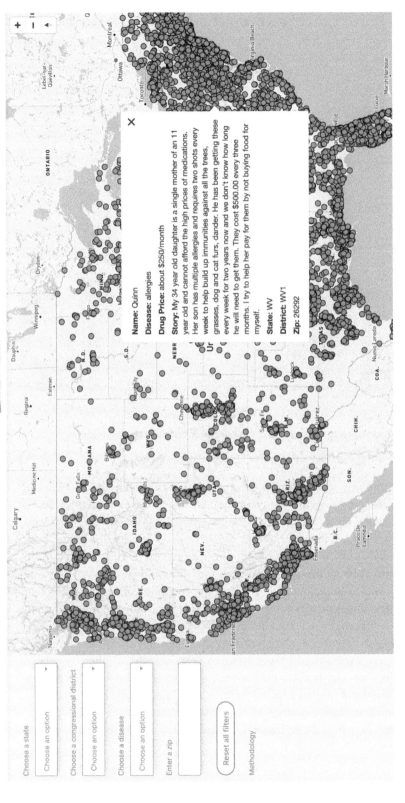

Fig. 4.2. Patients for Affordable Drugs' story map of the United States

ples where content is plentiful in today's digital world but attention is finite (Crogan and Kinsley 2012), suggesting that *strategic* content development and placement will be more useful for capturing the attention of key publics than mass uploads of user-generated material. Since the 2008 Obama election campaign, going where people already are online has become a key principle of online mobilization—particularly through social media channels—instead of expecting people to come to purpose-built sites (Chadwick 2011). Conversely, purpose-built sites remain the most popular platform choice for the advocacy organizations that publish crowdsourced stories "in bulk," except in rare cases.[1] Public-facing story repositories may strike a chord with existing supporters who are already familiar with an organization's work and motivated to go to its website, but they are unlikely to attract a sizable viewership beyond this, let alone generate the type of attention that is needed to have an impact on policymaking and controversial public debates more broadly. This raises a legitimate question about the quality of exposure that unfiltered stories published in bulk truly receive, and has a direct implication for empowerment, given that being heard is a fundamental component of expressing one's voice effectively (Dreher 2010).

This explains why most advocacy organizations—including those that maintain large public-facing story repositories—prioritize only a limited number of story ideas from crowdsourced collections and typically develop these into more complex narratives that are then strategically integrated into their websites and other online platforms (Dush 2017). As one interviewee who worked for Families USA, which has engaged in story banking for longer than perhaps any other Washington-based progressive organization, explained, when it comes to disseminating personal stories "there's danger in [prioritizing] volume: are you gonna sit and read that stack of stories, or are you gonna take the time to really listen to one story?" (Interviewee, Families USA, June 2018). In this context, it would be a mistake to assume that more selective approaches are inferior to the publication of "unedited" and "unfiltered" stories when it comes to storyteller empowerment. In interviews, many organizers described story development as a long-term "investment" in storytellers through training and other forms of support. For these reasons, it is essential to better understand the perspectives, needs, and experiences of grassroots storytellers in technology-powered storytelling.

From interviews with organizers, observation of storytelling advocacy practices, and a systematic review of story banking manuals and other "how to" materials, it is possible to delineate four main phases in contemporary storytelling for advocacy. These include (1) story collection, (2) development, (3) dissemination, and (4) evaluation. A range of digital technologies play increasingly important functions in each one of these phases, from the online forms used to harvest story ideas to the database tools that aid story selection and curation, and from the platforms used for dissemination to the analytics that inform evaluation. Technological choices are influencing the type and significance of input that grassroots storytellers have across these processes. We also explore to what extent these new approaches are supporting a diverse and representative range of voices, including those at greatest risk of marginalization in the broader cultural, social, and political context.

The amount of effort and resources invested into each phase of story advocacy varies a great deal between different organizations and campaigns. These practices also evolve alongside technological innovation, personnel turnover, and cultural changes. As an interviewee from a U.S. labor union involved in story banking explained, this change tends to be messy and typically results from "general hunches of how things went [in previous campaigns]" (Interviewee, ACFSME, June 2021) more than from systematic evaluations and the growing availability of digital analytics. While there are story banking manuals prepared by organizations with considerable experience in this field as was mentioned in chapter 3 (see the appendix for a complete list), as well as guidelines for more holistic approaches to story sharing developed by specialized U.S. consultancies such as StoryCorps, Story Center, and Working Narratives, advocacy organizations tend to borrow from many of these as they see fit, rather than sticking neatly to a single approach. Thus we used the four phases of storytelling advocacy campaigns as a useful framework for structuring the analysis in the rest of this chapter, outlining key trends to illuminate the variation between different practices that organizations have adopted across the entire process. Understanding their potential impact on the role of grassroots storytellers and their significance for representation and empowerment constitutes a useful way of grounding this analysis for the long term.

4.2 Capturing the Experiences of Storytellers and Organizers

To fully examine the opportunities and challenges associated with crowdsourced storytelling, we purposefully focused on the perspectives and experiences of people who are typically underrepresented in public discourse and might also face additional barriers to sharing their stories through technology. The importance of this approach to inclusion was corroborated during interviews with one of the most experienced story bank organizers, who noted that much of the digital [story] collection is tapping into blue [liberal] communities, into affluent communities, people who have time and the ability to mobilize. You're leaving behind people of color and rural communities who maybe don't have access to the Internet and those stories are getting untold and that's a problem. (Interviewee, Families USA, June 2018)

To address this issue, twelve in-depth ethnographic interviews were conducted in 2021 with individuals from marginalized backgrounds who had engaged with technology-powered advocacy storytelling. Ten participants were recruited through open calls posted on over two dozen social media groups and email lists (with membership ranging from a few thousand to hundreds of thousands) for people in the United States with experience of issues that have been the focus of prominent story-based campaigns in recent years, including healthcare (including Covid-19 and so-called long Covid symptoms), racial injustices, gender-based discrimination, women's rights, immigration, disability, economic inequality, and homelessness. This broadened the pool of participants beyond the organizations examined in this book. Potential participants completed a short questionnaire that focused on their recent experience with crowdsourced storytelling, in addition to useful demographics. In addition, a call for participants was also shared by some of the organizations examined in this book, which asked their storytellers to contact us directly if they were interested in participating. This generated two additional participants. This combination of recruitment methods helped minimize organizational bias while also incorporating the perspectives of storytellers who worked with some of the organizations we investigated in detail.

Crucially, the resulting pool of participants was very diverse with nearly all identifying with two or more marginalized groups or identities (e.g., black and disabled, transgender and immigrant, living in a rural area and chronically ill, and so on). Of these, seven had shared their stories online with one or more advocacy organizations, three had initiated the process but ultimately decided not to go through with it, and two were in the process of deciding whether they should do it. A more detailed overview of these storytellers is available in the appendix. In the interviews, we asked storytellers about their experience with story collection processes, any incentives, barriers, or concerns they encountered along the way, their relationship with advocacy organizations and their role in story development, as well as any consequences or outcomes of having (or not having) shared their personal stories.

These interviews provide a key perspective on the relationship between storytelling technology and key social and cultural factors, but they also need to be placed into context of the opportunities created by advocacy organizations to share stories. Thus we also undertook a systematic content analysis of ninety-six digital interfaces used to crowdsource personal stories and any associated permission policies used by the seventy-nine major U.S. progressive advocacy organizations we found to be engaged in story banking as of June 2021, as well as interviews with fifteen organizers in charge of these systems (see the appendix for more information). Together, these datasets offer a systemic overview of how organizations manage this point of entry and set expectations for storytellers. Most organizations tend to "mix and match" different approaches to each phase of storytelling. This makes for a complex, nuanced, and dynamic landscape that "tokenistic" to "participatory" models like those developed to capture citizen participation in the civic arena (Arnstein 1969) would struggle to understand adequately. The same organization can fall at different points on the tokenistic-participatory spectrum, depending on which phase of crowdsourced storytelling is examined and on the timing of analysis. Therefore notable examples of different practices—both good and bad—are highlighted here to analyze the empowering and disempowering mechanisms that lie at the intersection of organizational strategies and cultures, grassroots expectations of better representation, and technological changes that drive contemporary advocacy storytelling.

4.3 Story Submission Interfaces

Although the architecture of story submission interfaces may seem a trivial analytic starting point, in practice these tools have significant implications for storytelling-based advocacy. This is because as the main entry point for crowdsourced stories, online submission paths inherently have a path dependency effect on the entire advocacy storytelling process. By dictating what information is required, desired, or unnecessary (or even unwanted), they set expectations of what content aspiring storytellers should share with organizations. This influences what storytellers decide to share, but it also impacts on whether individuals share anything at all. Sharing lived experiences and personal information online leads to specific implications that may generate concerns in storytellers. These are distinct from concerns that people tend to have when they share their stories in offline advocacy settings, including for example in briefing with policymakers and press conferences, as the storytellers interviewed explained. In addition, the architecture of story submission interfaces also provides a window into what kinds of information story banks actually hold, which in turn informs story selection for further development, or direct dissemination.

There are three main questions that we applied to story submission interfaces. First, what kinds of information and types of content are required, simply encouraged, or discouraged? Second, what types of guidelines, if any, are provided to storytellers about crafting their submissions? And finally, what kinds of permissions and other policy documents, if any, accompany story sharing? In considering the implications of these steps, we have compared the systematic qualitative review of submission interfaces with the relevant experiences and considerations of storytellers to unpack the implications of organizational choices for story sharing and the story collections that support advocacy campaigns. This makes visible who has control over the narrative (both in its individual and collective aspects), what roles technologies play in these processes, and what can be done to address potential issues.

4.3.1 Balancing Privacy with Diversity

Two-thirds (66 percent) of story submission interfaces were hosted on the organizations' main websites, with the remaining one-third featured on separate websites that organizations had set up for specific campaigns. This corroborates the impression of story banking as increasingly embedded within the main tactical repertoire of digital advocacy from which U.S. organizations can draw regularly in their work rather than only at specific times and in connection with certain initiatives. While most of these submission paths were clearly labeled as part of advocacy efforts and placed within "get involved" and "take action" pages (42 percent), or website sections specifically dedicated to storytelling (11 percent), a full third was not immediately apparent and could only be located by searching the relevant websites. The location of this information matters. Less prominent or less clear submission paths may decrease the likelihood that new and inexperienced storytellers come across these opportunities, potentially increasing the weight of the voices of traditional or active supporters, who are typically more motivated to seek out opportunities to be active in organizations (Bimber et al. 2012).

Automated story submission forms embedded in organization and campaign websites—either custom-built or using commercial platforms such as Google Forms, Survey Monkey, and Phone2Action—were the most popular mode of submission. More than nine in ten submission paths included this option, followed by email submission, which was available for just over one-fifth of organizations. We analyzed how these forms were structured and what kinds of information they supported, required, or discouraged from aspiring storytellers.

A common minimum requirement was for aspiring storytellers to share their name, which was mandated by just over 80 percent of the forms analyzed. Nevertheless, that also meant that nearly one in five (19 percent) online forms allowed anonymous submissions. This opportunity for anonymous storytelling was somewhat surprising because, in the age of social media, authenticity—or at least the genuine appearance of it—has become an increasingly "central currency in the attribution of credibility" (Dencik 2021, 26) in political discourse. In interviews, organizers talked at length about the importance of authenticity. As a story editor from a disability rights organization explained, story-based campaigns "focus 100 percent on authenticity [. . .] the most important thing [in this kind of advocacy] is that you can really feel the voice of the storyteller coming through" (Interviewee, Rooted in Rights, July 2018). In addition, anonymous sharing also runs contrary to the "identifiable victim effect" that plays a pivotal role in boosting the persuasiveness of story-based appeals (Small et al. 2007). Thus stories without names or with made-up names may weaken the persuasiveness of advocacy storytelling, or even raise unhelpful skepticism in those reading or viewing them. On the other hand, anonymous story sharing was brought up spontaneously by a third of the storytellers interviewed, who saw it as an opportunity to make story advocacy more comfortable and secure for people from marginalized groups who "are already under such 'surveillance' in our society" (Storyteller G, June 2021). This gave an indication of the importance of the design of "safe spaces" for online story sharing according to the experiences of marginalized storytellers, discussed in more detail below.

Crucially, the vast majority of story submission paths (81 percent) did **not** include specific fields for sharing personal information such as race and ethnicity, gender identity, and age. Of the less than one in five organizations that provided specific fields for sharing this information, only three out of ninety-one mandated its submission. This is another interesting nod to privacy that may help advocacy organizations broaden their reach and support the collection of a wide range of material because it sets minimum requirements for initial story sharing, thus unburdening aspiring storytellers. At the same time, this approach also generates a lack of important demographic information within the technological context of story collection that relies on keywords and labels to organize and utilize digital databases. Given how organizations query databases to identify stories for development and dissemination, as was discussed in chapter 3, that storytellers generally are not offered the opportunity to include personal details with their initial submissions raises the issue of whether diversity can be properly factored into the story selection process at all. It is also important to be able to identify and highlight the intersectional nature of many issues and concerns by storytellers, which is particularly crucial for organizations that cut across different social groups. In general, blanket omissions or erasures of personal information from databases, even when done to aid privacy, may cause more harm than good as it reduces opportunities for appropriate social contextualization (franzke et al. 2020, 19).

One way to address this problem would be to have organization staff tag story submissions for key demographics in the process of checking them and organizing the database. Some organizations routinely do this in order to create their "own taxonomy [. . .] literally just reading every single story every single day and going through it to see what are the different themes" (Interviewee, AARP, June 2018), to make sure databases are usable. However, this is also potentially problematic because personal information entered by organization staff is based on assumptions that strip storytellers of the opportunity to self-identify and could be incorrect. Another approach that simultaneously injects useful information into story databases, respects privacy, and is more empowering for storytellers is to provide specific but not mandatory fields that enable them to "opt in" to sharing personal information, as some large organizations that have been leaders in story banking such as the ACLU, the NAACP, Planned Parenthood, and The Arc already do.

4.3.2 Setting Inclusive Expectations

Most organizations gave aspiring storytellers ample freedom in how they structured their initial submissions. There were three different approaches. At one end of the spectrum, there were "minimalists" that covered one-third of the story submission paths analyzed. Minimalist submission interfaces did not provide any specific guidance about story focus, length, or narrative structure. This approach enables a storyteller to share whatever they want. Yet, at the same time, it also does not clarify what exactly might be most useful to organizations, which in turn affects how prominent and "visible" a story will be in a database.

At the opposite end of the spectrum, there were organizations that took a highly structured "maximalist" approach. Maximalist submission interfaces, representing just over a quarter (28 percent) of those analyzed, asked story-tellers to share their stories by answering specific questions that were sometimes located on separate web pages. While this facilitates story classification in large databases at the point of origin, particularly for organizations that have a small staff, it has important implications depending on how potential storytellers use technology. Specifically, story submission forms with multiple questions on different pages are more burdensome for people who access the Internet primarily through mobile devices or have subpar connectivity. This includes not only marginalized user groups such as people of color (Atske and Perrin 2021) and people with disabilities (Perrin and Atske 2021) but also those in rural areas who still struggle with broadband service (Vogels 2021). For these people, story forms with multiple questions can be more difficult to navigate and complete, which in turn has implications for the diversity represented in story banks.

A final and more moderate approach, favored by 40 percent of the organizations examined, sought to avoid the downsides of the two poles outlined so far. This relied on the inclusion of only one specific prompt or a single guiding question on story forms. Here, the prompt or question served to direct storytellers toward valuable content while at the same time giving them considerable latitude to structure their submission as they saw fit. This relies on the question or prompt being sufficiently broad and not appear to be overly prescriptive, which was more common on submission paths posted on the organizations' main websites (66 percent), that were typically open to a broad range of stories, compared to those set up separately to support specific campaigns (34 percent).

4.3.3 Visual Content and Story Hierarchy

With regard to content and format, text submissions were virtually always (98 percent) allowed and required in more than three-quarters (77 percent) of the story submission paths. In contrast, video and photo submissions were encouraged by a relatively lower—but still substantial—number of organizations (20 percent and 31 percent, respectively) and were mandated by only two out of ninety-six. In interviews, organizers often stressed the role that powerful visuals play in boosting the persuasiveness of advocacy stories. A representative from Little Lobbyists, one of the two organizations that required at least one photo in every submission, linked this to a desire to build an especially effective collection of stories, as is discussed in detail in chapter 5.

For their part, storytellers seemed sensitive to the importance and potential impact of crowdsourced pictures and videos, including as opportunities to diversify visual representations in advocacy campaigns because, as one explained, "with any marginalized group, they're not represented in stock photos often [and], if you can get photos [through crowdsourcing] that's just invaluable" (Storyteller G, June 2021). At the same time, however, many also had strong reservations about sharing their pictures through online forms, which they characterized as risky. This was particularly common for storytellers who were part of social groups that are routinely stigmatized in society, such as migrants and LGBTIQ people, or feared being "found out" by family and friends who may disapprove of their identity or oppose something controversial they did. For example, one storyteller who had shared her experience of having an abortion commented about being "more careful when I first shared my story. I wouldn't give them [Planned Parenthood] a picture of me" (Storyteller D, June 2021). This echoes broader concerns that Internet users have about "context collapse" and identity management online—particularly on social media—meaning a reduced ability to control which information about the different aspects of one's lives other people are able to access (Vitak 2012).

In light of this, mandating a visual component clearly affects marginalized individuals' propensity to share information in ways that are likely to make the experiences represented in advocacy story banks less diverse. This is discussed in more detail with specific examples from disability advocacy in chapter 5. Moreover, the importance accorded to visual content has implications beyond the small minority of organizations that require photos or videos as part of each story submission. The one in four story banking organizations that allow—while not mandating—the submission of photos or videos on their story forms should be mindful of the fact that databases set up or utilized in ways that prioritize entries that include visual content over those that do not are likely to "bury" the stories of those more concerned about sharing this type of information, which are also some of the most marginalized in society. Thus the search for visual content can create an implicit hierarchy of story submissions that potentially excludes some storytellers and replicates underrepresentation problems that already plague public discourse not merely because of technical inaccessibility or other digital divide issues but also because of the complex social dynamics that surround these processes. Sharing is a foundational step in the advocacy storytelling process and dismissing or ignoring story ideas at this stage because of their text-only nature can reduce opportunities to tell compelling advocacy stories and contribute to exclusion of important voices from the public arena.

Taken together, these trends prompt some reflections on how organizations can create "safe spaces" for individuals—particularly members of marginalized groups—to share their stories online and for bridging the submission and story development stages in ways that are empowering for storytellers and simultaneously produce strategic value for organizations. A useful place to start in this process is to consider the significance and implications of the permission policies associated with crowdsourced online story collection.

4.4 Digital Appropriation Concerns

Before conducting interviews with aspiring storytellers, we had assumed that those who are on the fence about contributing to digital story banks, or ultimately decide not to do it, may simply be opposed to sharing their personal experiences under any circumstance. Yet our interviews painted a more nuanced picture in which storytellers weigh digital technologies heavily in their decision-making processes. For example, two participants recounted their positive experiences of telling their stories in physical settings such as face-to-face meetings with elected officials. However, they also expressed serious doubts about contributing their experiences to digital story banks. This is counterintuitive given that face-to-face advocacy is commonly regarded by scholars and practitioners as a more resource-intensive and high-threshold form of political participation compared to online advocacy. Crucially, these participants went on to explain that—because of their minority status and other personal circumstances—they perceived sharing their stories online to be riskier compared to doing so in person. One of these participants—a black, disabled single mother living in the southern United States with previous experience of homelessness—said:

> when it comes to storytelling in a database my concern would be they [advocacy organizations] would edit it, and often we as black women are not edited in a positive light. Maybe it's subconscious and not intentional, but they [the organization] would rewrite my words and it actually made me sound less articulate and all of these things. (Storyteller I, June 2021)

Comments like this underpin the role "authenticity" is perceived to play in these processes, especially if storytellers are concerned that their words may be edited to fit broadly held yet stigmatizing stereotypes in order to make their stories more compelling.

Interviews corroborated the impression that aspiring storytellers—particularly those with direct experiences of discrimination and voice appropriation—might see crowdsourced storytelling initiatives as problematic specifically because they are online. Comparatively, telling one's story in person to a specialized and limited audience can offer these storytellers a stronger sense of control over the narrative, wording, and framing used. Better understanding how aspiring storytellers perceive risk in digital story crowdsourcing is the first step toward trying to alleviate some of these concerns and eliminate barriers to sharing and collaborating digitally.

4.4.1 Reconceptualizing Risk

Exploring the permission policies associated with digital story crowdsourcing and considering storytellers' reactions to them revealed a mix of approaches, most of which focused exclusively on protecting the organization. In fact, 35 percent of the story submission paths reviewed here did not include any information about this at all, not even a link to generic website privacy policies. This lack of information leaves aspiring storytellers' basic questions about content ownership and decision-making around editing, publication, and dissemination unanswered. In other words, one out of three story collection initiatives was publicly construed as a "black box," which is likely to undermine trust in organizations and impede the crowdsourcing mechanisms on which this innovative form of advocacy storytelling is based. The remaining two-thirds (65 percent) included some form of permissions policy. Of these, only one in five distinguished between permissions to edit, curate, publish, and disseminate stories, while the other 80 percent bundled these together in order to secure maximum flexibility and protection for the organization.

In reflecting on the very broad scope of these permission documents, one storyteller offered an interesting parallel between online story collection forms and "blanket policies" that today are ubiquitously associated with social media platforms and to which people "are so accustomed to" (Storyteller H, June 2021). This hinted at the "normalization" of tick box permission and privacy policies in the digital world, implying that advocacy storytelling is increasingly aligned with that trend and derives some of its "rules" from it.

While this normalization trend mitigates the likelihood that broad permission policies would deter many from sharing their stories, its effect needs to be contextualized appropriately and considered within the individual circumstances of storytellers. This issue was not lost on the story bank staff interviewed for this book, many of whom said they felt conflicted about such broad permission policies. As an interviewee from AARP noted, there are "some serious legal ramifications of using people's stories; truthfully, a lot of the concern was the ramification for the organization" (Interviewee, AARP, June 2018). In discussing how permission policies were drawn up, representatives from several organizations said that extremely broad waivers were typically championed by legal teams, not advocacy or communication specialists. While story bank staff generally understood the need to ensure legal protections for the organization, they argued that it would be best to balance these with the need to build trust and lasting relationships with potential storytellers. Instead, they said, colleagues in the legal departments failed to realize that sweeping permission policies made it harder or even impossible to build trust with certain storytellers.

These issues were echoed in interviews with aspiring storytellers as women, black, disabled, poor, and less educated individuals, as well as those living in rural settings, were especially concerned about the potential of their voice being distorted, or their stories being taken out of context and disseminated in ways that may involve particular risks, as a result of signing off the rights to their own personal stories to participate in these processes. In discussing these issues, a disabled storyteller living in a rural community in the U.S. Midwest highlighted the need for advocacy organizations to better contextualize permission policies and story banking processes more broadly for aspiring storytellers. In particular, she said that "before you have somebody sharing their story, you should probably explain to them the vulnerabilities of what they're doing so that they're fully informed about what might happen" (Storyteller B, June 2021). She then explained that sharing one's story is

> more vulnerable for people [who live in smaller rural communities] than if you live in a larger city because in a larger city you're more anonymous, whereas here your family will find out through the grapevine. (Storyteller B, June 2021)

This storyteller and others who expressed similar sentiments hinted at the need for advocacy organizations to include information about risk for storytellers as part of their permission packages, which instead was missing from the policies that typically focused only on organizational risk.

Arguably, some of the information fields included in online submission forms implicitly signaled that, in practice, story banks tend to operate in more nuanced ways than is indicated by the letter of sweeping permission policies. While only one organization explicitly promised to contact storytellers before publishing their stories, virtually all of them (97 percent) asked storytellers to provide an email address. Over a third (34 percent) also included space to provide a phone number. This hinted at opportunities for storytellers to be consulted and provide input beyond their initial submission, which interviews with story bank staff revealed to be standard practice in many organizations. For storytellers able to read between the lines about likely follow-up, this may alleviate concerns and encourage them to share their experiences.

Yet to address this problem systemically, advocacy organizations should align how story editing, publication, and dissemination processes are represented in permission documents with the customs that regulate them in practice and suggest more interaction between storytellers and organizations that can be gleaned from reading their current policies. Greater transparency would foster better trust between aspiring storytellers—particularly those from under- and misrepresented groups—and advocacy organizations, which in turn could support richer and more representative story collections. To inform this process, the needs of storytellers and examples from the organizations that have implemented innovative, supportive, and transparent practices are highlighted below.

4.5 Bringing the Storyteller Back In

In discussing how digital storytelling can intersect with established disempowering dynamics, an organizer shared an example of a friend who sent his story to an advocacy organization that quickly

> put it out [online] in an ad and didn't tell him where it was gonna go and people in his community suddenly knew how he voted, what his health conditions were, and he just felt really taken advantage of. (Interviewee, Families USA, June 2018)

As was noted earlier in this chapter, this type of transactional storytelling is becoming rarer. Yet this example illustrates well how risk for storytellers stems from the interaction of technological factors (e.g., where online is the story published, shared, and commented on), social and political trends (e.g., stigma, media representations, community relationships), and personal circumstances (e.g., family relationships and those to whom the storyteller has disclosed their experiences or identity). Advocacy organizations reviewing their digital storytelling processes ought to standardize seeking permission to share story ideas with external partners, and consider ways to communicate these complex forms of risk, mitigate them, and support storytellers through the process. Reflection on the positive experiences and key demands that emerged from the interviews with both storytellers and organizers provided insights in the combination of technological and organizational practices with a view to creating digital "safe spaces" for personal story sharing, development, and dissemination. Three key areas emerged from our analysis that organizations should pay attention to.

4.5.1 Building Digital "Safe Spaces" for Story Sharing

A first step to make digital story sharing and development more inclusive is for advocacy organizations to develop and apply better situational awareness of the impact of technology-driven storytelling on individuals. This means understanding that online context collapse (Vitak 2012) affects each storyteller in specific ways depending on their background, story, and social connections. This can generate different concerns about advocacy storytelling, which are not static but evolve over time alongside changes in storytellers' lives, circumstances, and broader social trends. In addition to the issues raised by storytellers from small rural communities that were mentioned earlier, storytellers from immigrant Asian and Muslim communities interviewed for this book also expressed concerns over being unable to control exactly who would know about issues such as their political affiliation or gender identity through advocacy storytelling, and the fear that they may endanger important family and community relationships in the process. Furthermore, black women storytellers we interviewed were worried about sharing personal information through advocacy stories that might put them at heightened risk of discrimination from current and potential future employers. These examples signal the complexity of the intersection of technology, politics, and personal everyday life that characterizes digital advocacy storytelling for individuals. In addition, these issues are compounded by the fact that advocacy organizations cannot know preemptively about each storyteller's situation.

A useful strategy to address these challenges is to reconsider story sharing processes in light of these complexities, make them more flexible, and put storytellers at the center, rather than seeking to collect permissions "in bulk." Some forward-looking political organizations, including election campaigns

(Trevisan 2022), have begun this process as part of a broader push toward digital inclusivity. One particularly good example of this comes from the Polaris Project, an organization that focuses on human trafficking and uses the National Human Trafficking Hotline's website—which it operates—to collect stories of trafficking survivors (fig. 4.3).

The Polaris Project's straightforward, brief, and—crucially—accessible permission document is innovative in three main ways. First, it clearly "pauses" the story until the organization's staff has pursued further development of the initial story idea, which provides an opportunity to discuss and evaluate risk with storytellers. Second, it links to a separate, plain language document in Frequently Asked Questions (FAQs) format that explains what happens after someone clicks "submit," discusses confidentiality, and includes contact details for reaching story bank staff with questions or requests to delete one's information from the database. Third, as a first step, it enables anonymous sharing and minimizes the collection of personal information by requiring only an email address. Thus, through thoughtful solutions, there are ways to make crowdsourced advocacy storytelling become less transactional and more inclusive, including for people who have survived extremely traumatic experiences, such as human trafficking.

While anonymous sharing may not be suited to the needs of every organization, the other two steps align well with the approach of those that do not upload initial story submissions to their websites "in bulk," which, as was discussed above, constitute the vast majority of story banking organizations. As advocacy organizations acquire more experience with story banking and evaluate the implications of their systems, they may find this two-step model more beneficial than trying to get storytellers to sign blanket policies just in case, without a specific reason. In addition, another good practice that characterizes the Polaris Project's story form is that it acknowledges explicitly that sharing personal stories can be difficult, something that storytellers said was important for organizations to recognize but was almost never addressed in requests for online story submissions. This ability to empathize points to a second key area, that of storyteller support.

4.5.2 Supporting Storytellers: Checking In

Storytellers talked at length about their expectations for what should happen following initial story submissions, illustrating a range of experiences. There was a widely shared sentiment that, as one participant said, "the *good* organizations will do a partnership approach" (Storyteller B, June 2021) between

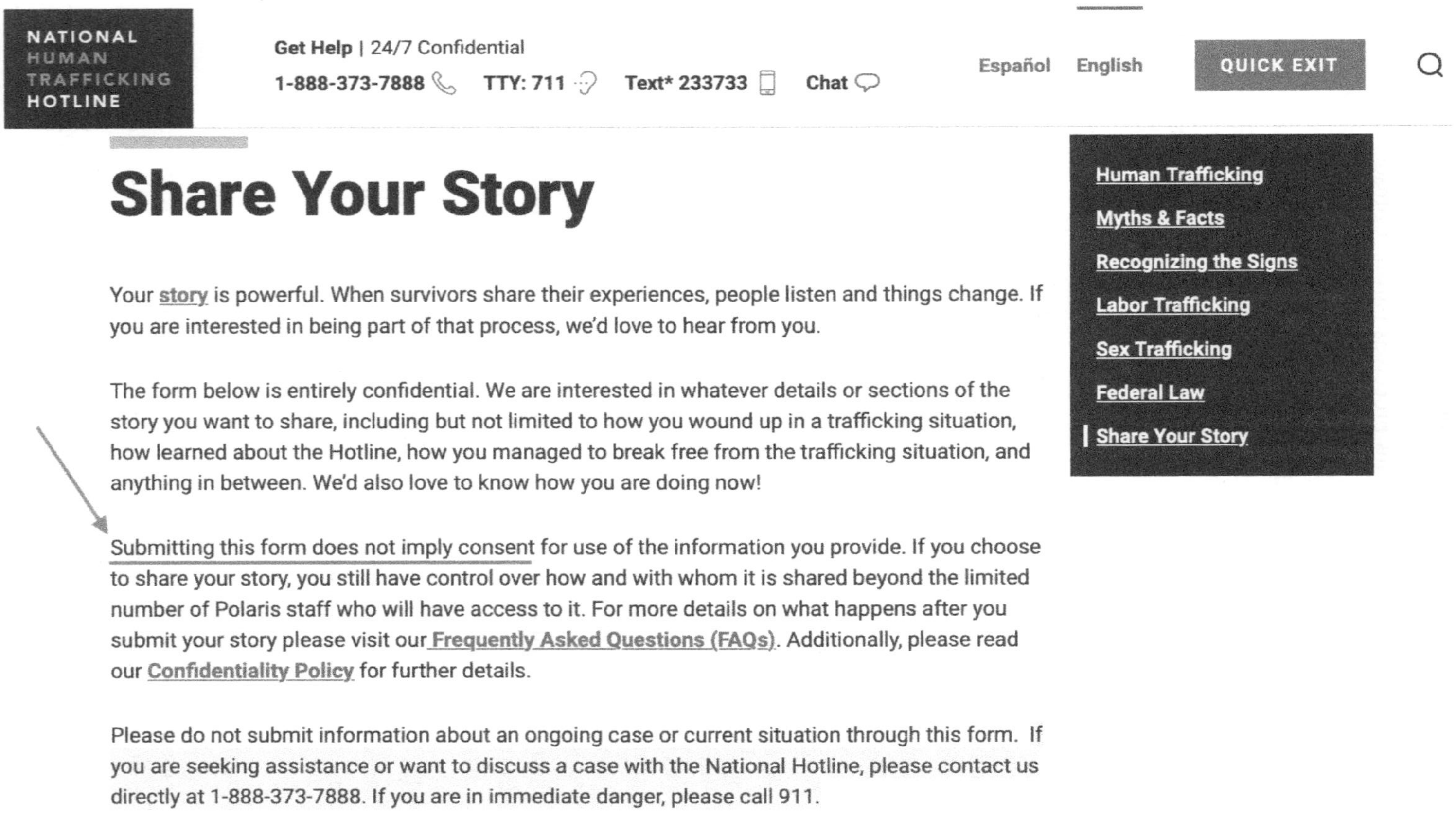
NATIONAL HUMAN TRAFFICKING HOTLINE

Get Help | 24/7 Confidential
1-888-373-7888 **TTY: 711** **Text* 233733** **Chat**

Español English **QUICK EXIT**

Human Trafficking
Myths & Facts
Recognizing the Signs
Labor Trafficking
Sex Trafficking
Federal Law
Share Your Story

Share Your Story

Your story is powerful. When survivors share their experiences, people listen and things change. If you are interested in being part of that process, we'd love to hear from you.

The form below is entirely confidential. We are interested in whatever details or sections of the story you want to share, including but not limited to how you wound up in a trafficking situation, how learned about the Hotline, how you managed to break free from the trafficking situation, and anything in between. We'd also love to know how you are doing now!

Submitting this form does not imply consent for use of the information you provide. If you choose to share your story, you still have control over how and with whom it is shared beyond the limited number of Polaris staff who will have access to it. For more details on what happens after you submit your story please visit our Frequently Asked Questions (FAQs). Additionally, please read our Confidentiality Policy for further details.

Please do not submit information about an ongoing case or current situation through this form. If you are seeking assistance or want to discuss a case with the National Hotline, please contact us directly at 1-888-373-7888. If you are in immediate danger, please call 911.

Fig. 4.3. Polaris Project's story permission policy

storytellers and their staff. This was also echoed in interviews with some of the organizations that invested substantially in story banks in recent years and pioneering consultancies, which talked about "building a relationship [with storytellers], developing their voice, helping them to have the skills they need to be their best advocate" (Interviewee, Resource Media, July 2018).

Specific approaches to story development varied between organizations. That being said, most of them typically involved a direct relationship between individual storytellers on one side and staff or external consultants on the other. This contrasted with workshop-based storytelling methods such as Story Circle (Hartley and McWilliam 2009) and others employed by community groups in recent years where peer groups play a central role in helping aspiring storytellers "find and refine an individual voice with feedback and affirmation from a collective" (Vivienne and Burgess 2012, 365). Nevertheless, organizers invariably stressed that it is crucial that stories are told in the first person by the storytellers themselves. One exemplar organization for the support it offered storytellers was the World Food Program (WFP). It strived to provide participants in its *Storytellers* program with ongoing skills training and opportunities for personal development in the long term, well beyond the moment their stories were published in the organization's social media pages. Even in this case, however, it was unclear whether this was the responsibility of the organization, and WFP representatives explained in an interview that this type of activity was funded through external grant money rather than the organization's core budget—a setup that mirrored early experiments with advocacy story banking as discussed in chapter 2.

Storytellers generally demonstrated a pragmatic attitude to story development, clarifying that they did not need or indeed expect to be necessarily involved in every aspect of it. Rather they talked about "options of level of involvement so that if people want to just contribute a story and be done with it that can be an option but sometimes you want to be part of more than just the [initial] story [submission]" (Storyteller G, June 2021). The most important factor across all these processes remains the ability of storytellers to be consulted and have the final say before a story is published. This resonated with previous research that identified different styles of participation in digital advocacy (Bimber et al. 2012). That said, while organizations tended to talk mainly about the need to move beyond practices that documentary filmmakers would call "extractive storytelling"—i.e., taking stories from individuals and communities without involving them in the process or without consulting them about editing and final cut (Marquez 2020; Wissot 2017)—it was clear that storytellers also thought about what happens both before and after story development. In particular, there was a widespread desire for organizations to follow up with storytellers where needed, for example when stories are republished through new channels or shared with other organizations.

Supporting storytellers before, during, and after story development clearly has resource implications for organizations. Nevertheless, interviews revealed that some important innovations in this area are possible at no or relatively low cost. One of these good practices involved creating opportunities for aspiring storytellers to connect with organizations in a stable and empathetic manner from the very moment they submit a story idea. This is a seemingly straightforward but surprisingly overlooked issue for advocacy organizations. Only 10 percent of the story submission interfaces examined included any contact information and as few as four out of ninety-six provided details for a specific staff member. In contrast, storytellers identified this as an important way to build relational trust that involved two parts. First, it was important for storytellers to be able to correspond with the same person who would know and understand the complexity of their situation. Second, storytellers pointed out the need to liaise with someone who truly empathized with their experiences, possibly because they had gone through something similar themselves.

As one black trans male storyteller explained, "it could be so welcoming knowing that there's somebody else [working with you] going through the same problem or the same situation" (Storyteller F, June 2021). Reflecting on this issue, another storyteller recommended that advocacy story banks be staffed by people "who may look or have shared experiences to folks that they're trying to recruit, [which] could really motivate somebody to share their story" (Storyteller D, June 2021). This suggests the need for a diverse story bank workforce, while story banking positions have tended to be filled by young, female, and white staff who recently graduated from college (Trevisan et al. 2020). Some of the storytellers we interviewed pointed out this discrepancy. For example, one said that "people who are collecting stories but haven't shared their own are young, they don't have the experience" (Storyteller B, June 2021). This type of change requires more intentionality in hiring decisions, rather than separate resources, and may help address issues of trust with a positive effect on the diversification of story databases.

4.5.3 Protecting Storytellers from Cyberbullying and Threats

Another set of measures to support storytellers more effectively relates to preparing for potential negative online interactions once a story is published. Here, storytellers identified three main priorities, including help with coping with abusive responses on social media (both public and private), managing stress related to recounting past traumatic experiences, and arranging advocacy events in ways that enable storytellers to prepare and recover as needed when telling difficult stories. Among these, the potential for dismissive or, worse, harassing and abusive online comments was top of mind for most storytellers. For example, one migrant storyteller who identified as black and queer explained that he "was really concerned about what people would say about me because I've seen people getting rejected and stigmatized, probably mostly because of their sexual orientation" (Storyteller C, June 2021). Two participants spoke about having endured a "torrent" of dismissive, negative, and abusive comments following the publication of their stories, which the advocacy organizations tried to resolve by removing that content altogether. Story removal may alleviate some of these problems, but it is also an extreme measure that simultaneously disempowers storytellers. This is an area in which organizations themselves admitted they were falling short by not having more proactive strategies in place, which was part of broader difficulties with following up with storytellers after story publication and dissemination, as is discussed in detail below.

Specifically, moderation policies for comments on stories posted online—on social media or other interactive websites—were mentioned by three different aspiring storytellers as something that would make them feel more comfortable sharing their experiences. Clear comment moderation policies, they said, would help organizations be more prepared and clarify expectations about support for storytellers. While specific guidelines may differ depending on the organization and population served, storytellers pointed out that it is important for those affected to be involved in their development so that they can capture all the relevant nuances and potential sources of negative interaction. For example, one storyteller with disabilities who felt their story had been dismissed by social media commenters because of a pervasive and persisting "hierarchy view of disabilities, that's a kind of 'oppression Olympics'" recommended organizations ask storytellers to be "part of a piloting to see how it [moderation] worked and then [have] a feedback loop [with storytellers] to improve it" (Storyteller G, June 2021).

4.5.4 Closing the Loop

A final phase of digital advocacy storytelling in which storytellers expressed an interest was less obvious: evaluation. Intuitively, this is not a part of the process where storyteller involvement would seem necessary, or maybe even valuable. After all, it could be assumed that impact assessment and strategizing the next steps are best left to professional communicators and organizers. Yet the interviews with storytellers pushed our analysis beyond this assumption and encouraged us to reconsider this phase from their perspective. This theme emerged organically from interviews and took on an unexpected significance as the study progressed. In particular, storytellers talked about how it felt important to them to know about their stories' impact, whether that is construed as policy change, public opinion persuasion, or support for someone going through a similar experience. Interestingly, storytellers said that it did not necessarily matter to them whether their stories were associated with a "successful" campaign. Instead, knowing how their stories were used served to validate their contribution and strengthen their sense of agency irrespective of the outcomes. This mirrored research on feedback loops in digital participation, such as online petitioning or crowdfunding, that does not necessarily attain policy or political change but still provides individuals with a positive and politically valuable experience that predisposes them favorably toward more participation (Wright 2016; Vromen, Halpin, and Vaughan 2022).

This is an area whose importance appears to be underestimated by organizations. In interviews, organizers generally recognized that there is room for improvement in this area and blamed a lack of resources for not communicating effectively with storytellers about what happens after their stories are published. However, they also did not recognize this as a priority. In contrast, storytellers identified this as something that mattered to them a great deal. In general, they described this part of the process as typically disheartening because in most cases "you pour out this information and then you hear nothing, you see nothing, you don't know if the project even wrapped up" (Storyteller G, June 2021). Storytellers pointed out the importance for organizations to "close the loop" as a way to boost retention and encourage further story sharing. As one participant explained, "when you speak to what this [story] is actually doing to not only me or the community or whomever I'm sharing it with, it helps you feel comfortable as a storyteller" (Storyteller J, June 2021). This resonates with previous research that found communicating outcomes—even when these are different from those that a campaign originally set out to achieve—is a key motivational component for keeping online supporters engaged and drive further engagement (Eaton 2010; Karpf 2016).

In interviews, storytellers were again pragmatic about why advocacy organizations have not done a better job of following up with them about the trajectory and potential impact of their stories. In addition to staffing and resource constraints, which were also mentioned by organizers, storytellers pointed out that "within politics, you have crunch time [. . .] you did X project, you finished it and, good, but you kind of put it out of your head because you're trying to win either a[nother] race, or change a bill" (Storyteller B, June 2021). These comments resonate with the current nature of story banking that, at least on the progressive side of the political spectrum, is used almost exclusively in ways that are reactive and short-term oriented (Trevisan et al. 2020). In light of this, developing better processes for "closing the loop" with storytellers can be regarded as part of the larger need for crowdsourced storytelling advocacy and story tech systems to be reconfigured as long-term strategy.

4.6 Conclusion

Overall, the practices and experiences examined in this chapter showed that crowdsourced advocacy storytelling is moving away from transactional models toward approaches that include more meaningful opportunities for storyteller involvement beyond initial story submissions. Although experiences vary, storytellers have generally demonstrated a pragmatic understanding of these processes and realistically do not expect—nor want—to be engaged directly in every step. Instead, they wish for opportunities to "check in" and provide input at key moments along the way. Moreover, concerns about how to effectively manage context collapse occupied a central place in how certain potential storytellers, especially those from multiply marginalized backgrounds and traditionally stigmatized groups, make decisions about participating in crowdsourced advocacy storytelling. Organizations that respond to these challenges in an inclusive storyteller-centered way will create better opportunities for storyteller empowerment. At the same time, they will also be able to build richer and potentially more effective story collections.

These findings underscore the importance for organizations to reconsider and contextualize storyteller risk, which is different online than in other settings as it results from a combination of technological factors, cultural, social and political trends, as well as personal circumstances. Not every organization has put the same amount of effort into planning for this, but those that do it best—for example, by setting minimum requirements for story sharing, outlining clear and flexible permission policies, and applying situational awareness to digital collection interfaces—are building new ways of elevating grassroots voices in influential ways. While the variation between organizations and the dynamic nature of these processes mitigates against developing a typology of effective digital crowdsourced storytelling, flexibility similar to that which allowed organizations to cater to a range of different participation styles (Bimber et al. 2012) has emerged with regard to the role and involvement of storytellers.

That said, there are some important caveats to this generally positive trend. Although in interviews organizers expressed a high degree of reflexivity on their practices, it was also clear that their work is limited by important factors that can—and in several cases do—generate storytelling processes that risk excluding and potentially disempowering some of the most marginalized voices. In interviews with organizers, these limitations were frequently ascribed to organizational factors—particularly differences of opinion between leaders, communication staff, and legal teams—and scarce resources. There are, however, innovative examples that show how some of these issues may be addressed not by necessarily throwing more money at them but rather by reviewing key steps and systems from the perspective of marginalized people and adapting technological interfaces for story collection, development processes, and how these are communicated to aspiring storytellers.

Arguably the most critical point in the digital storytelling process is initial story submission. This not only determines which stories are included in a database and which are not but can also affect the hierarchy of content in said database with knock-on effects on the entire process. As was discussed in detail above, even content that is not mandated but merely suggested or recommended, such as photos, can impact a submission's placement in this hierarchy. This tends to disadvantage storytellers from traditionally marginalized groups who, due to cultural, political, economic, or other reasons feel less comfortable than others about sharing their stories online. For many organizations, this is compounded by "blanket" approaches to storytelling permissions, which tend to raise concerns about possible voice appropriation and further erode trust among marginalized storytellers.

Some organizations, however, have begun to address these problems by considering the combined implications of technological factors, social and political trends, and personal circumstances on marginalized storytellers. This has informed relatively simple but thoughtful innovations in story collection interfaces that seek to address aspiring storytellers' concerns at the root by setting out clear expectations, contextualizing risk, and developing a customizable consent process. This approach signals a cultural shift within some pioneering organizations, which have looked at the advocacy storytelling process and the role that techno-social factors play in decision-making from the perspective of potential storytellers, not just their own. If others follow their lead, crowdsourced advocacy storytelling will be a step closer to fulfilling its potential for truly elevating community voices and empowering a broader range of individuals.

CHAPTER 5

Unexpected Narratives: Personal Disability Stories

Countless families—even sick little children, the Little Lobbyists–
bravely came forward to tell their [Affordable Care Act] stories. And
they made the difference.

Nancy Pelosi, Speaker, U.S. House of Representatives
Inaugural address, January 3, 2019

On October 5, 2010, President Obama signed bill S.278 into law. This piece
of legislation, better known as "Rosa's Law," replaced the terms "mental
retardation" and "retarded" with "intellectual disability" in federal health,
education, and labor statutes. "Rosa's Law" was a major achievement for
disability rights advocates in the United States. One factor that made this
policy success stand out in the U.S. disability community's decades-long
quest for dignity, inclusion, and empowerment was that the campaign that
led to it was strongly centered on the personal story of an eight-year-old
girl with Down Syndrome, Rosa Marcellino. One year prior, Rosa and
her family successfully petitioned the Maryland state legislature to pass a
similar bill after learning that Rosa had been legally labeled "retarded" at
school, which led to increased bullying and discrimination. This state-level
advocacy caught the attention of Democratic senator Barbara Mikulski of
Maryland who, together with Republican senator Mike Enzi of Wyoming,
spearheaded a bipartisan effort to establish similar legislation at the federal
level. This campaign prominently featured Rosa's story. Rosa and her family
sat in the front row at the presidential signing ceremony in the East Room
of the White House. Barack Obama personally thanked them for their advocacy and hugged Rosa. That very same evening, Rosa's story was broadcast

to millions of American households as the featured "person of the week" in ABC News' primetime program.

Despite being a remarkable success, the fact that the campaign for "Rosa's Law" was centered on a personal story was unusual for disability advocacy. Disability rights advocates have long been conflicted about using personal stories in their mobilization and persuasion work. There are several reasons for this, which are discussed below. The campaign for Rosa's Law occurred at a time of great excitement around the potential uses of social media in politics on the heels of Obama's 2008 election and was supported by PR and technology-savvy organizations operating in the intellectual disabilities advocacy and inclusion space such as Special Olympics. This chapter explores whether, with the advances in story tech and datafied storytelling discussed in previous chapters, disability rights organizations have changed their approach to personal stories. It analyzes story-based campaigns from Every Australian Counts, an Australian pan-disability organization that was pivotal to the establishment and implementation of the National Disability Insurance Scheme (NDIS), and Little Lobbyists, a U.S. organization for the rights of disabled children that played a central role in ensuring the Affordable Care Act and other legislation withstood repeated repeal attempts from Republicans during the Trump administration.

5.1 Disability Stories So Far

Following in the footsteps of the 1960s civil rights movement, U.S. disability rights activists have often used individual cases in legal advocacy to obtain court decisions that benefit many (Vaughn-Switzer 2003). However, they have typically avoided building large mobilization efforts around personal stories. Crucially, skepticism about the use of personal stories for advocacy purposes is rooted in a rejection of "victimizing" representations of disability that were commonplace in past nonprofit fundraising campaigns. For a long time, large nonprofits in countries like the United States, the United Kingdom, and Australia attempted to generate donations by using tragic disability narratives that elicit pity or sympathy from supporters (Barnett and Hammond 1999). A classic example of this were old March of Dimes advertisements built around emotionally charged imagery of paralyzed children that stressed how they would "miss many of life's good things" because of their disability and advocated for a "cure." This kind of narrative was steeped in a medical understanding of disability based on the notion that disabled people are deviant and need to be "fixed." Representations of disability have generally improved in recent years. However, pitiful and victimizing "charity case" narratives continue to be popular, including as Internet memes (Hadley 2016). This has generated a longstanding distrust of the use of personal stories among disability advocates.

Even when personal stories do not victimize people with disabilities, there is a concern that they could "privatize" problems that instead are collective and need to be addressed through system-wide and policy change, not individualized interventions. Individualistic frames are problematic for any organization that seeks to promote equality and diversity (Cooper 2004). This assumes a special significance in the disability rights movement, which is fundamentally driven by the social model notion that disability is a social construct generated by exclusionary barriers that need to be eliminated, not a "personal tragedy" deriving from medical conditions that should be cured (Oliver 1990). For these reasons, many disability rights advocates—particularly self-advocates—have systematically sought to "take personality out" (Trevisan 2017a, 194) of their campaigns, as a prominent activist explained in discussing the digital transformation of the U.K. disability movement in the wake of radical welfare reform proposals. Although a total veto on personal stories may seem extreme and arguably counterproductive, this tension highlights the importance for storytelling disability organizations to focus on representations that support equality of opportunity for people with disabilities rather than a "cure" for disability itself.

In addition, disability storytelling is hindered by the fact that many in the disability community can find it difficult to share their stories for multiple reasons. Besides disability stigma and concerns about having their stories appropriated or distorted, many people with disabilities are justifiably worried that they may be attacked—virtually or even physically—if they share their experiences publicly. Typically, media representations of disability have been "constructed using a technique of drama to add impact and emotion to elicit strong response from viewers" (Haller 2000, 281). This makes promoting disability stories that are less sensationalized and seek to be more representative while at the same time also command the attention of both policymakers and the general public very challenging. In addition, this has made nondisabled audiences disproportionately familiar with disability stories that have high dramatic value, elicit pity, and encourage charity, which some have come to expect.

People with disabilities who share stories that do not conform to these stereotypes and, instead, highlight positive experiences report being "frequently accused of exaggerating events or even outright lying" (Charlton-Dailey 2020). This is especially the case for people with disabilities who are simultaneously part of other marginalized groups or are marginalized within the disability community itself such as black people and other people of color, people with invisible disabilities, people with intellectual disabilities, and others. Although the disability community is inherently intersectional in terms of class, gender, race, and type of disability, a "hierarchy" of disabilities and overall lack of diversity has long existed in disability media representations. Typically, this has manifested itself in the overrepresentation of wheelchair users and white people (Haller 2000), as well as having the experiences of people with disabilities filtered through "expert" voices such as doctors and other medical staff (Kang 2013).

It is against this backdrop that this chapter examines how participatory technologies, crowdsourced campaigns, and political opportunity have incentivized some disability rights advocates to design story-centered campaigns in both the United States and Australia in recent years. Participatory technology offers specific affordances against some of the dilemmas and challenges outlined here. Through crowdsourcing, many stories can be collected and publicized simultaneously instead of focusing on a selected few, which could facilitate the representation of disability issues as collective. Direct dissemination through online platforms also enables greater community control over stories and—at least in theory—lessens the possibility of distortion and appropriation by third parties. Although the Internet access gap between disabled and nondisabled people continues to be a problem (Perrin and Atske 2021), recent improvements in accessibility have enabled many to share their stories who previously could not because of a number of barriers. This potentially increases diversity in stories and enriches disability rights campaigns with more compelling narratives.

In short, digital media provide disability advocates with opportunities to tap into storytelling in ways that are more ethical, strategic, and congenial to their goals. Just over a decade after the campaign that promoted Rosa's Law, the approach to storytelling in disability rights advocacy is being transformed. Examining these emerging practices helps reveal both the opportunities and limits of participatory technology and storytelling for groups that, like people with disabilities, have traditionally been unlikely candidates for personalized advocacy.

5.2 A Rapidly Shifting Context

Innovations in advocacy are rarely constrained by national borders, as we explored in chapters 2 and 3. Instead, technology and tactics diffuse between countries before being tailored to local political contexts in different ways. Thinking about the role of participatory technologies in disability rights advocacy, then, is enriched by thinking transnationally. This chapter profiles two prominent case studies from the United States and Australia in order to highlight features that we can observe both recurring and diverging across national contexts, and how the process of innovation across different countries is interrelated.

In some ways, disability rights advocates face similar challenges in the United States and Australia. In particular, media representations of people with disabilities are similar enough that the same conceptual framework has been applied to both countries and found similar results: dominant media representations too often rely on traditional framing around tragedy, pity, or deviance (Ellis et al. 2018; Haller and Zhang 2014). When disability rights advocates in both countries design their campaigns, they confront the same deficit of realistic and empowering representations in the media. Personal storytelling is a powerful way to provide alternative representations that both empower people with disability themselves and shape attitudes among the public and policymakers in order to expand the possibilities for progressive reform.

Yet the case studies in this chapter show how campaigners adapt strategy for the specifics of their home country, including the norms of the cultural and political context. Culturally, the push for new ways to frame disability in contrast to dominant media representations needs to resonate effectively with different key publics, making audience preferences an essential part of strategic planning. Politically, the opportunity structure for winning campaigns varies not only between countries but over time within countries. The presidential election of Donald Trump in 2016 created the threat that recent U.S. policy gains would be wound back, just as the election of a new Labor government in Australia in 2007 created the opportunity to campaign for ambitious reform. As we will show, although crowdsourced storytelling in general remains relevant, the kinds of stories that are told when defending the status quo are different to those used when generating momentum for change. This discussion is informed by two emblematic case studies: the Every Australian Counts campaign (EAC) in Australia and Little Lobbyists in the United States.

5.2.1 Every Australian Counts

EAC was launched in 2011 by a coalition of three large Australian umbrella organizations representing the different constituencies of disability policy: disability service organizations (National Disability Services), people with disability (Australian Federation of Disability Organizations), and caregivers (Carers Australia). A major report by the Productivity Commission in 2011 found that Australia's existing disability support system, based on a patchwork of different rationed programs, was "underfunded, unfair, fragmented, and inefficient" (Productivity Commission 2011). While this report focused on the economic costs of the status quo, EAC used storytelling to make words like "unfair" and "fragmented" real for the public. Such as the story of Shahni, who acquired a disability after hitting a power pole on her bicycle and struggled to qualify for help: if Shahni had hit a car instead she would have been eligible for support under the relevant state legislation, but only if the car was registered in the state of Victoria (Bonyhady 2014). Or Peter, who became paralyzed at sixteen years old after a swimming accident: even though Peter went on to become an award-winning youth development officer, he risked losing his job because as soon as he tried to use his paid care to work instead of staying at home, he lost thirty hours of support each week. The recommendation of the Productivity Commission, and the campaign goal of EAC, was a new National Disability Insurance Scheme (NDIS). The NDIS would operate as a cohesive system by providing all Australians with cover in the event of significant disability, no matter how it was acquired.

Two years after the Productivity Commission report and the launch of EAC, legislation enabling the NDIS passed the Australian Parliament. When then prime minister Julia Gillard introduced the NDIS legislation in 2013, she was moved to tears recalling the stories of two people she had met: twelve-year-old Sophie with Down Syndrome from Victoria and seventeen-year-old Sandy with cerebral palsy from Queensland. Sophie's and Sandy's mothers were both organizers in the EAC campaign. The success of EAC is remarkable not just for achieving broad political support under an unstable minority Labor government in a highly partisan parliament but because of the central role of personal stories in mobilizing both public sentiment and elite decision-makers. Following the introduction of the NDIS in 2013, EAC has remained active to advocate for people with disability and their caregivers during the controversial implementation of the scheme.

When EAC launched, its combination of personal storytelling and crowdsourced digital campaigning was innovative not only for disability rights campaigns but also the Australian advocacy landscape more broadly. The following years vindicated those innovations with some remarkable successes. First, in lifting awareness and support for major reform among the public, and second, in maintaining a broad cross-partisan base of support among political elites. That success is all the more remarkable in a decade of Australian politics characterized by political instability and policy paralysis—consider the five different Australian prime ministers over this period, none of whom managed to establish any durable consensus around Australia's policy response to climate change.

5.2.2 Little Lobbyists

Little Lobbyists was founded in 2017 by a group of parents of children with disabilities concerned about the repeated attempts by the Trump administration and Congress Republicans to repeal the Affordable Care Act (ACA), colloquially known as "Obamacare." This organization quickly amassed a considerable following and built connections with top U.S. lawmakers. In one memorable moment in January 2019, House Speaker Nancy Pelosi credited Little Lobbyists' children with helping "save" the ACA in her inaugural address. This was remarkable for an organization created less than two years prior and run entirely by volunteers with relatively little organizing experience.

Recognizing that children's stories can be particularly useful for connecting with elected officials and the news media, Little Lobbyists' organizers sought to use this advantage to involve other disability groups too. As one of their organizers said in a 2019 interview, many "disability rights organizations really struggle with having access [to legislators]," and Little Lobbyists "try to make room for other disability rights groups at the table" if they "are invited to a meeting and see that other disability groups are not present." While disabled children's families are the primary "engine" of Little Lobbyists, this approach has enabled them to quickly develop close relationships with very established U.S. disability self-advocacy organizations. They enjoy a very good reputation in the national disability grassroots community, which has led to some important collaborations with long established disability advocacy catalysts such as the American Association of People with Disabilities (AAPD). For example, a 2022 joint campaign focused on pushing the Center for Disease Control and Prevention (CDC) to reconsider its communication about Covid-19 to be more respectful toward disabled people. This sets Little Lobbyists apart from other parent-oriented organizations that have been criticized by disabled advocates in recent years for alleged voice "appropriation" practices (Parsloe and Holton 2018).

Crucially, technology was central to the very creation of Little Lobbyists, whose founders first met through Facebook groups for families of children with complex medical needs. Without these opportunities to connect virtually—one of the organizers explained—they would almost certainly never have met. As researchers of health- and illness-related online communities have noted (Vicari 2022; Vicari and Cappai 2016), this highlights the importance of social networking platforms for mobilizing and organizing communities that face significant barriers to coming together in person and participating in more traditional forms of grassroots action. This is particularly relevant for children with disabilities, whose voices are at an especially high risk of exclusion from public debates due to their doubly marginalized status as both children and disabled people.

In light of this, threats to the ACA provided a fundamental catalyst for political activation within these networks. This mirrored an increasingly established pattern in disability rights advocacy—and digital grassroots advocacy more broadly—for which crisis spurs digital innovation in both new and established groups, as shown previously by the renewal of U.K. disability rights advocacy following a radical reform of state welfare (Trevisan 2017a) and immediate reactions to Donald Trump's shock election in the United States (Trevisan 2018). From the start, Little Lobbyists' strategy was centered around crowdsourced stories. In line with the story tech trends discussed in the previous chapter, Little Lobbyists collected stories through an online form. As with EAC, stories were then developed and disseminated through multiple online channels—particularly Instagram—and incorporated in direct advocacy efforts targeted at elected officials.

5.2.3 Comparing Disability Advocacy Stories between Countries

These two campaigns are both innovative, high profile, and emphasize the central role of personal storytelling. The two cases also show the divergence between political and cultural contexts. EAC intervened at the agenda-setting stage to proactively build support for a well-defined policy goal (the establishment of a National Disability Insurance Scheme). Conversely, Little Lobbyists was primarily oriented toward protecting existing legislation—the ACA—and its ancillary provisions—for example, Medicaid expansion programs. Given the prominence of visual storytelling for each of these organizations, our research triangulates semistructured interviews with campaign leadership with the analysis of personal stories disseminated through YouTube and Instagram. EAC interviews were conducted when the campaign achieved its policy goal of establishing the NDIS in 2013 and again in 2019–2020 to discuss storytelling during the scheme's controversial implementation. Little Lobbyists interviews were carried out in 2019 after the Republican attempt to repeal the ACA failed.

The qualitative analysis of personal stories focused on the narratives that these organizations promoted during their most intense campaign periods (2013 and 2017–2019, respectively). For EAC, we examined a collection of twelve YouTube videos that profiled individuals advocating for the NDIS in Australia. For Little Lobbyists we analyzed the 297 Instagram posts it published between 2017 and 2019, 60 percent of which (n=177) featured personal stories of children with disabilities. These were collected through the Crowdtangle platform for academics. All the posts were manually coded (using separate codes for images and the corresponding text) for several variables focusing on personal elements (e.g., people and setting, whether disability was visible or mentioned), narrative structure (e.g., voice, sources, and public narrative elements), and political elements (e.g., calls to action, references to policy and policy effects, and politicians mentions). More details about this process are in the appendix.

5.3 Technology and Disability Stories

A useful starting point to understand the role of personal stories in today's disability rights advocacy is the sociotechnical architecture that has enabled these campaigns to collect, archive, organize, and disseminate stories. As was outlined in previous chapters, each organization tends to develop its own approach to story tech within a general trend that favors crowdsourcing methods. Although there continue to be barriers to digital participation for people with disabilities, and barriers which are experienced unevenly within the community, the two campaigns profiled in this chapter demonstrate the central role of new participatory technologies in prompting an innovative approach to disability storytelling.

5.3.1 EAC's Email List

For EAC, the search for new ideas was built into the design of the organization itself. While the coalition of major organizations representing the sector provided the funding to launch the campaign, they contracted a professional communications consultancy—Essential Media Communications—to assist with advocacy operations. Essential Media Communications were not specialists in disability advocacy but had prior experience on a wide range of other progressive campaigns such as the highly effective Australian Council of Trade Unions (ACTU) "Your Rights at Work" campaign on industrial relations in the lead up to 2007. Therefore these consultants brought a model of campaigning informed by innovations in the broader advocacy environment, rather than the history of disability rights advocacy in particular.

This meant that EAC showed all the hallmarks of a digital native campaign, in contrast to the established NGOs that funded it (similar to the distinction between MoveOn.org and older issue-specific NGOs described by Karpf (2012). The campaign consisted of a small core of paid staff connected digitally: a "virtual team" (Interview B, EAC, July 2013) with each paid organizer wholly responsible for one or two Australian states, communicating with each other primarily online and via weekly phone hookups. This small core organized a much broader and looser database of supporters. Membership of the campaign only required signing up for updates through the website or signing a hardcopy postcard supporting the campaign, requiring little in terms of financial or other resources but also signifying little at the outset in terms of the depth of commitment felt by those supporters. Instead, the goal was to quickly amass a large database of supporters that could be mobilized and tracked through low-cost digital communications. In 2011, EAC set a goal of gathering one hundred thousand supporters, reporting back to member organizations about the progress toward the goal; when it was achieved, the campaign then set a subsequent goal of two hundred thousand supporters in 2012. Like other digital campaigns, EAC's engagement strategy revolved around monitoring the response of supporters through data generated by online communications like open and click-through rates, and using that data to tailor messaging and priorities. In the words of one of the EAC staff, "we really tracked our list pretty hard. We've cut it and diced it a dozen ways" (Interviewee A, EAC, June 2013).

One important reason for EAC's digitally savvy strategy was so that they could use their online supporter database to crowdsource powerful personal stories. After EAC had launched, they commissioned a website from another U.S.-based digital consultancy that enabled supporters to submit short videos sharing their own story and promoted this collection effort through their list. Many of the videos were then redistributed through EAC's social media platforms, reaching a number of people beyond the expectations of campaigners, and a smaller subset of stories were developed into high-quality videos published over YouTube and Facebook, such as the campaign's playlist of "Our Stories" on YouTube. The ability to crowdsource personal stories from their supporters' list was both a strength and a potential limitation of EAC. Email subscribers are a particularly valuable asset to any advocacy organization because they have shown enough interest and commitment to sign up for regular updates and calls to action. This could make them especially motivated storytellers. At the same time, however, this also restricts the range of potential storytellers—and therefore stories—to those on a campaign's list, who are more likely to be specific types of people more interested in politics than average and not necessarily representative of the community at large. In comparison, Little Lobbyists took a different approach to their crowdsourcing strategy, which enabled them to reach and engage with a larger set of potential storytellers beyond their core supporters.

5.3.2 Little Lobbyists and Story Banking

Little Lobbyists also made crowdsourcing a centerpiece of its storytelling strategy. In this case, crowdsourcing reflected the reactive nature of this group rather than a more deliberate attempt to plan a proactive campaign like in the case of EAC. In the scramble to stop the ACA from being repealed, crowdsourcing enabled Little Lobbyists to collect many compelling stories very quickly. As a Little Lobbyists' organizer explained in an interview, this group's strategy moved rapidly from initial in-person efforts by its founders, who live in the heavily Democratic Washington, D.C.-Baltimore area and "brought [to the U.S. Capitol] letters and photos from friends [with kids with disabilities] who live in other [Republican-dominated] states and weren't able to contact their legislators" (Interviewee, Little Lobbyists, November 2019) to digital story crowdsourcing.

The technology used by this group to collect and catalogue personal stories followed the typical "arc" that was outlined in chapter 3 and evolved very rapidly, supporting a fairly systematic approach to storytelling. Within three weeks from the beginning, Little Lobbyists' story collection efforts moved from email correspondence to a Google Form, and eventually to a custom-made form that was built on Wufoo, a web package by online survey giant Survey Monkey, and constituted the centerpiece of its website's "Join Us" section (fig. 5.1).

One of the most useful features of this platform, a Little Lobbyists' organizer said, was its search function that supports looking up the database

Tell Your Story

Children with complex medical needs and/or disabilities deserve to be seen, heard, and supported. Telling their stories is central to our mission – we take them with us when we visit legislators and we share them on our social media to create awareness. If you're the parent or guardian of a kid like ours, we invite you to share your story here and join the Little Lobbyists.

1 Tell us about yourself and your child. 2 Tell us about your child's health care needs. 3 Tell us about your child's educational needs. 4 Tell us about your child's accessibility needs. 5 Welcome to Little Lobbyists!

Tell us about yourself.

Let us know where you're from and how we can get in touch.

Your Name *

First   Last

What is your relationship to the child *

Enter **2** to **50** characters.   *Currently Used:* **0** *characters.*

Please confirm: *
  I am this child's parent/legal guardian and am
  authorized to share the information submitted in

Fig. 5.1. Little Lobbyists' story collection form

for "stories with keywords in different states, different diagnoses, different needs, and different levels of [health] insurance [. . . to] find stories that illustrate that need in the most easy to access, easy to understand way" (Interviewee, Little Lobbyists, November 2019). In addition to standard contact information, Little Lobbyists' form asked aspiring storytellers to enter separate narratives on healthcare, education, and accessibility needs. This guidance sought to ensure that the stories collected were closely related to the organization's priorities. This intention to steer story flow through website design set Little Lobbyists apart from many other organizations discussed in this book that essentially let storytellers write about whatever they wanted in their online collection forms. Little Lobbyists' approach is strategically advantageous as it can generate a more coherent story database that can be used to create a more unified voice, avoiding the fragmentation and lack of focus that plagued other crowdsourced disability advocacy initiatives in recent years (Trevisan 2018). In addition, Little Lobbyists' collection form also mandated the submission of at least one photo of the child at the center of the story. The ability to support photo archiving was another key reason behind the selection of the Wufoo platform given the centrality of children's photos to this organization's advocacy strategy, as is discussed in detail below.

Overall, this system characterized Little Lobbyists as a story banking organization in line with the principles described in chapter 3. While this group was mostly interested in stories about a well-defined set of issues and oriented toward the short term, it also archived any other submissions it received for possible future use. This signaled a technological setup that could support a long-term pivot and substantial story bank expansion, should Little Lobbyists decide to take that route in the future. That said, the way in which this group designed story collection enables some important considerations about the relationship between participatory technologies, on one side, and organizational structure and resources, on the other.

Whereas large multi-issue organizations like the Center for American Progress can afford to invest considerable amounts of money to create dedicated story bank teams, smaller organizations run by volunteers such as Little Lobbyists benefit from technologies that save time and make decision-making as straightforward as possible. This is particularly important for organizations whose workers juggle competing priorities and demanding personal circumstances, as in the case of Little Lobbyists' "leadership who [. . .] take care of their child[ren]'s complex medical needs and disabilities" (Interviewee, Little Lobbyists, November 2019). In this context, database search algorithms can take on even more influence than usual given the little time available and the need to identify useful stories quickly. Similarly, the mandatory photo submission and the request to provide narratives on three different issues constitute an attempt to "preselect" the most committed storytellers and high-quality stories. This approach has noteworthy limitations, mainly that it sets a relatively high entry threshold for storytellers, which defies common story banking practices that typically simplify, streamline, and lower participation thresholds. This has implications for inclusion, particularly for members of minority groups who may be more concerned about sharing photos and personal information in an initial submission, and increases the probability of missing important and possibly very impactful stories. At the same time, however, this tells us that story banks have affordances for smaller and less resourced organizations, too, albeit slightly different from the ones enjoyed by larger organizations.

From these initial considerations, the practice of crowdsourcing personal stories online emerged as a centerpiece of disability rights campaigns by both EAC and Little Lobbyists. However, there are some nuanced but important differences that point to the influence of contextual factors on storytelling technologies in disability rights advocacy. In particular, EAC focused inward by tapping its supporters' list for stories. In contrast, Little Lobbyists looked outward by using a highly structured, publicly available online form to engage a potentially much larger range of storytellers while keeping contributions relevant and their number manageable for a relatively small organization. These technological choices show that there can be important variations in crowdsourced story campaigns that derive from their interaction with local factors, long-term goals, and other circumstances. Here, participatory technology is shown not to be a given that supports the same outcomes for everyone everywhere. Instead, it is adapted to specific circumstances where even small tweaks can have significant repercussions.

5.4 The Roles of Disability Stories

The extent of the acknowledgment of the role of crowdsourced stories of disability in changing policy was shaped by local cultural, political, and media contextual factors, as well as the intended outcomes of each campaign itself.

5.4.1 Building Support for a New Disability Policy

For Australian disability rights advocates, stories offered a way to problematize the status quo and make the case for change. The problems were already well-known among policy networks, and the years leading up to the campaign's launch in 2011 showed an emerging consensus around the solution of a National Disability Insurance Scheme (NDIS). In 2008, Kevin Rudd's newly elected Labor government held a national "2020 Summit" calling for long-term reform ideas for the country's future. Disability advocates were able to get the idea for the NDIS included in the report of the Summit's discussions, and the government commissioned the Productivity Commission report the following year, specifically examining the option of a national insurance scheme.

The "2020 Summit" neatly encapsulated the mix of opportunities and threats faced by disability rights campaigners. The main opportunity was a newly elected progressive government with political capital and an appetite for substantial reform. As the following years would demonstrate, the NDIS as a policy reform required effort far beyond Australia's three-year electoral terms and across partisan divides. Yet the Summit was full of many exciting ideas for reform. Many of these, though, did not go any further than the idea stage while others led to short-lived policy interventions. To take one example, the Rudd government's so-called Mining Tax—a levy on profits from the mining of nonrenewable resources—was inspired by the Summit but proved immediately controversial and went on to be almost immediately repealed after a change of government in 2013.

How then were disability rights advocates able to avoid the fate of other policies at the "2020 Summit"? Advocates understood they needed more than just the right policy solution. If the NDIS was going to be able to survive the polarized, unstable environment of Australian politics, then the sophisticated policy work underpinning the NDIS would need public demand and a broad base of cross-partisan support in the parliament. Yet the campaign's own polling told them that before EAC launched, fewer than one in ten Australians supported an increase in funding to disability services (Australian Broadcasting Corporation 2013).

Campaigners attributed this low support in large part to lack of awareness of the issues faced by disabled Australians among the broader electorate, rather than calculated indifference. As one campaigner argued, disability has

> often been a crisis that happens in silence in people's homes [. . .] we were really confident that once the general population and our politicians understood the realities, that we were always going to win. It was just about making sure that that reality, that story got told. (Interviewee B, EAC, July 2013)

For EAC, winning meant making sure the real stories of living with a disability were told. To do that, the campaign crowdsourced stories via email, asking supporters to share their experiences of why they needed the NDIS. Crowdsourced narrative content was developed into further public campaign material, helping to increase campaign reach and mobilization among the general public. For example, in the EAC campaign's YouTube channel all the stories are told in the first person by people with a disability or their caregivers. An EAC organizer reflected on this crowdsourcing attitude, where the campaign functioned primarily as a platform for supporters to author their own stories:

> we saw what our job was is to provide the opportunity for those people to tell their story on their own terms. That's very important to us, we didn't tell the story for them. They told their own stories. (Interviewee C, EAC, February 2020)

As our qualitative analysis revealed, the most common backdrop for these stories was people's homes, interspersed with B-roll of the storytellers moving about their daily lives. Far from reinforcing the stigmatizing, unrealistic portrayals of people with a disability in the media as exceptionally heroic or exceptionally tragic, EAC videos told everyday stories full of challenges embedded in mundane realities. These stories' main purpose was to highlight the gap in fairness experienced by people with disabilities. As an EAC organizer explained, the campaign had a strong hunch that this value would resonate with Australian audiences because "in Australia, the sense of fairness is very engrained" (Interviewee C, EAC, February 2020). Thus fairness—or, better, lack thereof—was seen as a culturally appropriate and strategically beneficial value to highlight through stories in Australia, particularly compared to the United States where "it's a different set of circumstances and a different frame of reference," an EAC interviewee who had worked in the United States said. This assumption was made early on in the campaign and informed many of its strategic choices, including its name and the ways in which personal stories were framed.

For example, in the video "Claire's Story" (fig. 5.2), Claire Anderson shares her experience of living with muscular dystrophy. Speaking directly to camera from her home, she describes a series of daily challenges, made worse by a lack of proper support. She talks about the difficulty in preparing dinner by herself when chopping vegetables leaves her too exhausted to eat, and the frustration of waiting for funding to make her own front door accessible after her arm loses its strength to lift her key, leaving her vulnerable to a dangerous incident with an intruder. Claire's story invites the audience to identify with her and experience the lack of fairness by considering what they would do if they could not eat dinner or lock the door of their own home, and in the act of sharing her story she transforms her private experience of powerlessness into a public act of advocacy. In 2013, following two years of campaigning, public support for increased public funding to disability services had climbed to a staggering 78 percent (Australian Broadcasting Corporation 2013).

These crowdsourced stories were also delivered directly to elite decision-makers. Campaign correspondence, public events, and private lobbying were all structured around people with disabilities sharing their stories, exploiting the ability of stories to communicate complex advocacy framing to policymakers even when they have limited attention and expertise (Davidson 2017). This shift toward crowdsourced and distributed storytelling maximized the campaign's strengths (e.g., extensive digital contact lists and motivated supporters) while mitigating its weaknesses (e.g., sufficient funding for national advertising campaigns in competition with other policy areas).

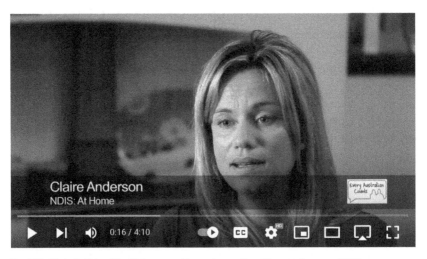

Fig. 5.2. Claire's Story, YouTube post, Every Australian Counts, January 2011

5.4.2 Reaching across the Aisle: All-American Liberty and Freedom Stories

EAC faced an uphill struggle in trying to push a new issue onto the public agenda and build consensus for urgent change. Yet the proactive nature of its campaign also gave it considerable latitude over how to represent the issues at hand. In contrast, Little Lobbyists faced the opposite problem. As its founders became mobilized to oppose Republican attempts to repeal the ACA in 2017, the terms of engagement were largely set for them by others. In the United States, healthcare is a polarizing issue that is regularly depicted and interpreted through a partisan lens, especially since the ACA was passed (Gollust et al. 2017). Republicans have long framed the ACA as the beginning of a slippery slope toward "socialized medicine." In particular, their messaging focused on provisions such as the "individual mandate," which imposed a federal tax penalty on those who opted out of having health insurance and supposedly infringed upon the fundamental American value of liberty and individual freedom.

This not only put Little Lobbyists—and the rest of the disability and health advocacy community—in a reactive position that limited their options, but it also dragged them into a challenging debate with potentially polarizing ideological overtones. To compound this issue even further, to stop repeal efforts disability rights advocates needed to find ways to put pressure on Republican lawmakers, who at the time held the majority in both the House of Representatives and the U.S. Senate. This involved both targeting elected officials directly and reaching out to independent and possibly Republican voters in the districts of said lawmakers, with the 2018 midterm elections looming as the debate went on.

To meet this challenge, Little Lobbyists created a collection of stories that emphasized the same values highlighted in Republican rhetoric, including liberty, independence, and the freedom to pursue one's life ambitions. At the same time, however, these stories simultaneously turned the overarching Republican narrative on its head by presenting the ACA as the vehicle for achieving—not curbing—freedom and independence. This strategy echoed a tactic employed by story-based disability rights campaigns in the United Kingdom a few years before (Trevisan 2017b), which also retained the rhetorical structure put forward by conservative actors but simultaneously hollowed it out and replaced its content with lived experiences that formed a direct counternarrative.

Little Lobbyists' stories were shared with voters through a range of social media platforms, with a particularly noteworthy set of one hundred Instagram posts specifically designed to target voters in the run up to the 2018 midterm elections using the #HealthCareVoter hashtag. In addition, they were also formatted as "profile sheets" to be then shared in meetings with elected officials and candidates across the country. As a Little Lobbyists' organizer explained in an interview, this process involved both coordination from the center and a certain degree of freedom given to local campaign "ambassadors," who could access both pre-prepared profile sheets through

> Google Drive so that people can find them there if they have a meeting in [, for example,] Pennsylvania with their legislators they can go print out the Pennsylvania people forms and a template for [capturing] every story that [. . .] fits your area [. . .] and create a [new profile] sheet. (Interviewee, Little Lobbyists, November 2019)

Little Lobbyists' story-focused Instagram posts framed the ACA's various provisions—sometimes in combination with the Americans with Disabilities Act (ADA) and the Individuals with Disabilities Education Act (IDEA)—as enablers of liberty in two main ways. First, over 70 percent of the stories linked these measures to enhanced opportunities for children with disabilities, their families, and others in their networks to live independently, pursue important life ambitions, and contribute to the economy and society. In a majority of posts, these positive effects went beyond individual children and were shown to also benefit other family members (7 percent) and society more broadly (45 percent). Maisie's story (fig. 5.3), a post

littlelobbyists ✓   ···

littlelobbyists ✓ 82/100 Maisie, age 5 months, Virginia
Maisie recently discovered smiling and now loves to smile, especially in the morning and when her dad makes funny sounds. She loves grabbing her toys on her play gym and going for strolls. She loves being walked around her house to look at the art on the walls. Maisie spent 88 days in the NICU and GI floor of the hospital before coming home for the first time. She was born with #JejunalAtresia, her small bowel never developed in utero. Only 3 in 1 million babies are

♡ ◯ ◁   ◻

Liked by   and **others**
October 18, 2018

☺ Add a comment...

Fig. 5.3. Masie's Story, Instagram post, Little Lobbyists, October 2018

about a five-month-old girl from Virginia with short bowel syndrome, was a typical example of this as it explains that ACA-programs such as Medicaid expansion allow her family "to focus on her quality of life and development, knowing that the basic care she needs to survive is covered. Maisie can't attend daycare because they are not allowed to care for her central line [that delivers her nutrition]," but Medicaid allows her parents "to continue working because we have access to nursing care for her [at home]."

Second, Instagram stories regularly highlighted the risk of losing one's liberty and independence, should the ACA ever be repealed or significantly curtailed. One especially frequent strategy—used in 45 percent of Instagram stories—was to frame this concern as a financial risk associated with a set of ripple effects that would give families no choice but to place their children in institutions in order to receive medical care, or quit work to be able to care for them at home. Take for example Asah (fig. 5.4), a two-year-old from Missouri with multiple complex conditions, for whom cuts to Medicaid would mean losing "his nursing care and may have to return to the hospital or need to live in a rehabilitation hospital." Similarly, Evie (fig. 5.5), a six-year-old girl from Ohio with Down syndrome, and her brother Jack, who is autistic, "are getting a great education in their public schools and [. . .] with support they [one day] can be employed, tax paying citizens. But, without Medicaid, [. . .] may lose the independence we're working hard to teach them, and they're working hard to gain."

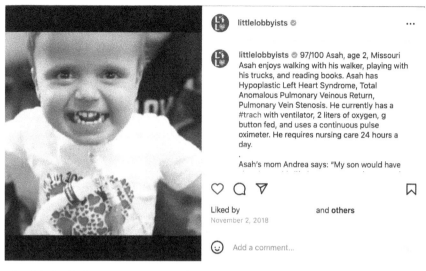

littlelobbyists ✓ ···

littlelobbyists ✓ 97/100 Asah, age 2, Missouri
Asah enjoys walking with his walker, playing with his trucks, and reading books. Asah has Hypoplastic Left Heart Syndrome, Total Anomalous Pulmonary Veinous Return, Pulmonary Vein Stenosis. He currently has a #trach with ventilator, 2 liters of oxygen, g button fed, and uses a continuous pulse oximeter. He requires nursing care 24 hours a day.

Asah's mom Andrea says: "My son would have

Liked by   and others
November 2, 2018

Add a comment...

Fig. 5.4. Asah's Story, Instagram post, Little Lobbyists, November 2018

littlelobbyists ✓ · Following ···

littlelobbyists ✓ Edited · 279w
72/100 Evie, age 6, Ohio
Evie is tiny but mighty! She loves dancing, gymnastics, horseback riding, new friends, fashion, fruit snacks, playing with her dollhouse, helping her mom, giving hugs, and putting her big brother Jack in headlocks. Evie has #downsyndrome, sleep apnea, and strabismus and gets lots of sinus, ear, and eye infections. She's had 7 surgeries so far, including: open-heart surgery, surgery on her airways, and ear tubes. She uses a CPAP, wears bifocals, takes medications and needs frequent sleep studies. Thanks to her individualized education plan (IEP), Evie attends kindergarten in an inclusive public school classroom where she's

Liked by   and others
October 8, 2018

Add a comment...

Fig. 5.5. Evie's Story, Instagram post, Little Lobbyists, October 2018

Strategically, these were smart moves as these types of stories do not require readers to espouse a new set of values. More simply, they invite them to recognize and identify with shared foundational values that are at the core of the American psyche. This is the same principle that informed one of the key messages in Kamala Harris's 2024 presidential campaign, which was also centered on freedom. According to social psychologist Jonathan Haidt (2013), there are six pairs of moral foundational values that support persuasion and, by extension, inform effective advocacy storytelling. These include: care/harm; liberty/oppression; fairness/cheating; loyal/betrayal; authority/subversion; and sanctity/degradation. Liberty/oppression is part of a triad of value pairs—together with care/harm and fairness/cheating—that are viewed positively by audiences across the ideological spectrum. This makes Little Lobbyists' choice to highlight the role of the ACA in promoting personal liberty a smart strategic move for engaging directly with difficult to persuade but politically essential audiences (conservatives) while staying on common ground that makes likely supporters (liberals) feel sufficiently comfortable.

Because "American conservatives [. . .] sacralize the word *liberty*, not the word *equality*" (Haidt 2013, 204), this also shows that framing stories around fairness, like EAC did in Australia, would have been a nonstarter for Little Lobbyists. In doing so, it serves as a cautionary reminder that crowdsourced storytelling strategies must consider their intended audiences carefully and account for specific cultural and political factors in order to be successful. In particular, there seem to be opportunities for using bipartisan values such as "liberty" to reach "unexpected validators [. . .] who agree with your specific issue but come from the opposite side of your political or social spectrum" (Matthews et al. 2017, 314) as the centerpiece of a strategy that emphasizes "common ground" to overcome the strategic disadvantage of being in opposition.

5.5 New Representations of Disability

Another key question that relates to the use of personal stories in disability rights advocacy centers on how disability itself is represented. This is particularly important given the stigma that is often associated with disability, which represents a challenge to advocates seeking to mobilize internal and external publics. Is disability highlighted in any specific way in crowdsourced advocacy stories? How is it integrated with other aspects of everyday life? Is it explicitly mentioned or only hinted at indirectly? Both EAC and Little Lobbyists' stories sought to present people with disabilities holistically, but with some important differences and shared limitations.

5.5.1 Disability "Stories of Us"

Many different kinds of storytelling, from court testimonies to theater productions, work by creating intuitive and emotional understandings of the lived circumstances of the storyteller. Successful advocacy storytelling adds an important step where those individual circumstances come to stand in for a wider group of people. This is the stage in Marshall Ganz's public narrative framework (Ganz 2011) where the narrator explicitly links their "story of self" to a "story of us." The majority of stories by both EAC's and Little Lobbyists' campaigns made this step, linking individual accounts to the wider disability community and signaling that "stories of us" perform an essential role across different countries, their political structures, and cultures.

For example, in EAC's "Robert and Mary's Story" video, Mary Mockler talked about the daily difficulties caring for her adult son, Robbie, who acquired a severe disability after a serious brain hemorrhage at birth. In the video, Mary first shared her "story of self," discussing the realities of helping Robbie shower and get into bed without the support of grandparents who had become too elderly themselves to help. Mary then explicitly links this personal experience to a "story of us" by talking about the broader community of people with disabilities, their families and friends. As she said in the video:

> The number is 700,000 people with severe disabilities in Australia. They have carers, they have families. There are a lot of people touched with disability. There are a lot of people who know someone in a family living with a disability. So, I think we are all touched by this.

Storytelling in advocacy, then, involves a deliberate entanglement of individual and shared experience. The personal alludes to a shared collective experience, at the same time as the scale of that collective experience underpins the dramatic significance of the personal story. This is particularly important in disability rights advocacy because of the need to counter the old-fashioned but still widely held idea that disability is a personal issue best addressed at the individual level through some sort of "cure." That said, the allusive quality of this relationship between the personal and the collective complicates story selection for advocates, who need to consider what is the relationship between individual accounts and the experience of millions of other people with disabilities. In Mary and Robert's story above there is certainly a common thread, both in the explicit naming of "disability" as a shared identity and in the articulation of the universal right to basic dignity. The story is also full of the kind of divergent specificities that are central to its narrative richness (such as the way in which Robert acquired his disability and his changing needs as he and his parents grew older).

For Little Lobbyists, 57 percent of story-based Instagram posts connected individual stories to collective struggles and used the first plural person "we." This emerged as a key strategy to build community and address the stigma that many families of children with disabilities have internalized. In interviews with Little Lobbyists' organizers, they stressed time and again that "educating" other families who "are teachable about the fact that challenges in their lives come from lack of resources, not from disability" (Interviewee, Little Lobbyists, November 2019) was a paramount goal of their storytelling work. This speaks to the role of personal stories and lived experiences in facilitating mobilization among people with disabilities in countries such as the United States, where the medical model of disability and its disempowering tenet that people—not environments—should be "fixed" or "cured" continue to be predicated in a good portion of the media (Haller et al. 2010).

One implication of Little Lobbyists' focus on internal publics was that its stories were less likely than EAC's to mention "disability" explicitly. Over one-third of Little Lobbyists' Instagram story-centered posts included a detailed account of medical and healthcare needs. However, these same stories made no explicit reference to "disability." This is an important difference. As a Little Lobbyists' organizer explained, this was due to the fact that "in their stories, people talk about health care before disability [. . .] people are scared of the word disability" (Interviewee, Little Lobbyists, November 2019). U.S. disability self-advocates are proud of their disability identity. In recent years, they have been vocal in their opposition to alternative wordings such as "preexisting conditions" that obfuscate disability and have encouraged opinion leaders—including presidential candidates—to use the word disability through hashtag campaigns such as #SayTheWord on Twitter (Andrews et al. 2019). Yet mobilizing and organizing emerging publics around an identity such as disability, which for many people continues to have negative connotations, is still a challenge. In this context, Little Lobbyists' experience shows that organizers play a fundamental role in balancing crowdsourced story content that reaches new supporters by sidestepping disability with representations that seek to promote this identity more actively.

5.5.2 Empowering Disability Stories

One central concern for Little Lobbyists was to promote stories that centered on disability and medical conditions but at the same time provided well-rounded representations of disabled children and their families as individuals who lead fulfilling lives within strong local communities. This was particularly noteworthy for an organization focused on medical needs and healthcare issues, and shows an ability to use crowdsourcing to move past "personal tragedy" stories that is beneficial both strategically and as a contribution to individual and collective inclusion and empowerment. That said, given the societal stigma that typically surrounds disability and the negative impressions it contributes to, creating holistic stories that would resonate with external publics was no easy task. Thus, Little Lobbyists stories were cleverly designed to live beyond the immediate policy battle and simultaneously function at "the micro level [. . .] when there's a piece of legislation [. . .] or something happening in a particular state" and the "macro level [. . .] to achieve awareness [. . .] that [disabled] kids are just kids like anybody else" (Interviewee, Little Lobbyists, November 2019).

Photos were especially central to this type of innovative representation. Most Instagram posts depicted children and their families in settings that underscore individual agency such as home and outdoors (45 percent), as well as lobbying and rallies in places such as Capitol Hill (22 percent). In contrast, medical settings such as hospitals, which frame disabled people as passive patients, were virtually absent from photos (2 percent). Although a majority of the stories included a fairly detailed description of complex medical conditions (52 percent), all of these were also accompanied by an account of everyday life such as playing sports, attending school, enjoying music, and spending time with family and friends. Furthermore, more than three-quarters of the pictures showed children and their families smiling or otherwise projecting happiness. These representations demonstrate a determination to ensure that children are not "defined by disabilities" and, Little Lobbyists' organizers said, generated an overwhelmingly positive response on social media with only occasional criticism from a limited number of users that pointed out a supposed dissonance between disability and happiness rooted in old-fashioned stereotypes.

5.5.3 Diversity and the Limits of Crowdsourcing

One way in which disability rights advocates deal with the challenging issue of representation is by telling different kinds of stories. For example, in the eleven EAC videos there were seven different kinds of disabilities mentioned explicitly. Similarly, Little Lobbyists' Instagram posts represented a very diverse set of disabilities with over one-quarter featuring people with multiple disabilities. Visual representations were also balanced between clearly visible disabilities (49 percent) and invisible disabilities (45 percent), with a majority of pictures (53 percent) showing no assistive equipment. These representations contrast with typical media coverage, which rarely focuses on invisible disabilities, and defy the traditional "hierarchy of disabilities" that continues to favor wheelchair users in disability imagery (Haller 2000; Rees et al. 2019).

In addition to including a broad range of disabilities, representing the diversity of lived experiences of people with disabilities also means accounting for a complex interplay between disability and other dimensions such as age, gender, race, ethnicity, culture, and more. It seems inevitable that, even when advocacy campaigns approach that task with the best of intentions, they will struggle to meet every supporter's legitimate desire for representation. In line with the sociotechnological dynamics discussed in the previous chapters, participatory technologies have a complex effect on the representational challenge of storytelling in disability advocacy. In some ways, these technologies are a powerful way to expand the scope of storytelling: digital crowdsourcing enables many different people with different lived experiences of disability to tell their own story, meaning less representational weight has to rest with any one individual. However, these same technologies can create new issues that are concealed by the apparent openness of digital platforms, as was the case for both the campaigns examined here.

For example, an organization like EAC might email a crowdsourced call for stories to their supporter database and receive thousands of responses. Yet, since all those sharing their stories have self-selected to do so, it can be difficult to know which barriers to participation are creating biases in the resulting sample. In the EAC YouTube channel there was no clear representation of Culturally and Linguistically Diverse (CALD) Australians among any of the storytellers. This was an issue that campaigners referenced unprompted in interviews, saying that cultural and linguistic diversity is

> something we're still trying to do better. But I think that's not an uncommon problem across different forms of campaigning, is that people who have multiple forms of disadvantage, often find it difficult to participate in public. (Interviewee C, EAC, February 2020)

In light of this, one could assume that open crowdsourcing that goes beyond email lists such as that carried out by Little Lobbyists could yield a more diverse set of stories. Yet, Little Lobbyists' representatives said, other facets of diversity—particularly race—were not very well represented in their story database. This illustrated the complex interplay—discussed in chapters 3 and 4—between the technological design of story collection initiatives and the associated level of risk as perceived by marginalized people, and poses an important challenge to the accurate representation of a community that is deeply intersectional. To address this issue, Little Lobbyists' organizers said that if they "have a family who's involved [in the database] and [. . .] represent more diverse communities, [they] really try to engage with them and [. . .] make sure [they] represent everyone" (Interviewee, Little Lobbyists, November 2019).

Overall, this provides an important confirmation that online crowd-sourcing, by itself, does not automatically generate more diverse stories. Instead, crowdsourcing personal stories can create gaps in the representation of a campaign's constituency, and those gaps can concentrate around precisely the demographics that face the most barriers to participation through their multiple and intersecting forms of disadvantage. Across different countries, technology works in tandem with underlying socioeconomic factors, which can make it particularly difficult for multiply marginalized voices to emerge. Given that the impressive scale of participation in crowdsourced storytelling can simultaneously reinforce and conceal representational biases, a proactive approach from storytelling organizations—especially the work of story brokers and curators—remains essential to ensure that story-based advocacy adequately reflects the diversity of the communities it seeks to help.

5.6 Disability Stories, Politics, and the Policy Process

Storytelling in disability advocacy is shaped not just by representational dynamics but by the strategic demands of the political context. Specifically, what is the key policy battle and what stage of the policy process is being negotiated? Sometimes campaigners want to put a new problem on the political agenda and propose specific solutions. At other times they have to influence the implementation of a policy that is already being rolled out, or defend a beneficial reform that is under threat of being wound back. As ideas emerge, agendas are set, and solutions are selected, enacted, implemented, and evaluated in continuous cycles (Birkland 2020), advocates need to navigate changing opportunities and constraints. As the two campaigns in this chapter demonstrate, these contextual factors also shape the kind of stories told by disability rights campaigners, and the publics they prioritize.

5.6.1 From Problem Definition to Policy Implementation

When EAC was launched in 2011, its strategic goal was clearly to raise the political salience of disability services reform. The campaign saw its main challenge as a lack of public awareness of the problems in the existing system. As one campaigner summarized:

> unless you were a person with a disability or a family member, people in the general community really didn't understand the kind of discrimination, the kind of barriers, the lack of support that people with disability experienced. (Interviewee C, EAC, February 2020)

This political context shaped a form of storytelling that was often unflinching in its portrayal of negative lived experience. Storytellers shared their raw emotions and used them as a call to action for other Australians to emotionally engage themselves, such as Claire asking "why is my purpose and my quality of life—why isn't that important?" While EAC's overall theme appealed to widely shared positive values that *Every Australian Counts*, the campaign's personal stories communicated the gap between those values and the status quo.

After the NDIS was legislated in 2013, the strategic priorities of EAC shifted and so too did the stories they told. Only one video on the EAC YouTube channel is dated after the NDIS legislation passed. Titled "NDIS—Live Your Life" there are some striking differences: the video is jointly branded with the logos of EAC and the NDIS itself, signaling the campaign's reorientation as a coproducer of policy alongside the independent statutory National Disability Insurance Agency. The tone of storytelling in the video is different too: instead of the pain and difficulties shared in stories calling for the NDIS, these later stories show much more positive emotion about the success of the fledgling scheme. For example, one of the narrators, a young girl called Siobhan, uses assistive technology to generate this speech:

> I don't have to have mum do everything now and that's really awesome. . . . Life's never been better really. I feel really awesome and excited about the future knowing I'll be in charge of who supports me to do what and when."

Just as EAC used stories to put the problem of disability services reform on the political agenda from 2011 to 2013, in the following years they also used stories to represent the value of the scheme as it was being implemented.

This is not to say that storytelling after 2013 was exclusively positive. At various points there have been significant issues around the implementation of the NDIS, unsurprisingly given the complexity and scale of the reform. This means that EAC has needed to advocate for their constituency in specific aspects of the rollout of the NDIS, while still maintaining support for the scheme as a whole. For example, EAC in 2020 ran a campaign called "Tipping the Balance," which asked their supporters to share personal stories—both positive stories about what was working well for them and negative stories about what needed to be improved. The overall message for the campaign was to "Tip the Balance" toward the positive rather than negative stories. As one EAC campaigner reflected about the difference between storytelling after the NDIS legislation passed:

> the role of the campaign again has been to give people with disability and their families a platform, and an opportunity to say "Here's the bits that are working and that's great. Here's the bits that are not, and here's what I want done about them." (Interviewee C, EAC, February 2020)

Naturally, the more nuanced message of EAC during the implementation phase is less suited to a public mobilization campaign, given the complexity of the assessments and the detail of the policy changes being canvassed. Instead, the campaign has addressed its storytelling more directly to political and bureaucratic institutions. For example, a standing parliamentary committee on the NDIS has met since 2013 and held several public inquiries—at the time of writing there are four current inquiries around themes like implementation issues, planning, and the NDIS workforce. EAC campaigners responded to an initial lack of individual submissions to these inquiries by crowdsourcing personal stories from their supporters and submitting them directly to the committee. In the most recent instance, EAC crowdsourced one thousand personal stories and submitted them all to the committee along with a public summary. Even though EAC has continued to emphasize personal storytelling and has continued to use crowdsourcing to do so, they have increasingly emphasized elites responsible for policy implementation as a key public.

5.6.2 Positive Stories to Protect Existing Provisions

While EAC's experience highlights the use of crowdsourced storytelling during the problem definition and implementation phases of policymaking, Little Lobbyists' strategy speaks to its application beyond the traditional policy cycle, focusing on a specific instance in which established legislative provisions came under attack. In this context, the urgency that typically surrounds threats to important legislation such as the ACA may tempt campaigners to focus on negative stories of loss and pain. Yet the controversial use of tragic representations of disability in previous campaigns has evidenced that such narratives harm empowerment and independence prospects for people with disabilities in the long run (Doddington et al. 1994). Thus, it is interesting to note that the vast majority of Little Lobbyists' Instagram stories successfully escaped the dualism between positive and negative representations by carefully balancing references to potential risks—such as the potential loss of freedom and independence, as was discussed in detail above—with highlighting the positive effects of the ACA.

Here, disability itself or living with a disability were virtually never represented negatively, with less than 1 percent of the posts showing people crying or appearing sad. Instead, ACA "success" stories were highlighted that supported the policy and at the same time promoted the idea that, with the right kind of support, people with disabilities lead happy and fulfilling lives. Jack's story (fig. 5.6)—a post about a thirteen-year-old boy with cerebral palsy and other developmental disabilities from Georgia—was a good example. He was pictured during a football game and Medicaid was credited for enabling him to become a "confident middle-schooler" who looked forward to one day "working, paying taxes, and living [. . .] in an inclusive community setting."

The positive framing of stories like this one shows that the immediate policy context is only one of the factors—albeit an influential one—that inform the use of personal narratives in crowdsourced campaigns. The long-term consequences of storytelling also matter a great deal as these narratives have the potential to outlast specific policy battles and inform notions of disability in public debates and collective imagery beyond specific provisions. Thus, Little Lobbyists' approach shows the ability to learn from past experiences and adapt important strategies to better support the overarching goal of disability inclusion. Furthermore, this type of positive framing can also help reach and mobilize internal publics who otherwise may be fearful that their stories could be cast under a tragic light, helping to grow the network of potential storytellers. This last point on key publics is central to how disability stories are inserted into political and policy debates, and it deserves specific attention.

littlelobbyists ⊘   ⋯

littlelobbyists ⊘ 52/100 Jack, age 13, Georgia
Jack loves to swim, play on his iPad, tease his
friends and watch football with his buddies. Jack
also has cerebral palsy and other developmental
disabilities. •
•

While Jack's family has private insurance, their
plans have had limits and high deductibles that
made his care unaffordable. Fortunately, Jack
has been on the Katie Beckett Medicaid waiver
since he was 2 years old. Jack's Medicaid
coverage is crucial - it covers medical and

♡ ⚪ ◁   🔖

Liked by   and **others**
September 18, 2018

☺ Add a comment...

Fig. 5.6. Jack's Story, Instagram post, Little Lobbyists, September 2018

5.6.3 Depoliticizing Stories to Persuade Key Publics

It is interesting to note that almost none of Little Lobbyists' story-centered Instagram posts included references to partisan politics or politicians. In particular, Donald Trump and his administration—despite being fully behind the attempted ACA repeal—were never mentioned in conjunction with a personal disability story. Similarly, although the Instagram account featured several photos of Little Lobbyists' advocates with top legislators including Democrats such as then House Speaker Nancy Pelosi and then Senate Minority Leader Chuck Schumer, as well as high-ranking Republicans such as the late Arizona Senator John McCain, these images were kept separate from posts focusing on personal stories. In interviews, Little Lobbyists' organizers described this separation between personal stories and party-political content as a deliberate attempt "to remain nonpartisan [although] it's hard sometimes" because "healthcare and disability rights have become more progressive issues [over time]" (Interviewee, Little Lobbyists, November 2019).

Importantly, this approach set Little Lobbyists apart from other recent instances of crowdsourced disability rights advocacy in the United States, particularly the January 2017 virtual Disability March whose posts focused largely on Donald Trump, leaving very little space for personal stories and substantive issues (Trevisan 2018). In contrast, Little Lobbyists' approach echoed the model established by high-profile action platforms such as Change.org whereby the most successful petitions are typically framed in personal terms without ideological or overtly political references (Karpf 2016; Vromen et al. 2022).

This has the potential to strengthen story-based advocacy in multiple ways. First, it avoids overshadowing the message and narrative arc of personal stories with partisan content. Second, it helps to attract a broader range of readers by deemphasizing the partisan nature of the issues at stake. Here, Little Lobbyists strategy exemplified a simple but effective way to maximize the effectiveness of crowdsourced stories to reach and mobilize both external (independents and Republicans) and internal (other families new to political advocacy) publics. In other words, it avoided the pitfalls of initiatives structured around a rejection of specific leaders, parties, or ideologies that tend to generate powerful but also heavily politicized messages that preach to the choir and do little to reach new supporters. Instead of prescribing a target (the Republicans or Trump), Little Lobbyists' stories used allusion to guide viewers to "imagine" those responsible for the attacks on disabled children, which has been shown to strengthen the persuasive power of storytelling (Polletta et al. 2011). This also ensured that personal stories were set up to deliver on one of the things they do best, which is to persuade those who are on the fence or on the other side of the political aisle (Gooch 2018), while emphasizing the fundamental role that digital curators and communication managers perform in ensuring that crowdsourced stories are used in ways that are as effective as possible. Although any story editing and curation needed to avoid distorting stories as they were intended by the storytellers, a responsible management of crowdsourced content was essential to navigate the complex space of political opportunities and constraints that surrounds them.

5.7 Looking Ahead: Personal Stories for Disability Rights Advocacy

Crowdsourced personal stories played a central role in the success of both the disability rights campaigns discussed in this chapter. This demonstrates the potential of crowdsourced storytelling strategies for fueling progressive advocacy and policy change for groups traditionally associated with disempowering media representations that have previously been conflicted about including personal stories in their campaigns. At the same time, the analysis also shows that underlying cultural, political, and organizational opportunities and constraints fundamentally influence both the shape and success of crowdsourced storytelling campaigns in the area of disability rights. In this context, organizers perform a central role in successfully navigating these environments to ensure that crowdsourced stories reach, resonate with, and persuade key publics. In turn, this again puts a spotlight on the need for story curators to possess relevant professional skills and, at the same time, also be grounded in the communities they advocate for, as initially highlighted in chapter 4.

Little Lobbyists focus on internal publics shows that personal stories can address chronic barriers to effective and large-scale mobilization within groups that experience widespread societal stigma, which can lead many to resist calls to action based on identities such as disability. This also exposes the reality of crowdsourced story-based campaigns that, to make sure they can scale up engagement and attract a sizeable number of good quality stories, need to find a balance between emphasizing basic commonalities in life experiences and communicating a strong sense of identity. This is particularly important in the U.S. disability community where, due to persistently stereotypical disability representations, many have internalized stigma in ways that make it difficult for them to positively associate themselves with a disability identity. This led Little Lobbyists' storytellers to be consistently open about their medical challenges and healthcare needs, while mentioning "disability" less frequently in their accounts. Comparatively, a campaign like EAC that involved a smaller number of storytellers drawn from a specific and generally more engaged constituency found it easier to build bolder and more explicit connections to disability identity in its stories.

Another important takeaway from this chapter relates to the use of crowdsourced disability stories at different stages of the policy process and the related need to reach and persuade different external audiences. Both EAC and Little Lobbyists approached crowdsourced personal stories and the technology that supports their collection, organization, and deployment not as fleeting gimmicks but as systemic innovations with a long-term outlook and value across the different stages of the policy process and beyond.

Throughout the decade of EAC's evolving advocacy, crowdsourced storytelling has been a common thread. When EAC needed to help members of the public understand the severity of the problems in the previous system, videos such as those on the "Our Stories" YouTube channel provided a powerful window into the lived experience of people with a disability. When EAC needed to consolidate the support of key political elites, these stories were brought to direct lobbying meetings, and as this chapter described previously, those stories then frequently made their way onto the floor of parliament. And when EAC needed to influence the implementation of the

NDIS—highlighting significant problems while maintaining the critical importance of the scheme overall—they crowdsourced stories of both positive and negative experiences to feed into public inquiries. The varied uses of personal stories over the advocacy life of the EAC campaign points to the durability and versatility of storytelling in disability rights advocacy, and its likely central role into the future.

Comparatively, Little Lobbyists' experience shows how personal stories of disability can be used to protect controversial legislative provisions at a time of political turbulence and with an important election approaching. Personal stories constitute a particularly effective way to reach and persuade independent and conservative lawmakers and voters, which is key to achieving strategic success in this context. For these reasons, Little Lobbyists' strategy demonstrates the importance of "depoliticizing" stories to let compelling personal narratives shine and boost their persuasiveness. Relatedly, emphasizing culturally specific and widely held moral values such as liberty in the United States and fairness in Australia emerged as a key element in disability advocacy storytelling. This distinguished these groups from the larger multi-issue organizations discussed in previous chapters that paid less attention to value-laden storytelling and have approached crowdsourced stories as tools to respond rapidly to breaking news and intervene in the political information cycle.

One important limitation encountered by both organizations was a certain difficulty in gathering diverse stories. EAC's and Little Lobbyists' stories showcased a very broad range of disabilities, which contrasted with the usual "hierarchy" of disability media representations. However, their representatives pointed out that other aspects of diversity—particularly racial, cultural, and linguistic diversity—were represented less effectively in their crowdsourced story collections. This confirms that crowdsourced story collection, by itself, does not generate more diverse representations and reminds us that technology does not operate in vacuum. Instead, as was discussed in the previous chapter, its impact is both enhanced and constrained by underlying social, cultural, political, and economic factors. This is exemplified here through the lens of disability. In particular, difficulties in gathering diverse disability stories extended beyond persistent inequalities in Internet access and suggest that stigma, which often makes people hesitant about sharing their story on public forums, affects the intersectional disability community unevenly with a deeper impact on those who are simultaneously part of other minority groups. As this pattern emerged in both countries, it suggests that this issue of intersectionality transcends cultural and political systems. There is a risk that crowdsourced story campaigns will reproduce inequalities in disability representations if organizers and story curators do not adopt a proactive approach to enhancing the diversity and representativeness of their campaigns.

Overall and despite its limitations, crowdsourced storytelling has opened a new chapter in disability rights activism. Participatory technologies and culture are squarely at the center of these trends. Moreover, a group that once lagged significantly behind others in digital advocacy is now an important example of advocacy storytelling innovation. This speaks more broadly of the opportunities that lie in engaging the community and preparing stories that deviate significantly from stereotypical representations for groups that historically have been conflicted about integrating personal narratives in their advocacy repertoire.

CHAPTER 6

Datafied Storytelling's Double-Edged Sword in Marriage Equality Campaigning

In 2017, Australians were asked to vote to on whether same-sex couples should be able to get married, and nearly two-thirds of those who voted said "Yes." This unusual (and constitutionally unnecessary) vote emerged after years of parliamentary gridlock where politicians had become increasingly out of step with public sentiment on this issue. The resulting national campaign was bitterly fought as it moved from Parliament house to the arena of public opinion and mobilization. Personal stories became one of the main sources of ammunition used by both sides of the debate. The Australian campaign was also heavily shaped by learning in other countries. The Australian Marriage Equality (AME) campaign hosted discussions with activists from both the United States and Ireland to learn from their experiences (Greenwich and Robinson 2018). AME's executive director, Tiernan Brady, had even worked as the political director for Ireland's Yes Equality campaign in the lead up to their 2015 referendum.

AME campaigner Adam Knobel has talked publicly about "one of those moments where your stomach just drops," when the crucial postal ballots arrived in mailboxes across the country five days earlier than expected (*#15 Marriage Equality*, n.d.). The campaign's response to this crisis was fairly representative of their overall approach: they asked supporters to step up by sharing selfies on social media with their personal stories of why they were voting yes. Over the following days, hundreds of thousands of Australians took up that call to action, turning a crisis into an opportunity.

Yet behind the powerful energy of this mass, collective storytelling effort lay a shadow, articulated by a different kind of story filtering out. Edie Shepherd, cofounder of Blackfullas for Marriage Equality, wrote about the gap between the "growing narrative of the respectable cis white gay couple who want the white picket fence and who is just like you" (Eades and Vivienne 2018, 8) and "the pain, the struggle, the bravery and the triumph for so many queer, trans and gender diverse people in defending the validity of their existence" (21). That pain is evident in some of the subsequent research that has found that the national vote significantly increased psychological distress for LGBTIQ Australians (Casey et al. 2020; Ecker et al. 2019; Verrelli et al. 2019). An ambivalence settled into the collective memory of the marriage equality campaign, documented in contrasting records of what had taken place. As Karp (2018) reported the following year, the exultant victory narrative of *Yes Yes Yes: Australia's Journey to Marriage Equality* (Greenwich 2018) sat alongside the archive of struggle and pain in *Going Postal: More than 'Yes' or 'No'* (Eades and Vivienne 2018). This ambivalence sets the scene for the organizing metaphor of this chapter: the double-edged sword. While datafied storytelling was a route to agency, self-expression, and political power, the campaign also curated stories for the public discourse that added to a wider narrative that left some queer Australians feeling invisible and invalidated.

The key to a double-edged sword is that one edge is implicated in the other. In part, the two edges in the marriage equality case reflect trade-offs common in strategic political decision-making, which are technology-independent and tap into longstanding debates between reformist and radical wings of activist (and specifically queer) communities. For the Australian Marriage Equality campaign this manifested in the tension between their strategic goal to persuade the majority-straight electorate to support a change to the law and their responsibility to articulate the diverse subjectivities of the LGBTIQ community.

We see our contribution in this chapter as pointing out the way datafication operated alongside questions of political strategy to bind the two sides of the sword even more tightly together, and sharpen their edges. Toward the end of the chapter we detail how the precise technological affordances that gave the campaign political power also brought specific challenges, as seen on three distinct levels: first, increased scale in story collection necessitated increased selectivity on the part of campaigners and a shift in agency away from storytellers; second, increased reach in story dissemination brought with it an increased emphasis on audience responses; and third, the positive feedback loops that optimised both supporter and staff behavior also narrowed the field of possibilities for which stories were being told. In sum, AME's highly successful campaign demonstrates the difficult trade-offs involved in crowdsourced and datafied storytelling, and offers insights into the dynamics of new forms of advocacy beyond the specifics of this individual case.

6.1 The Politics of Queer Storytelling

The politics of queer storytelling follows dynamics that will be familiar from those sketched in the previous chapters of this book. Stories become political when they publicly articulate the previously private subjectivity of the storyteller (Jackson 2013); and like the disability rights campaigners in the previous chapter, part of campaigning for queer rights involves making the invisible visible.

Yet, at the same time, queer storytelling also has its own history and contradictions, encapsulated most clearly in the trajectory of the "coming out" story. Ken Plummer (1994) described how the increasingly public circulation of formulaic coming out storylines toward the end of the twentieth century served both to establish the collective identity of Western gay and lesbian communities and reinforce somewhat restrictive narrative tropes for the expression of that identity. In Plummer's view, such stories followed a fairly linear narrative arc, from troubled childhood through to a moment of crisis, followed by resolution in self-actualization through membership of the LGBTIQ community; his prediction was that in the future such authoritative "modernist tales" would give way to a new politics defined by "the delight of differences" (Plummer 1994, 148). Nevertheless, subsequent research has continued to show a tension between formula stories and the capacity for queer self-expression. For example, Sara L. Crawley and K. L. Broad (2004) wrote in their study of storytelling in student organization panels at U.S. universities that

> Most important, we see our work as a caution to progressive movements making use of formula stories. While formula stories like the coming-out narrative remain politically efficacious in some sense, they also limit the possibility of narrating queerness and complexity. (Crawley and Broad 2004, 69)

As recently as 2020, Dominique Adams-Santos noted that the narrative strategies in Black women's coming out stories on YouTube ranged from those appealing to respectability norms to those pushing back against them with "intimate candour" about queer sexual desire, as well as those alternating between the two styles (Adams-Santos 2020). Optimistically, the technologically mediated proliferation of queer storytelling in the context of shifting social norms has opened up space for new storylines; a more pessimistic view notes the ongoing power of narrative tropes to constrain as well as enable queer self-expression.

For the purposes of our case study of the AME campaign we highlight three themes from existing research. First, storytelling has always been central to the exercise of power for queer people through enacting and publicly articulating subjectivities that have historically contended with erasure. Second, there are longstanding tensions between the regulating power of narrative tropes and a more deconstructive counter-impulse, such as expressed through ambivalence around coming out storylines. Third, changes to the technological mediation of these narratives have been an important part of their evolution, in particular since the growth of social media over the past decade. In the rest of this chapter, we draw these three strands together to shed further light on how datafication processes represent a potentially new development in the evolution of queer storytelling.

6.2 The Australian Marriage Equality Campaign

Although Australia's national vote on marriage equality was finally held in 2017, its first seeds were planted thirteen years earlier. When the Australian Parliament, under conservative prime minister John Howard, passed the Marriage Amendment Act 2004 and reinforced the legal definition of marriage as a union of a man and a woman, a majority of Australians supported the legislation. However, the position of LGBTIQ Australians themselves was reasonably divided: some critiqued the institution of marriage as patriarchal and heteronormative; others called for a greater focus on more materially grounded inequalities that existed for unmarried or "de facto" same-sex couples (such as in taxation law, access to healthcare, and so on). In fact, it was only after the Howard government passed its 2004 legislation and made marriage a symbolic marker of (in)equality that it was elevated as a political priority for LGBTIQ activists, leading for the first time to the creation of multiple national-level organizations campaigning for marriage equality (Bernstein and Naples 2015). By 2017, there was a high degree of coherence among LGBTIQ activists, who were desperate to win the political battle that had been running for the past thirteen years, despite that the historical desire for marriage among Australian LGBTIQ activists—in the absence of such a salient symbolic battle—had been less clear.

The period of 2004 to 2017 can be summarized as a drawn-out period of parliamentary nonresponsiveness in the face of rising public support for legislative change (the first poll showing majority support for marriage equality was in 2007). Importantly, 2016 saw the election of a proequality Liberal/National Coalition prime minister (Malcolm Turnbull), a proequality opposition leader of the Labor Party (Bill Shorten), and many proequality members of Parliament and senators. Nevertheless, the combination of strong parties, weak governments, and hardened opposition among well-placed conservative veto players stymied a parliamentary solution to the impasse (Vaughan 2019).

Another key dynamic playing out over these years was the diffusion of marriage equality internationally, both as policy reform and a rights norm (Vries-Jordan 2021). In the United States, marriage equality was both lost and won in different popular votes, from 2008's bruising Proposition 8 referendum in California to the first successful popular state votes in 2012. Activists' experiences in these early campaigns, such as the effectiveness of negative messaging around risks to children, would be directly fed into strategic messaging of campaigns in other countries like Ireland and Australia. These messages nevertheless had to be tailored to specific cultural contexts: U.S. campaigners have reflected how, for example, language around equality resonated much more successfully in Ireland than it had in the United States (Zepatos and Meeker 2017).

By the time of the 2017 vote in Australia, there was a wealth of this kind of messaging research to draw on, and some of the strategic decisions of the AME campaign, like avoiding a focus on same-sex parents, can be explained partly through this transnational diffusion of prior learning. Australian campaigners learned not just from the messaging research of other marriage equality contests but also from the technological innovations happening in campaigning more generally. As one key memoir reflects, when devising their strategy "the team . . . hit the phones to talk with campaigners around the world, including people working on the United States (U.S.) primaries deploying the newest campaign technologies" (Greenwich and Robinson 2018, 197). The Australian campaign can therefore be seen as influenced by two distinct learning processes: strategic messaging in marriage equality campaigning and story tech innovation.

On August 9, 2017, the Liberal/National Coalition government announced a nationwide postal ballot would be conducted by the Australian Bureau of Statistics as a noncompulsory quasi-plebiscite to break the parliamentary gridlock and resolve the issue once and for all. In the subsequent campaign more than twelve million Australians—almost 80 percent of the population—returned a survey, with 62 percent supporting a change to the law to allow same sex couples to marry.[1] Our case study focuses on how this shifting political context shaped the role of digital storytelling for the structurally marginalized LGBTIQ community. Specifically, the calling of a nationwide postal ballot to resolve the issue of marriage equality on August 9, 2017, was a critical juncture, which shifted the political context from a more institutionally oriented lobbying campaign to a more public-facing mobilization and persuasion campaign.

In this context, we analyzed the role of digital storytelling in AME's campaigning, how this changed following the shift to a public vote in 2017, and how the shift to a more public-facing campaign influenced the representation of storytellers in AME's campaign. To analyze the shifting relationship between political context and digital storytelling, we used a mixed-methods approach that drew on two main sources of data: first, we conducted a quantitative content analysis of all AME's communication on Instagram from January 1, 2017, to November 15, 2017, encompassing the precampaign period before the public vote was announced, and the formal campaign period itself. We selected Instagram as a highly popular social network site in Australia being used by 45 percent of Australians in 2018 (*Sensis Social Media Report*, 2018); although the AME campaign used a variety of different social media channels, we chose Instagram because of the likelihood that the platform would emphasize personalized and affect-driven storytelling. Data was collected via the CrowdTangle platform for academics, which provided complete historical data of all the public account's posts as well as metadata around user engagement, such as likes and comments. These 245 Instagram posts are coded for the presence of storytelling, as well as a range of more specific variables like the identity of storytellers and dominant frames, using a slightly tweaked version of the coding scheme developed for the chapter on disability campaigns (more information about this is available in the appendix). Second, we also report on semistructured interviews with four key campaign staff who were directly involved in the collection, curation, and dissemination of stories in AME's campaign.

6.3 Crowdsourcing and Promoting Marriage Equality Stories

The following results section presents combined analysis of the campaign's Instagram data, as well as interview data from campaign staff, integrated along thematic lines. Findings are organized in two sections corresponding to the chapter's two core themes: first, an examination of the significance of storytelling in AME's campaign, and second, analysis of the dynamics of representation for storytellers.

Fig. 6.1. "Nick and I . . .", Instagram post, Australian Marriage Equality, September 2017

6.3.1 The Significance of Storytelling for AME's Campaign

First, what did storytelling actually look like in AME's campaign? In figure 6.1, we have included a screenshot of one of the posts on the campaign's public page.

Several features in this story effectively illustrate campaign strategies that are themes throughout the chapter, such as the positive emotion conveyed through the image and the frames of romantic love and equality that run through the story text ("All we want is to be treated equally under the law"). The narrative begins with the personal, at the start of the relationship: "Nick and I met thirteen years ago as students at Sydney University, we fell in love and now we've been together for ten wonderful years." The story then builds to a broader sense of the present challenge and collective agency: "We were planning a huge party for our ten-year anniversary with friends and family, but instead we joined 30,000 other Australians to march for equality in Sydney!" AME campaigners reported that in total they crowdsourced around 15,000 of these kinds of personal stories for use in their campaign.

Analysis of AME's Instagram account demonstrates that storytelling played an ongoing role before and after the shift to a public nationwide vote, although the intensity of storytelling increased significantly in this final campaign period. Figure 6.2 shows that while 11 percent of precampaign posts contained storytelling, this increased to 24 percent for the campaign

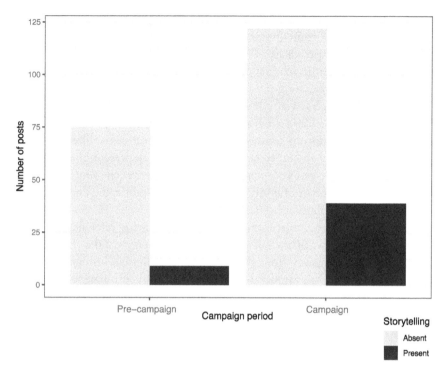

Fig. 6.2. Salience of storytelling in AME campaign

period.[2] This suggests that AME saw personal stories as useful narrative "ammunition" to target the voting public.

As in the other case study chapters that examine specific storytelling campaigns, we applied a reasonably strict definition of personal storytelling: a story had to include narrated details about events (a beginning, a middle, and an end, which could be implied or alluded to) and/or characters, told in order to make a point. For example, there were many posts sharing photos of campaigners taking part in actions, attending events, or holding up "Yes" campaign material. While this helped to construct a broader narrative of the campaign as grassroots, we did not code it as containing personal storytelling unless the accompanying text provided story-oriented biographical detail from one or more of the activists. The kind of posts that did not contain storytelling had varied purposes such as documenting events like public forums and showing volunteers supporting the campaign. As the year progressed, posts also performed an important information-distribution function: AME tried to raise awareness about deadlines for enrolling to vote, deadlines for putting ballot papers in the mail, and outcomes of critical events like court challenges to the postal vote itself.

Closely analyzing the posts that contained storytelling, some clear similarities in form and content emerged. Stories generally focused on sharing the personalized experiences of "everyday" individuals: stories were overwhelmingly narrated in the first person (78 percent) and 81 percent of storytellers had no preexisting public profile, sharing their experience as private citizens (examples of storytellers who did have a public profile included actor Hugh Jackman and an Australian reality television personality in a same-sex relationship). In contrast, politicians and institutionalized politics were almost entirely absent. In fact, the only politician present in any of the storytelling content was Independent MP Alex Greenwich, who is openly gay and acted as cochair of AME, and he appeared in the same image as one of the other storytellers.

Crucially, there were no examples of politicians being referenced or targeted directly in text or images. This reflects a strategy on the part of the campaign to move away from the polarized and divisive history of party politics on the issues, similar to the way disability campaigners in the United States avoided referencing Trump and the Republicans in their story-centered posts, as discussed in chapter 5. One AME organizer explained in an interview that they "wanted to make sure that it [the campaign] represented a very specific vision we had for Australia, which is progressive, but not in a partisan way" (Interviewee A, AME, June 2020). The focus on everyday citizens taking action for the people they love is illustrated in figure 6.3: the storyteller relates that she is taking action for those close to her: "It breaks my heart to think that my sister, my housemate and half of my closest friends don't have the same rights as I do." She emphasizes the desire to "win this" by making calls for the campaign, but agency and in this case "responsibility" lie at the level of the individual citizen rather than partisan elites.

In interviews, campaigners largely discussed the increasing importance of storytelling for the campaign (as visualized in the above figures) in terms of the strategic political context. They generally referred to themselves as political outsiders in relation to institutional politics, as summarized by one interviewee: "storytelling was the only way we could leverage power. We had to build people and make things difficult for the politicians" (Interviewee B, AME, July 2020). Not only were they institutional political outsiders, but they also differentiated themselves from other more established nongovernmental organizations (NGOs):

> There are certain NGOs that have stable funding and have been around for a long time and have a brand name. That means they have a type of power that they can leverage to achieve their outcomes.

amequality ✓ · Follow

amequality ✓ "It breaks my heart to think that my sister, my housemate and half of my closest friends don't have the same rights as I do. They're in incredible, loving relationships that aren't seen as equal under the law. This campaign isn't about me, but I do have a responsibility to do everything I can to fight for equality for the people I love, and so should you. Everyday I'm fighting as hard as i can to win this, and ensure my LGBTI friends and family are supported, loved and eventually, equal. I signed up to, and have been making calls as

Liked by   and others
September 15, 2017

Add a comment...

Fig. 6.3. "It breaks my heart . . . ," Instagram post, Australian Marriage Equality, September 2017

Meaning they don't necessarily have to adapt, or that's why they haven't adapted. . . . We're a smaller NGO . . . asking people to share stories and putting those back out online helps bring people toward you, build a community, get you that power you need to change. (Interviewee B, AME, July 2020)

AME therefore viewed itself as distinctive in being established as a stand-alone campaigning organization focusing on the single issue of marriage equality. This created challenges in terms of establishing new organizational structures, rapidly building public legitimacy, and finding avenues for influence; it also created opportunities to innovate, experiment, and devolve agency to supporters in ways that may be less appealing to larger "brand name" organizations. The urgency of the time-limited campaign, and the pressure to succeed in a high-stakes public vote, further drove the campaign's willingness to experiment. Storytelling for AME was a strategy to organize and exercise power in light of an unresponsive institutional political system, and in the absence of alternatives available to more established advocacy groups.

There are, however, particular features to advocacy around LGBTIQ politics that also shaped the prominence and character of AME's storytelling. Reflecting on the individualized and personalized quality of the storytelling, campaigners noted the distinctive role of visibility and invisibility in LGB-TIQ identity, particularly in dynamic response to structural oppression. Part of the task of LGBTIQ activism historically has been publicly articulating its existence as a subjective position. In the words of one interviewee from AME:

> The LGBTI person, the story that you have to tell about your aware-ness of the world being unfair is essentially your coming out story and experience, which is then a complex story which involves you, your family's reaction, and other people's privacy. It's a much more com-plex story to tell, which is why the people who did it throughout the campaign are phenomenally brave and important . . . but it does feel that LGBTI storytelling for politics is a little different . . . for LGBTI people it's less visible. You often have to start "in" and then go "out." (Interviewee A, AME, June 2020)

This issue-specific centrality of sharing personal experiences is reflected in the composition of storytelling present in AME's Instagram content. When coded using Ganz's (2013) framework of differentiating between the story of self, story of us, and story of now, the largest focus in AME's campaigning was the story of self (90 percent of posts, compared with 49 percent contain-ing a story of us and 59 percent containing a story of now). This personaliza-tion and individualization are reinforced by the visual dimension, where the majority of storytellers are depicted posing for a portrait or looking directly into the camera (69 percent); the next most commonly depicted action was mailing a postal vote ballot (8 percent).

6.4 The Challenges of Representation

Turning to the second theme on the representation of storytellers in the AME campaign, we examined three key variables coded in the Instagram dataset: racial diversity, sexual orientation, and gender identity.

6.4.1 Racial Diversity

Regarding racial diversity in the Australian context, we attempted to code whether (1) storytellers explicitly referred to a Culturally and Linguistically Diverse (CALD) identity; (2) CALD identity was signaled in other ways, such as through visual cues; (3) storytellers explicitly referred to white racial identity; or (4) there was an absence of visible minority representation. As shown in figure 6.4, the vast majority (88 percent) of storytellers did not include visible minority representation. Only two stories made explicit reference to a nonwhite racial identity, one from a First Nations drag queen and another from a Chinese lesbian couple.

It is clear that the lack of racial and cultural diversity in storytellers in AME's campaign is not reflective of the composition of the Australian community, as in 2020 more than two million Australian residents, or almost 10 percent of the population, had been born in just five Asian countries (India, China, the Philippines, Vietnam, and Malaysia—see ABS 2021), not to mention the wider cross-section of the Australian-born community with diverse cultural and linguistic roots. Of course, it is likely that some of the storytellers who were coded as "Unclear" will have diverse racial and cultural backgrounds. However, we argue that if that identity is not signaled through textual or visual cues then it fails to achieve the objective of representing diversity visibly in a campaign's content.

One AME campaigner reflected that the lack of diversity resulted not from the strategic decisions of the campaign but rather the structural barriers to participation, which presented unevenly across different cultural cleavages. In language reminiscent of that used by the disability rights campaigners quoted in the previous chapter, they said that

> it's sometimes not, you know, [. . .] you can't be as diverse as you like. I mean, we certainly try to include ethnic diversity, but that was hard just finding people. A lot of ethnic backgrounds are more [. . .] there is a lot more homophobia in some of those communities and so it was harder for people to want to come forward and share their stories and so those are always a struggle to be ethnically more diverse, because certainly we were trying to do that. We weren't avoiding that, but that was just you know, it's probably whiter than you would want it to be if you were really thinking about it broadly. (Interviewee D, AME, August 2020)

The results of the nationwide vote did in fact demonstrate that there was some relationship between a high "No" vote in local communities and immigrant populations. McAllister and Snagovsky (2018) analyzed national voting data, broken down by electorate, to conclude that the strongest predictor of an electorate voting "no" overall was a large number of recently arrived immigrants (McAllister and Snagovsky 2018). Arguably LGBTIQ members

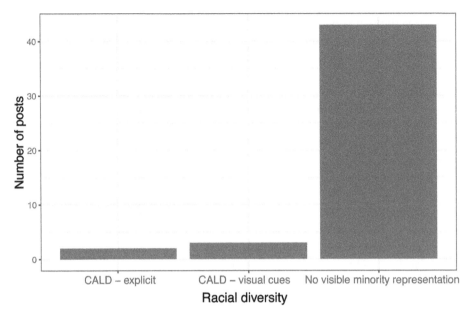

Fig. 6.4. Racial and cultural diversity of AME storytellers

of racial and cultural minority groups, if they did experience multiple forms of discrimination based on their intersectional identities, may also have been particularly keen to achieve representation in AME's reform campaign.

6.4.2 Sexual Orientation and Gender Identity

We also coded for the diversity of LGBTIQ identity presented in Instagram story-centered posts. We included two distinct codes, separately recording sexual orientation and then gender identity. For sexual orientation it was challenging to code confidently according to traditional identity labels in the community (e.g., "gay," "lesbian," etc.) since those often require explicit self-identification on the part of the individual. For example, a male-presenting storyteller referring to a male partner could potentially be gay, bisexual, or queer. We therefore focused more narrowly on same-sex versus opposite-sex orientation and coded (1) if the storyteller made explicit reference in the text to a same-sex relationship or same-sex attraction, (2) if this was not explicit in the text but made apparent such as through visual cues, (3) if the story-teller explicitly referred to opposite-sex relationship or attraction, or (4) if we were unsure based on the visual and textual information.

Figure 6.5 visualizes the results, which show a reasonably even spread across the different categories. Altogether just over half of storytellers could be understood as same-sex attracted either explicitly (31 percent) or implicitly (22 percent), with the remainder either explicitly straight (27 percent) or unclear (18 percent).

At one level, it is surprising that there is almost as much explicit articulation of opposite-sex attraction as same-sex attraction. Yet this can be better understood when considering AME's particular status as a marriage equality campaign rather than an LGBTIQ organization. In fact, campaigners were very deliberate on this fact, saying:

> We had a marriage equality community, and our marriage equality community was taking action for marriage equality. The [LGBTI] organizations themselves, most were quite supportive and aligned because of the sudden realization that it wasn't an LGBTI campaign and therefore it was a completely different constituency. (Interviewee C, AME, July 2020)

Importantly, AME viewed its primary constituency not as the LGBTIQ community but as people supporting marriage equality, who would have to be majority-straight in order to achieve the necessary public support to win the national vote. Viewed from this perspective, "diversity" came to be mobilized toward a different meaning for the campaign, as expressed here:

> it was also about ensuring that we could get as much diversity as possible in the stories that we were putting out, so that we accurately reflected the majority view of as many communities as we could, rather than just Sydney, Melbourne, LGBTI communities. (Interviewee C, AME, July 2020)

In this sense diversity is used to indicate the straight, regional, and rural supporters of marriage equality, which may not have seen themselves represented in existing portrayals of LGBTIQ advocacy. This operationalization of diversity is mobilized for strategic and instrumental reasons—in order to motivate public support ahead of the national vote—and not primarily to rectify an injustice for those underrepresented (straight, regional) communities.

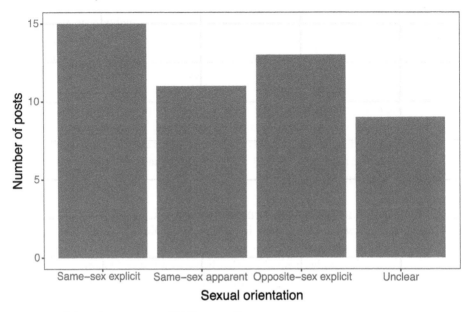

Fig. 6.5. Sexual orientation of AME storytellers

6.4.3 The Invisibility of LGBTIQ Identity

When same-sex relationships were the focus of the campaign's storytelling, it is remarkable how consistently language associated with LGBTIQ identity was avoided in favor of neutral tropes that could apply equally to queer or straight relationships. For example, we found only one explicit textual identifier of LGBTIQ identity (one reference to a storyteller identifying as lesbian) across the entire dataset of story-centered Instagram posts. In every other story about same-sex relationships, storytellers' same-sex orientation was usually made obvious through photographs or the couple referring to each other using gendered names ("Nick and I," "Vanessa and Kelly") or terms associated with relationships more broadly ("partner," "love of his life," "their sons' relationship"). The strategic motivation behind this form of storytelling was recognized by some interviewees, who explained that

> with marriage equality, we were looking for people who had had really beautiful love stories, and that really just kind of reflecting the kind of just Western standards of romance stories there . . . by showing those stories, the stories of people who have been seen as outside the mainstream, in a narrative structure that is extraordinarily mainstream,

it sort of brought our strategic goal of normalizing. (Interviewee A, AME, June 2020)

Yet some campaigners expressed their difficulties with this strategic logic of "normalizing" LGBTIQ relationships. For example, another campaigner said that "it was not representative of the LGBTIQ community . . . it's almost like de-gaying us, you know, making us, just getting rid of anything gay and making us as normal, straight appearing as possible" (Interviewee C, AME, July 2020). Here, the tension emerges again between the strategic imperative of political storytelling as a tool for mass persuasion and motivation on one side and the normative goal of using storytelling to enable visibility and self-articulation for traditionally marginalized groups on the other. This dynamic was even more clear in the case of two specific groups: the trans community and queer parents. We coded stories for the presence of any explicit references to gender identity—either cis or trans. Nowhere in our dataset of story-centered Instagram posts were there any such references, leading to an absence of the concept of gender identity in AME's storytelling. This is particularly striking given that the trans community was one of the main targets of the opposing "No" campaign's public messaging. For example, a public ad about boys being told they could wear dresses in schools was used in a scare campaign about the threat of "radical LGBTIQ sex and gender education programs" in schools (Palin 2017). Similarly, we coded for the presence of children in AME's storytellers. In our dataset, children never appeared with LGBTIQ storytellers, but they did appear three times as part of the families of explicitly straight equality supporters, and once with storytellers whose orientation was unclear.

One interviewee explained that this lack of representation was largely driven by research conducted by AME at the start of the campaign, drawing on the experiences of similar marriage equality mobilization efforts in Ireland and the United States. Specifically, they explained that AME "didn't do justice to specifically those two communities, the trans community and the gay parent community, because [. . .] that was sort of the biggest fear in [. . .] all of the focus groups" (Interviewee B, AME, July 2020).

Reflecting on the opposing "No" campaign's public ad mentioned above, we can start to observe two conflicting campaign strategies. While the "No" campaign wanted to shift the terrain of the debate toward issues of gender diversity and children's welfare, the "Yes" campaign tried to maintain a focus on cis-gendered, adult, gay, and lesbian relationships that closely paralleled the dynamics of straight relationships. For gender diverse Australians and rainbow families, there was potential hurt and erasure from both campaigns.

6.5 The Double-Edged Sword

The previous section reported overall findings about AME's digital storytelling. First, stories were increasingly important as the campaign moved toward a public vote. Second, stories generally provided a personalized and individualized perspective on the debate. Third, stories presented a reasonably narrow representation of same-sex relationships as analogous to heterosexual romance, without reference to more controversial issues like parenting or gender identity.

In light of these insights, it is useful to focus on the question of how AME's storytelling campaign leveraged story tech, crowdsourcing, and datafication, and how this generated the specific opportunities and challenges introduced previously. Specifically, three affordances played an observable role. These included: increased scale of story collection through crowdsourcing; increased reach in story dissemination through platformed distribution; and reinforcing feedback loops for supporters and campaigners. These dimensions of storytelling are summarized in terms of opportunities and risks for marginalized communities in table 6.1.

The first key incentive for digitized story collection and datafication was increased scale. AME was a young, growing campaign organization that found itself at the center of a highly salient public debate, culminating in the sharp increase in public attention as the national postal vote was announced. Instead of relying on campaign staff or known activists to source stories, then, the campaign broadcast crowdsourced calls for supporters and members of the public to contribute their own narratives by email and website collection forms. Yet as the campaign increased the number of leads for potential stories—and therefore the chance of finding high-quality stories for campaign material—they had to apply filtering criteria to sort these leads. Campaigners described how stories would be filtered into multiple categories, with a middle-range category targeted for a photo and quote for social media, while the most powerful narratives would be tagged for film development or media talent.

Various criteria were applied in this filtering process, including the effectiveness and clarity of the communication style, the level of personal emotional connection (as opposed to more abstract argumentation), and some element of hopeful action potential at the end. However, these filtering decisions were largely made on strategic grounds. As one campaigner reflected:

> someone whose response [to story collection requests] was "this government's fucked, they're fucked, this is all stupid." [. . .] It's not that that person's story is not worthy, it's that when you're making a time cost analysis, there's a lot of work to move that person into a productive space for sharing a story. The other element of that is, there's no point in having everybody stuck in anger. [. .] It had to have that kind of hopeful end, in order to encourage people to take action and build that community. (Interviewee A, AME, June 2020)

These words suggest that campaigners viewed their decision in strategic terms as a response to the crowdsourced nature of their story collection. After all, the "time cost analysis" is directly related to asking thousands of individuals to share their stories, knowing that the limited number of staff and distribution opportunities can only directly develop a small subset of them for future communications. These strategic calculations have a clear rationale in terms of audience responses ("in order to encourage people to take action"), and the campaigner is at pains to stress that these strategic decisions are not a moral evaluation of the "worthiness" of the person's story. Although AME campaigners did not use the term story bank in interviews, their system effectively worked like one. Once initial leads were tagged, the database could be used to identify the most promising storylines for each strategic objective through search. Here, agency in decision-making about which stories are ultimately shared with a public audience shift between technological systems and intermediary campaigners, as the scale of story collection increases.

Table 6.1. The double-edged sword of datafied storytelling

Power of datafied storytelling	Risks for marginalized communities
Crowdsourcing enables increased scale of story collection	Increased need for selectivity and a shift in agency from the storyteller to intermediaries
Platformed distribution increases reach in story dissemination	Shift in priorities from articulating storyteller subjectivity toward aligning with audience preferences
Positive feedback loops optimize storytelling by supporters and campaigners	Narrowing field of possibilities for self-articulation

The second key incentive for using story tech and crowdsourced storytelling was increased reach in the dissemination of stories via digital platforms. With the shift to a postal vote campaign, suddenly the audience to persuade was comprised of the entire Australian electorate, rather than a particular set of politicians or institutional decision-makers (incidentally, this also provides an interesting contrast with the Little Lobbyists' U.S. case study reviewed in chapter 5, where moderate policymakers, both Democrat and Republican, represented a key target audience for crowdsourced personal stories). Digital platforms provide an ideal distribution mechanism to broadcast to this diffuse audience, particularly with the possibilities of viral social reach. Yet as soon as the intended reach for a narrative includes this kind of broad cross-section of the electorate, the mass preferences of those diffuse audiences acquire greater weight in shaping the form that storytelling takes. As one campaigner noted with reference to the 60,000 to 100,000 voters in each Australian federal electorate division:

> we try to sneak in a bit more diversity than perhaps is in that 60,000, 100,000 people, but nonetheless, the goal is to make those people feel like we are reflecting them. [. . .] That doesn't actually necessarily need to be those people themselves, but just people that they do respect, and not the people that they don't. (Interviewee C, AME, July 2020)

In this way, the broad reach of story dissemination also brings with it a weight of mass audience preferences, which exerts a tension against the political preferences of campaigners and the marginalized communities whose interests they are advocating for. Campaigners imagine who the "people that they do respect, and not the people that they don't" are, and in doing so anticipate and to some extent replicate norms about which voices are worth listening to.

The third key advantage of story tech and crowdsourced storytelling for AME were positive feedback loops for both campaigners and storytellers. For campaigners, the availability of data analytics in digital communication technologies as discussed by Karpf (2016) provided continuous feedback. Campaigners received a wealth of detailed information about which kind of stories achieved the best responses in terms of aggregate metrics such as likes and shares, which therefore shaped their future decisions about curation and story development as described previously. Yet individual supporters were also embedded in positive feedback loops: over the course of the campaign individuals observed the kind of stories being distributed by AME through their social media channels, and so came to learn which narrative themes, formats, and tropes were appropriate to this "genre" of storytelling. Sometimes this involved stylistic elements (like a focus on personal narrative rather than political polemic, and a focus on longer rather than shorter stories), and sometimes it involved the demographic profile of the storytellers themselves. In the words of one campaigner:

> Once we started displaying the stories that we were looking for, those were the responses being filled in the form. [. . .] We started putting out stories of parents, grandparents, and siblings, that's when we started to get stories back from parents, grandparents, and siblings. (Interviewee D, AME, August 2020)

The AME campaign therefore involved a chain of multiple positive feedback loops: from public audience to campaigners via data analytics, and from campaigners to individual storytellers through the modelling of genre-appropriate stories. In this way, even though stories were being crowdsourced by self-selecting individuals sharing their own experiences, over time the datafied nature of the storytelling process directed the shape that these stories took, with significant weight given to the ultimate strategic goal of influencing public audience responses. It is important, however, not to overstate these relationships as deterministic. Campaigners were agents who also engaged critically with the ethics and politics of mass audience preferences, as demonstrated by this recollection of the role of racial diversity:

> if we put a film out, and the image, the thumbnail was of someone of color it had a lot less views. I didn't know what was going on. I didn't understand until our editor pointed it out to me, 'cause I kept saying, "Why is nobody watching these films?" and she said, "It's because Australia is just racist." So that was [. . .] well, my attitude was like fuck it, you know? Sorry. You gotta get over your shit. (Interviewee C, AME, July 2020)

Here it is clear that there are times when even though audience preferences can be clearly perceived by campaigners, there can be a desire and capacity to contradict those expectations, even if this comes at a strategic cost (in this case, "a lot less views"). When to conform to these mass preferences, and when to challenge them, are challenging and important questions, and yet they remain largely invisible in the pipeline of technology-powered advocacy storytelling.

The metaphor of the double-edged sword illustrates how technological affordances bring a complex bundle of effects along with them. Crowdsourcing, datafication, and story tech more broadly may mean increased scale of story collection, reach in distribution, and optimization of storytelling over time; yet they also shift the agency toward intermediaries and audiences in the curation and development of those stories.

6.6 Conclusion

This chapter has used the case study of the Australian Marriage Equality campaign in 2017 to sketch a "double-edged sword" for marginalized communities in the possibilities of datafied storytelling. AME invested heavily in crowdsourced storytelling as part of their ultimately successful political strategy: stories made up a large part of their communications, increasingly so as the campaign moved to a public vote, and provided the tools to mobilize a majority-straight electorate to support greater equality for LGBTIQ people. Yet, partly as a result of these strategic pressures, and partly as a result of structural barriers to participation, the representation of storytellers in this campaign did not reflect the diversity of the LGBTIQ community, at times deferring to the preferences of its intended audience. Storytellers were overwhelmingly white, queer relationships were largely communicated through neutral romantic tropes and terminology to draw an analogy with straight relationships, and trans people and queer parents were entirely absent from these stories.

Through this case study, we argue that three mechanisms that provide the incentives for datafied storytelling also contain the seeds for these tensions between campaigners and individual storytellers. Increased scale in crowdsourced story collection improves the quality of story leads for campaigners—but also increases the need for selectivity that shifts agency away from storytellers toward campaigner intermediaries. Increased reach in digital dissemination means greater impact in persuading the voting public—but also a greater perceived weight given to diffuse audience preferences. Feedback loops that optimize storytelling on the part of both campaigners and storytellers improve the impact of stories over time—but narrow the field of possibilities that storytelling can offer as a form of self-articulation in response to audience cues.

This chapter adds to existing critical analyses of the role of storytelling in politics, such as Sujatha Fernandes's (2017) argument that they individualize structural grievances. The contribution of this chapter is to highlight the specific set of opportunities and challenges for advocacy organizations brought by digital communication technologies. The Australian Marriage Equality case also demonstrates, however, the critical and reflexive position that citizens and campaigners can take in response to the datafication of storytelling. AME campaigners reflected actively on the ethics of representation in their advocacy, and in multiple cases appeared to carry lessons from their experiences into subsequent advocacy work; and the aftermath of the vote saw citizens generating their own critical accounts and archives of the perspectives that had been underrepresented by the campaign's discourse. It remains to be seen how the "double-edged sword" of datafied storytelling develops over time, including whether the dimensions we outlined here apply in other cases and country contexts. From the vantage point of our project, the uneasy tensions between exercising political influence and enabling representation are unlikely to be resolved any time soon—and the ongoing evolution of technology-powered storytelling is likely to play an important part.

CHAPTER 7

Frontline "Heroes"

*Unions and Essential Workers' Stories
during the Pandemic*

As we have seen in previous chapters, the use of compelling personal stories in digital campaigns is now a normalized strategic activity for advocacy groups. Yet the success of storytelling campaigns often rests on the promotion of a positive cause for social change and can be more difficult to enact for groups that seek to challenge and disrupt system-wide, material conditions. The Covid-19 pandemic introduced unique circumstances for advocacy organizations as mobilization and promotion of political causes relied primarily on digital campaigning. At the same time, in both Australia and the United States many paid workers faced significant challenges during the pandemic. This included the loss of employment, work shifting from in-person to online or becoming hybrid, or the workplace itself becoming a space of heightened health and economic risk. Essential workers, ranging from health and care workers to those in retail and supply chains, often encountered increased levels of health risk, in-person abuse, and increased job precarity and financial insecurity.

In light of this, this chapter looks at how labor unions were active during the first two years of the pandemic in both defining and promoting positive stories of essential workers to advocate for broader industrial and policy-level change. We analyzed whether there was evidence of large-scale story collection and dissemination by unions though social media and demonstrate that essential worker stories were mainly used to buttress existing union campaigns on job security and low-paid work. This reinforces that the practice of digital unionizing focuses on government and media influence, and to a lesser extent membership-focused communications. During the pandemic these communicative approaches were used to broaden the idea of the "essential worker" in the public imagination to include low-paid workers in several sectors, including retail, supply, and distribution, who kept both countries functioning. This was a different strategy to primarily making material demands on the state, or claiming grievances on behalf of union members alone. Instead, the use of crowdsourced storytelling *from* workers *to* workers and the broader public was key for changing the narrative about workers' variable and often inequitable experiences during the pandemic.

7.1 Unions, Digital Organizing, and Storytelling

Jen Schradie (2021) argued that studies of digital unionizing that focus predominantly on Internet-based mechanisms for mobilization fail to understand the current role of unions. Instead, she suggested that more emphasis needs to be given to class, community, and context. What she means is that any understanding of a recent union campaign ought to be grounded within the broader geographical and historical context for union organizing in a particular area or industry, as well as an understanding of class capacity, solidarity, and engagement with digital technologies more broadly. In this chapter, we use the distinct context of the 2020–2021 pandemic where most union campaigning and organizing needed to shift online, away from local workplace and geographic community contexts.

Unions are fundamentally different from the other organizations we have analyzed so far in this book, many of which are digital native—that is, their digital strategy underpins their direction and tactics. Instead, unions are at their core member-driven organizations built around organizing workplaces to advocate for improving working conditions and providing advisory and support services for low-paid or disadvantaged workers. As a result, unions have been slower to adapt to new technologies and organize online (Dencik and Wilkin 2020) and have had a tendency to use digital media to broadcast key messages to either recruit new members or mobilize existing members (Frangi et al. 2020; Hennebert et al. 2021; Houghton and Hodder 2021). There have also been concerns among some traditional unions about media-focused activism that arguably centers on "public image, public relations and symbolic power at the expense of worker and community organization" (Dencik and Wilkin 2020, 1734).

Despite that digital organizing has been found to be incidental and/or underdeveloped as part of union strategy, there is new research with evidence of unions using social media technologies to both extend their reach and their own relevance as political campaigners. This includes moving beyond their existing membership to build support for collective bargaining power (Uba and Jansson 2021) and to build engagement and attention for core industrial causes and the situation of workers. Panagiotopoulos (2021) argues that social media has fundamentally changed the perspective unions have on how new connections and interactions happen through digital organizing, and how they understand (or imagine) the audience for their social media posts. He summarizes three core tendencies. First, union social media use has led to engagement with either atypical or less visible union members, such as women, young people, or part-time workers (see Thornthwaite et al. 2018 who also found that women union members were more likely to actively engage with union Facebook pages). Second, social media provide opportunities to distribute and democratize conversations among members and lead to ad hoc networking or strengthening of weak professional ties. Third, social media broadens the audience beyond union members to potential members or other targets of messages, including other unions or sympathetic NGOs, employers, the general public, and government (Panagiotopoulos 2021). The overarching point here is that unions have the opportunity to use social media to promote core messages, ideas, and stories into a broader political discourse that will be sympathetic to their core constituency: low-paid, disadvantaged workers. By not focusing on union members and union sympathizers alone as their imagined audience they remove themselves from being the center of the story to instead focus on creating public empathy with the struggles of workers for workplace and socioeconomic equity.

Australia and the United States can both be classified as liberal industrial regimes with decentralized collective bargaining coverage, a close relationship to the more labor-oriented political party (the Australian Labor Party and the U.S. Democratic Party, respectively), but minimalist interactions with unions as social partners of the state (Uba and Jansson 2021). To a large extent, unions facing membership decline, and exclusion from a social partnership and corporatist-style negotiations with governments over industrial policy, have needed to explore both new forms of unionizing, less driven by traditional membership models based on fulltime workers and using industrial power for collective bargaining or strikes. This focus has necessitated expanding their discursive power via messages to a broader public audience (Pasquier and Wood 2018), as well as a response to the realities of the contemporary labor market where the biggest growth has been in insecure contract work and "gig work." Thus there have also been notable incidences where storytelling and crowdsourced forms of storytelling have been used when unions intersect with new digital organizations that use social media-based campaigning.

For example, this was seen in Our Walmart, an independent workers association campaigning for fairer pay for retail workers (Pasquier and Wood 2018); the Fight for $15 campaign to attain higher minimum wage guarantees in the United States for precarious fast-food workers (Dencik and Wilkin 2020; Frangi et al. 2020); the emergence of born-digital worker-focused groups, such as Co-worker, the online platform that campaigned on worker safety, sick leave, and hazard pay issues during the pandemic; and SumOfUs, the corporate focused version of international online campaigning organization Avaaz. SumOfUs is an example of social movement or community unionism: it campaigns for workers' rights and for fair and sustainable supply chains worldwide, targeting campaigns to corporations and government. Ostensibly it looks like the merger of a progressive environmental campaign organization with traditional union concerns: it campaigns on sustainability, civil liberties, and animal rights, *as well as* worker rights and economic justice, privatization of public services, trade and finance deals, and shareholder advocacy. It is within the increasingly crowded progressive digital campaigning ecosystem that unions are trying to gain media and public attention, as well as both collect and disseminate the stories of low-paid, disadvantaged workers.

A recent study by Però and Downey (2022) argues for the idea of "communicative unionism" built on the discursive power that new, independent unions might have to change prevailing views of fairness in workplaces. This is a shift from the broadcast or top-down form of distributing core union messages, to the more personal, brief, visual, and emotive style of social media posting that people-to-people storytelling strategies encapsulate (Pasquier and Wood 2018). "Indie unions" have emerged over the last decade as a grassroots phenomenon in the United Kingdom, consisting of precarious low-paid, migrant workers in the service sectors, such as outsourced cleaners, porters, riders, sex workers, and security guards from more than sixty-seven different national backgrounds. They emerged largely because of the inadequate treatment that these workers received in mainstream unions. Notable Indie unions include the Independent Workers' Union of Great Britain, the United Voices of the World, and the Cleaners and Allied Independent Workers Union, which are all now legally registered trade unions that represent, organize, and bargain for (and with) low-paid precarious migrant workers (Però and Downey 2022, 7). There is a discursive lineage between the Indie unions and campaigns that organized workers in the United States like Our Walmart and Fight for $15. Però and Downey (2022) found that the media strategy of U.K. Indie unions focused successfully on "secondary stakeholders," beyond workers themselves, and that this "'outward' framing is intended to resonate with mainstream ideas of fairness, decency, dignity, and respect populating the public arena, so as to generate discursive power and boost workers' overall negotiating leverage" (Però and Downey 2022, 16).

Also important here is a long-held perception that unions find it difficult to engage with an intersectional discourse and framing of marginalization and insecurity in the workplace. That is, unions have typically focused on white working-class men as their core constituency when, in reality, most low-paid workers are now women and/or people of color. Part of the importance of campaigns such as Fight for $15 is that, despite support for organizing from the Service Employees International Union (SEIU), they did not label themselves as union campaigns and built coalitions with other movements such as Black Lives Matter. As Tapia and coauthors (2017) pointed out, the Fight for $15 movement still used material inequity and economic frames in their organizing, but "their model differs from traditional union organizing in that they recognize that economic identity cannot be the sole focus, and that workers' multiple identities matter when considering not only their economic experience, but also their social and political experiences" (p. 503). This intersectional experience being reflected in public debate does the discursive power work for unions and those advocating on behalf of low-paid workers, demonstrating that the workplace intersects with all dimensions of worker's lives and experience.

In Australia, the vast majority of unions are members of the umbrella body for unions, the Australian Council of Trade Unions (ACTU), which coordinates union campaigns across the country, represents workers in a range of government and/or international forums, and supplies industrial and policy research support to unions. Due to the dominance of the ACTU and its members, it has been rare for new, low-paid worker-focused groups, such as the U.K. Indie unions, to emerge. One interesting exception is the Retail and Fast Food Workers Union (RAFFWU). This started in 2016 as a deliberate competitor to the dominant union in the sector, the Shop, Distributive and Allied Employees Association (SDA), which it saw as more conservative and beholden to employers. RAFFWU has used digital campaigning to organize precarious workers in areas historically difficult for unions to organize within, such as McDonald's, small business retailers, and Apple stores. However, RAFFWU has little structural power, is not a union registered under the Fair Work Act, and can be excluded from industrial bargaining between employers and workers. As a result, its membership base remains small, at around 10 percent of that of the SDA.

The broader debate in Australia around the increasing precarity of work contracts, as well as routine underpayment or "wage theft," opened up spaces for new digital and personalized, story-driven campaigning. Recently the charge of wage theft in Australia transitioned from mainly focusing on immigrant workers in the agricultural sector to include low-paid hospitality and service workers, and this breadth fostered high-profile, media driven campaigns for fair pay (Clibborn 2020). For example, there were several digital petitions (using the union-run petition platform Megaphone) and personal story-led campaigns by hospitality workers against well-known employers, including a television celebrity chef who ran several restaurants in Melbourne. The discursive power of ideas such as wage theft already primed the broader Australian public about the systematic inequities in low-paid and precarious work and this made space for a broader focus on essential workers during the pandemic.

Unions in both Australia and the United States have a long history as organized, industrial representatives of workers and as actors within politics, which is a core part of their own legitimating story. They are also influential actors within progressive social change movements and have been involved in digital organizing coalitions and providing establishment funding for new organizations, like GetUp! in Australia (see Vromen 2017). However, when they collect personal stories online, it is less clear cut whether they are genuinely crowdsourcing new content from members and workers or simply adding digital collection onto existing strategies aimed at organizing or servicing their membership, such as creating online member profiles or advertising events. There is evidence that the individual stories of high-profile union leaders are increasingly being promoted and disseminated as part of broadening the audience for union campaigns and gaining media attention. Unions and union leaders in both Australia and the United States ably and interactively use both Facebook and Twitter, and, to a lesser extent, Instagram and Tik Tok, to promote messages, memes, and campaigns.

The most senior union leader in Australia, the Australian Council of Trade Unions (ACTU) National Secretary, Sally McManus is adept at both legacy and social media engagement, with nearly 130,000 followers on X/Twitter and 42,000 on Facebook. Her strategy is a shift from what has generally been found in earlier research: union leaders mainly use social media to distribute union media releases and set talking points to shape public debate, rather than actively engaging in debate itself (see Hennebert et al. 2021). As we discuss below, union leaders such as Sally McManus in Australia and Liz Shuler, president of the American Federation of Labor and Congress of Industrial Organizations (AFL-CIO) in the United States, were important actors both working with and against governments to change the dominant storyline about workers during the pandemic, as well as guiding public opinion about appropriate and worker-safe policy interventions.

7.2 Workers and the Pandemic in the United States and Australia

In the first stage of the Covid-19 pandemic in 2020, Australian unions participated in a revisiting of a corporatist or tripartite arrangement with government and business in attempts to rapidly respond to the pandemic and accompanying economic crisis (Gavin 2022). Australia shut its borders to the rest of the world, instituted hotel quarantines, and locked down large sections of industry, such as hospitality, food, and entertainment, as well as supporting work from home protocols for most people in desk-based, white-collar jobs (around 50 percent of the working population). New economic provisions were adopted to support those newly out of work, such as doubling welfare payments and also supporting businesses to keep their workers employed through a wage subsidy program called JobKeeper. Through this 2020 tripartite policy arrangement Australia did not really experience the Alpha or Delta waves of Covid-19 in the same way as Europe, the United Kingdom, and the United States; and both the extent of illness and deaths from Covid-19 were comparatively small.

However, in mid-2021 the major Australian cities moved into lockdown again while attempting to rapidly vaccinate the population. The effects of the pandemic hit the Australian economy, with significantly more job losses, a lack of cooperation between government, industry and unions (Gavin 2022), and disagreement over plans on how to reopen the national and state borders and the major industries that had been shut down. By November 2021, 80 percent of the adult population were vaccinated, and it was agreed that at least state, and slowly national, borders would open, and many people would be able to return to work. After this point, there was less social distancing or masking being mandated in public places, and with increased mobility many more Australians caught the Omicron variant of Covid-19. In early 2021, Covid-19 was mainly spreading in workplaces, by early 2022 this was mainly happening within families and in social situations generally, but also still in workplaces. To a large extent the workplace and working environment is at the center of our collective imagination of how people responded to the spread of Covid-19. There is still much to reflect on about the Australian pandemic situation and its long-term effect on work and well-being (Shergold et al. 2022). Suffice to say that by late 2022, while sadly

15,000 Australians from a population of 25 million died of Covid-19, this can be compared favorably to much higher per capita death rates in the United States of over one million deaths in a population of 330 million (World Health Organization, n.d.).

In the United States, leadership changed midway through the pandemic from an antiunion Trump Republican administration to a more labor sympathetic government under Democratic president Joe Biden. For example, essential workers were discussed in the 2020 U.S. presidential campaign with union criticisms that the Trump administration had not done enough to protect essential workers (Brooks 2020). Earlier, a newly constructed legal category of essential workers had been used in August 2020 in the United States to force teachers to go back to classroom-based work (Westwood 2020). One of Biden's flagship campaign promises was the American Rescue Plan, which he eventually signed into law in March 2021 and contained $1.9 trillion federal funds for economic stimulus (*American Rescue Plan*, n.d.). A core plank of this plan in its original version was raising the minimum wage to $15 per hour (by 2025) in response to the Fight for $15 and union campaigns mentioned above to lift more workers out of poverty, although eventually this was dropped from the final bill. Biden also campaigned on increasing protections for essential workers that expanded the category and particularly focused on low-paid workers at risk of catching Covid (*Joe Biden's 4-Point Plan for Our Essential Workers*, n.d.).

Over time, it is harder to see that essential workers became a distinct and settled legal category in the United States as state-based laws and approaches varied so much. Though it is notable that in Congress new legislation was launched by the Democrats in May 2021 to ensure citizenship for low-paid essential workers, many of whom were immigrants and without any citizenship rights (*S.747—117th Congress (2021–2022)* 2021). There was also a federal fund for bonus or hazard pay for frontline workers (Lieb 2021). While most healthcare workers could access this hazard pay, retail workers were added at a later stage in some places, as well as those working in law enforcement and prisons.

Overall, what we can see is that the pandemic context in both countries was important in changing how the general public discussed, understood, and experienced paid work. It provided a unique opportunity to change the dominant discourse about low-paid and essential workers needed to keep both the economy and society functioning in a time of crisis. Former divides between blue-collar and white-collar work, high-paid and low-paid work, or service work versus knowledge work became less clear cut. The main divisions in work during the pandemic were threefold. First, there was work that was still able to be undertaken and was not shut down or furloughed altogether leading to job losses, for example the live entertainment industry or flight industry where workers were largely out of work. Second, there was work that could be done at home or mediated via online platforms, for example the rapid shift in professional work that once relied on in-person interaction, such as seeing a doctor and the use of telehealth or legal proceedings that moved online, and largely the delivery of university and school education all went online. Third, there was the socially and economically essential work that needed to continue in-person and in workplaces.

Within this framework, essential work was not uniform because it is both low-paid and high-paid, it is both professional and low skilled, it is also both visible and invisible. Essential work ranged from high-profile healthcare workers such as nurses and doctors working on the front line of the pandemic to blue-collar workers in factories, in manufacturing or construction work, to service economy work in retail and supermarkets. Reconceptualizing paid work in this way also helps to see the opportunities for unions to campaign in new ways for the rights of low-paid workers to fair and equal treatment within their workplaces, especially when their members were essential workers at risk of catching illness, such as nurses and retail workers. It also reveals the expanding policy advocacy role for unions in arguing for a new, publicly driven economic and social safety net.

7.3 Media Attention to Essential Workers

To contextualize our analysis of personal stories of essential workers disseminated by unions, we initially conducted a review of how major newspapers focused on this category. For this, we used the media database Factiva and searched for mentions of "essential worker" in the headline or first paragraph of major newspapers in both Australia and the United States between March 1, 2020, and March 1, 2022. For the entire period, this returned 187 Australian articles (in the *Sydney Morning Herald*, the *Age*, the *Australian*, the *Australian Financial Review*, the *Daily Telegraph*, the *Herald Sun*); and 262 U.S. articles (in *The Wall Street Journal*, *The New York Times*, *U.S.A. Today*, *The Washington Post*, *Los Angeles Times*). The word clouds[1] in figures 7.1 and 7.2 provide an initial overview of the relative frequency of the words used in newspaper coverage of "essential workers" in the two countries.

While these word clouds provide only a somewhat rough overview of this collection of articles on essential workers during the pandemic, they give a

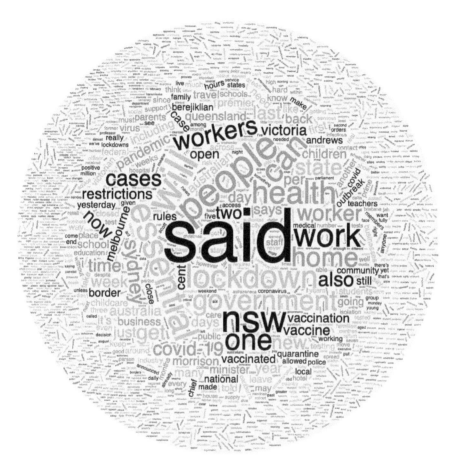

Fig. 7.1. Words used in Australian news articles about "essential workers"

sense of the discursive framework applied to the issue of essential workers that surrounded personal stories. In particular:

- "Government" was far more prominent in the Australian dataset by comparison with the U.S. data set, where both "government" or "administration" are absent. One likely explanation for this is that it reflects the different views on the role of government in the United States and Australia during the pandemic. That is, Australians expect and normalized a greater role for government intervention compared to the United States, where there remains greater skepticism about government intervention, particularly with regard

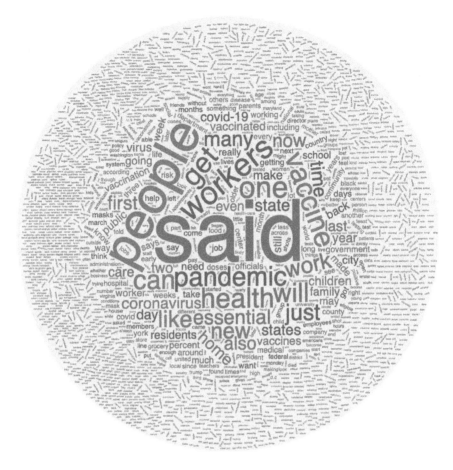

Fig. 7.2. Words used in U.S. news articles about "essential workers"

to intervention in everyday lives and actions, such as mandating mask wearing.

- Correspondingly, the names of key leaders such as Australian Prime Minister "Morrison," and state premiers "Andrews," and "Berejiklian" are all reasonably prominent in Australia, while no U.S. leaders' names appear so prominently in the U.S. data, including presidents Trump and Biden.
- Last, in terms of direct interventions into the pandemic, "lockdown" is very prominent in the Australian articles, while "vaccine" is very prominent in U.S. ones, largely reflecting the different strategies focused on by the two countries over 2020–2021.

Our qualitative analysis of this media dataset also found that "essential worker" was a generic term mainly used in the news media early in the pandemic for those who were unable to work from home, but initially also encompassed those who kept doing their jobs, either at home or in person. Rapidly, however, essential workers changed to mean only those who were frontline workers, or rather those still working but not able to work from home. This varied from healthcare workers dealing with Covid-19 every day to also include service workers such as those in retail, law enforcement, and city infrastructure. Over time in both countries a more industrial and legal definition, and debate, over the category of essential worker emerged, especially when it came to accessing payments, vaccinations, or freedom of movement.

In the Australian news during 2020, essential workers predominantly referred to those who were not able to work from home and were still working on the frontline and at risk of catching Covid-19. In late March 2020, when restrictions on movement and workplaces were first announced in Australia, then prime minister Scott Morrison made an important speech referring to all workers as "essential workers" and that the policies he would use would be predominantly about keeping people at work throughout the crisis ("Scott Morrison's Full Statement on the New National Coronavirus Restrictions" 2020). The practical definition of frontline and essential workers quickly broadened beyond healthcare workers to include other workers such as those in essential retail like supermarkets and garbage collectors (Dunn 2020).

However, by the lockdowns of 2021 in the major cities of Sydney and Melbourne, the category of an essential worker became much more of a defined legal category. For example, in terms of the permits that were needed for movement of essential workers to travel beyond the limitations of a 5–10km lockdown boundary from their home. Essential workers on the frontline were also prioritized in access to vaccination by mid-2021. In late 2021 and early 2022, after all local lockdowns and border closures were lifted, most of the news media discourse on essential workers focused on legal issues or restrictions on movement such as quarantine if ill with Covid, and capacity to go to work. One significant debate challenged the definition of essential workers and the amount of time they were expected to home quarantine if ill, to cope with a supply chain crisis in particular ("Unions Call for Urgent Talks with Scott Morrison over Isolation Rules" 2022).

By late 2020, in the United States the semilegal category of essential worker was being used regularly to define who needed to be at work and in the workplace, and it was also being used to allow people to travel internationally. One of the core differences between Australia and the United States was the polarized nature of the discussion about both Covid-19 and how to manage the pandemic. That is, in 2020 there was near unanimous support across Australia's political elites on the reality of Covid-19 and support for international and state border and local area lockdowns. This unity did not exist to a large extent in the United States as there was significant tension between the Centre for Disease Control and Prevention (CDC), infectious diseases experts such as Anthony Fauci, and the Trump administration (Behrmann and Santucci 2020).

A significant media-led debate in the United States was on the concept of frontline workers, meaning those dealing directly with the public, versus essential workers that encompassed all those who had to be at work. However, the terms came to be used interchangeably in both advocacy for occupational health and safety in the workplace, as well as access to vaccines. One *New York Times* article reported that, by the end of 2020, at least ninety million workers in the United States were defined as essential to keeping the country going, and this became more relevant as a debate ensued about who should be first in line to receive vaccinations at a point where supply was limited. The authors asked:

> Should the country's immunization program focus in the early months on the elderly and people with serious medical conditions, who are dying of the virus at the highest rates, or on essential workers, an expansive category encompassing Americans who have borne the greatest risk of infection? (Goodnough and Hoffman 2020)

The most important points being recognized by the media and attributed to union advocacy at this point is that nonhealthcare frontline workers were also essential to keeping the economy and society functioning. Many of these people were also vulnerable, especially those in retail and food processing, and who were poorer, more ethnically or racially diverse, and older than the general population (Rowland et al. 2020). More contentious within media coverage were proposals for hazard pay for workers on the frontline or compensation and protection when they fell ill with Covid-19 (Witte et al. 2021).

Throughout early 2021 most media reporting on essential workers was about two core issues: access to vaccinations and the need for more government assistance to low-paid workers and the newly unemployed. New president Joe Biden refocused the public debate on his recovery plan and minimum wage increases at this point, and many states were following suit. It is notable that by late 2021, once mass vaccinations were achieved in both countries and lockdowns were more or less nonexistent, the political debate over responding to the pandemic from the point of view of workers receded. For example, in the May 2022 Australian election campaign and the U.S. midterm elections of November 2022 (Smith-Schoenwalder 2022) there was barely any mention, by the major parties in both countries, of essential workers or even the effects of the Covid-19 pandemic on workers, despite that rates of Covid-19 illness and death continued to be significant in both countries.

7.4 Unions' Story-Centered Campaigning

As we outlined above, during 2020 the news media and high-profile political actors were important for broadening the idea of essential workers beyond healthcare workers and included low-paid workers within public debates. Yet it was the role of unions in sharing the personal stories of low-paid workers that provided recognition that they were vulnerable during the pandemic and also *essential* frontline workers. There was evidence in the media analysis above that from early to mid-2020 it was predominantly unions promoting the idea of workers who were truly "essential" during the crisis, especially during city-wide lockdowns. This framing quickly became accepted and mainstream in both Australia and the United States.

To analyze the sharing of personal stories undertaken by unions we collected a Crowdtangle dataset of public Facebook posts by all major unions in Australia and the United States for a two-year period during the pandemic. Initially, we built a list of unions, combining the fifty-six members of the AFL-CIO and forty-six members of the ACTU, and narrowed to focus on the eighty-six unions who had active Facebook pages during the time period. We then searched the posts for the use of the word "story," leading to our final sample of 587 posts from sixty-three unions. After coding our "story" dataset using the same criteria we applied to identify story-centered posts in the other case studies included in this book, we found that 263 posts (45 percent) from fifty-seven of these unions presented a story about an individual worker or a group of workers. This means that two-thirds of *all* unions in both countries told personal stories about workers at some time during the pandemic, suggesting that it is a relatively mainstream tactic for union-led Facebook communications now.

Fig. 7.3. Proportion of story-centered Facebook posts by union

The word cloud in figure 7.3 contrasts the number of story-centered Facebook posts from sixty-three different unions from both countries. The larger the font, the bigger the proportion of story-centered posts from that union in our dataset.

This reveals that a range of blue-collar and white-collar unions, as well as those advocating for both workers doing essential work and those who lost their jobs during the pandemic, published personal workers' stories during the pandemic.

We also coded story-centered Facebook posts for type of story, call to action (if any), and kinds of grievances alluded to. In addition, we recorded the total engagement rate of these posts measured as the combined ratio of shares, comments, and reactions in relation to the number of page followers.

7.4.1 Essential Worker Story Types

As was noted above, 45 percent of the posts we analyzed disseminated a personal story from a worker. The other 55 percent mentioned the word story in the post, which included posts asking individuals to tell their story (i.e., engaging in story collection) and posts noting a historical event or commemorative moment such as workers' roles in Black History Month.

The most frequent of all story types were those that featured a union member's personal story (see table 7.1), meaning that 39 percent of personal story posts articulated the identity of union members. In terms of engagement, these posts were second while posts that featured a personal story expressing gratitude toward workers were those with which users interacted most frequently by a reasonably large margin. Specifically, these "gratitude" stories generated 2.5 times more engagement compared to posts that relayed a union member's personal story. Several examples incorporating both story types can be seen in the posts of BCTGM International, where "action shots" of individual workers are shown accompanied by a description of them at work and an expression of thanks such as

> Local 68 member Kennita Jones keeping bread on the shelves in Baltimore via Schmidt Baking Co.! 🍞.THANK YOU for your hard work, Sister. Stay safe! (BCTGM International Facebook post, April 7, 2020)

An important point here is that unions delivering personal stories in their posts were more likely to focus *generally* on workers during the pandemic, and essential workers in particular, than they were to focus on eliciting solidarity with union members alone. This is a useful tactic for broadening the personal focus on who were essential, frontline, workers during this time; and the most popular posts discursively suggest that we should all display empathy via gratitude for worker service and sacrifice in a time of heightened risk.

Some posts referred more explicitly than others to the pandemic and its impacts. Posts that told a story of how workers had been directly impacted by falling ill with Covid-19, while relatively infrequent, recorded the third-highest rate of engagement of all story types. By contrast, posts that featured

Table 7.1. Union story types

Story type	n	Proportion of all posts (%)	Proportion of "story" posts (%)	Engagement rate
No story	321	55	-	2.63
Story	266	45	-	5.72
Union member's personal story	102	17	39	9.21
Struggle story	81	14	31	3.38
Inspirational story	46	8	17	3.41
Gratitude toward workers story	31	5	12	23.10
Take action story	28	5	11	3.34
Union supporting workers story	23	4	9	2.68
Working during Covid story	21	3	8	0.81
Impacts of contracting Covid story	7	1	3	4.31
Memorial for deceased worker story	7	1	3	2.86

Note: Some totals add to more than 100% because individual posts can include more than one story type.

a story about the physical conditions faced by workers who were on the frontline during Covid-19, particularly healthcare workers, generated the lowest amount of engagement by a relatively large margin and, importantly, were the only story type with a lower engagement rate than posts with no stories at all. Stories relating to workers' struggles and challenges,[2] inspirational stories, and stories describing a worker taking action to improve their working all had about the same rate of engagement.

Of the posts that did not include a personal story, 38 percent represented a call to workers to share their own stories, and 6 percent invited people to engage with some form of storytelling (e.g., by providing a link to a story featured in a news article). A large proportion of other, nonstorytelling posts included status updates expressing support for workers from marginalized groups, such as in relation to Australia's National Sorry Day, Pride Month, Women's History Month, "Juneteenth," and the Black Lives Matter movement.

Looking at the data by country, we noted that both Australian and U.S. unions were equally likely to feature personal stories of workers in their posts

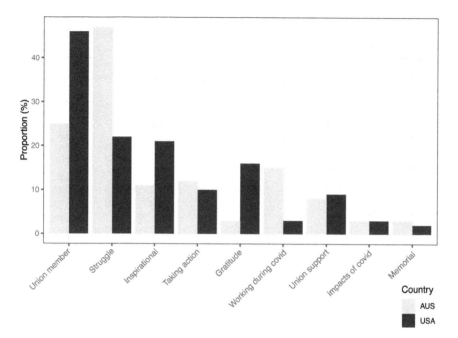

Fig. 7.4. Story types by country

(48 percent and 44 percent, respectively). The most frequently used story type among U.S. unions was on union members' personal lives (46 percent of story posts); by contrast, this story type was only used in half as many posts by Australian unions (25 percent) (see fig. 7.4). The most common story type among Australian unions' posts were those relating to workers' struggles (47 percent); this story type was seen less than a quarter of U.S. posts (22 percent).

Overall, U.S. unions' story-centered posts were characterized by more positivity than those of Australian unions. There were substantially higher proportions of inspirational stories and stories of gratitude in U.S. posts compared to Australian posts. Conversely, Australian unions' posts included higher proportions of stories relating to workers' struggles and experiences working in frontline roles during the pandemic compared to U.S. unions' posts. While a majority of union member *personal* stories were positive and uplifting in both countries, they were again by a higher margin in the United States compared to Australia (78 percent and 59 percent, respectively).

Table 7.2. Calls to action

Calls to action featured in posts	n	Proportion of all posts (%)	Proportion of "call to action" posts (%)	Engagement rate
No call to action	171	29	-	3.81
Call to action	416	71	-	4.14
Share your story	177	30	43	5.95
Engage with storytelling content	93	16	22	3.17
Access resources	65	11	16	1.27
Share/like post	49	8	12	4.32
Contact representatives	42	7	10	4.85
Sign petition	22	4	5	6.56
Attend rally/protest	15	3	4	4.88
Donate	7	1	2	4.05
Don't share/like post on government computer or while undertaking work for government	3	1	1	5.07
Join union	2	0	0	2.31
Other	29	5	7	3.83

Note: Some totals add to more than 100% because individual posts can include more than one story type.

7.4.2 Calls to Action

About 70 percent of posts featured one or more calls to action. In addition, posts with calls to action received more engagement than those without such calls. The most common types of calls to action were those that invited workers to share their own stories (see table 7.2). Most of these invitations to share a personal story focused on the experiences of essential workers during the pandemic. For example, some sought examples of workers being mistreated or overlooked by relief policies, as well as examples of workers taking positive actions in their working lives. A substantial number of calls to share personal stories also focused on workers' positive experiences as union members. For example, in the United States the Retail, Wholesale and Department Store Union asked people, "What was your #UnionYES moment? Share your story with us!" and the International Brotherhood of Electrical Workers asked, "How has the #IBEW changed your life? Tell us your story!"

This shows that unions also actively engaged in the established preference for crowdsourcing and large story collections that we have discussed throughout the book, and even attempted to involve potential storytellers beyond their membership. These "share your story" posts also generated substantial engagement levels, with the second-highest number of average post interactions per follower count, immediately after posts that asked people to sign a petition. Petitions appeared in only twenty-two posts overall but were the most likely to be shared or engaged with; they were also much more likely to be used in Australia compared to the United States and were particularly focused on a campaign to maintain the federal government's welfare safety net—JobKeeper—for Australian workers who lost work during the pandemic.

The next most common call to action were those that invited people to engage in storytelling content, such as by following a link to a newspaper article or website that included a story. These, however, generated only moderate levels of engagement compared to other types of calls to action. Interestingly, only two posts in the entire dataset encouraged people to join a union, perhaps because many Facebook page followers are likely to be union members already. Calls to action in the "other" category included suggestions to follow links to feel good/inspirational content and to news stories that may be of interest to workers, and to apply for job openings.

Looking at the data by country, calls to action were similar across the unions of Australia and the United States. However, U.S. unions were more likely to ask their followers to share their stories, while Australian ones were substantially more likely to call on followers to sign a petition (see fig. 7.5).

Some calls to action linked to campaign specific sites, which hosted petitions or story submission interfaces. For example, this was the case for posts from Australia's United Workers Union, which represents more than 150,000 workers within forty-five industries and was formed by merging two unions in 2019: United Voice and the National Union of Workers. The former had long been known within the union movement for its innovative adoption of story-based campaigns. During the pandemic, it ran a "JobKeeperForAll" campaign website that called for more government financial support to workers affected by pandemic lockdowns and business closures. This site showcased only thirteen text-based stories for about six months in 2021 and no videos. Clearly, this union was interested in story crowdsourcing but prioritized other distribution channels over its campaign website. This echoed our finding in chapter 4 that websites are not the primary distribution channel for many advocacy campaigns.

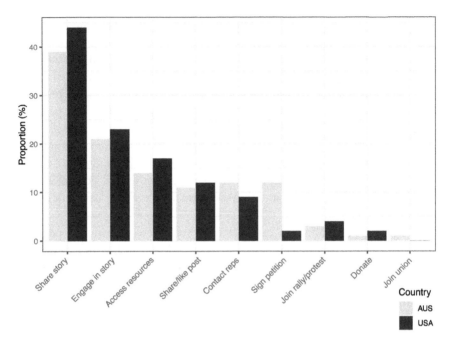

Fig. 7.5. Percentage of posts including calls to action by country

7.4.3 Grievances

We also coded the posts in the story dataset to determine whether griev-ances were mentioned and, if so, what the primary grievance was. We found that 37 percent of all posts suggested a grievance of some kind, with the most common relating to a lack of job security (18 percent of all grievance-including posts), unfair working conditions (14 percent), lack of access to Covid-19 income support (12 percent), and the need for fair wages and compensation (12 percent). Detailed results are in table 7.3.

Compared to those that did, posts that did not mention a grievance were 20 percent more likely to be engaged with, and this may largely reflect the importance of gratitude and hero narratives in pandemic related storytelling posts (see table 7.4). The two grievance types that generated most engage-ment focused on lack of access or limited access to Covid income support (42 percent more engaging than posts without grievance) and lack of job security (35 percent more engaging).

Looking again at differences between countries, Australian unions were twice as likely as U.S. unions to refer to a grievance, with 60 percent of Aus-

Table 7.3. Grievances mentioned in story-centered posts

Grievance type	n	Percentage of all posts	Percentage of "grievance" posts	Engagement
No grievance	372	63	-	4.30
Grievance	216	37	-	3.40
Lack of job security	38	6	18	5.75
Unfair working conditions	30	5	14	4.18
No/limited access to Covid income support	25	4	12	6.11
Need for fair wages/ compensation	25	4	12	3.40
Lack of worker safety	22	4	10	3.24
Discrimination against marginalized workers	22	4	10	1.18
Impact of Covid on workers and society	20	3	9	1.83
Struggling health/aged care system	16	3	7	1.44
Other	17	3	8	1.30

Note: Some totals add to more than 100% because individual posts can include more than one story type.

tralian posts mentioning a grievance compared to 31 percent of U.S. posts. The biggest differences in terms of the types of grievances expressed across the two countries were in relation to unfair wages and compensation (17 percent of Australian and 5 percent of U.S. grievance posts), the struggling state of health- and aged-care systems (11 percent of Australian posts and 3 percent of U.S. posts), and discrimination against marginalized workers (16 percent of U.S. posts and 5 percent of Australian posts) (see fig. 7.6).

Overall, our analysis of story-centered campaigning on Facebook by unions in Australia and the United States demonstrated that unions were actively sharing personal stories of workers during the pandemic to elicit empathy with those working on the frontline, as well as draw attention to inequities. Stories and requests to share stories drew attention to grievance issues such as job security and unfair wages for low-paid workers, as well as pandemic-specific scenarios around worker safety, working conditions, and access to some form of pandemic specific income or health support. Storytelling as story-sharing tends to be used in a positive sense, to generate feelings of empathy and solidarity *between* workers—or *for* workers via "give thanks to our heroes" tropes. Yet there is an inherent tension between these affirming messages and the increasing attention to a lack of fairness in essential workers' workplaces and their direct struggle with ongoing inequity and

Table 7.4. Examples of posts featuring a grievance

Grievance type	Post Example	Union (country)	Date
Lack of job security	Aged care worker Sherree lives in fear knowing one less shift could send her spiralling into poverty. This is her story. The Morrison Government's industrial relations bill is targeting working people like Sherree, and their families. Sign the petition and email your MP via the links below to tell this Government: hurting workers won't heal the economy. Petition:	Australian Unions (AU)	14 March 21
No/limited access to COVID income support	Today the first impacts of the Federal Government's cuts to JobSeeker will be felt hard by people across our country struggling through this pandemic. Next week, cuts to JobKeeper kick in. Now, more than ever we need a government that will put us first. We want to hear how these cuts will impact you, so we can send a message to our government that we deserve better. Share your story: https://www.jobkeeperforall.com.au/	United Workers (AU)	25 Sept. 20
Need for fair wages/ compensation	Like and share if you agree that our hard working causals deserve their wages for the work they do NOT gift cards. Story below	NTEU (AU)	6 March 22
Impact of COVID on workers and society	"Retail giants Macy's, Kohl's and Gap have furloughed thousands of workers as the coronavirus crisis deepens, and more stores will 'absolutely' follow, according to CBS News business analyst Jill Schlesinger." Have you or someone you know been affected by this? Share your story in the comments below.	Working America (US)	2 April 20

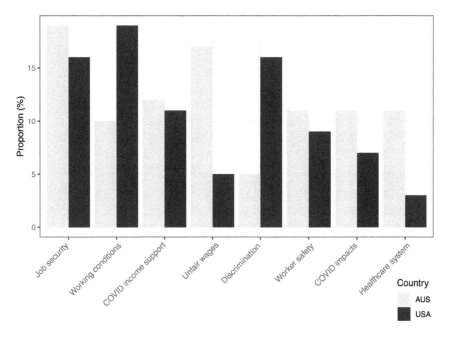

Fig. 7.6. Grievances mentioned in posts by country

precarity. There was a distinct similarity between the storytelling undertaken by unions in Australia and the United States, without there being evidence of direct diffusion of messaging or framing. The differences between the two countries seem to largely reflect the differences and experiences of the pandemic, and particularly the timeline: with lockdowns being used more extensively in Australia to contain the virus in 2021, and an overarching approach to rapid vaccination and no lockdowns of the population in the United States from late 2020.

7.5 Story Framing by Union Leadership

Given the similarities in digitalized and crowdsourced storytelling between Australian and U.S. unions we found, it is useful to consider how the main union federations (ACTU and AFL-CIO) and core union leadership in both countries also framed stories about the experiences of essential workers during the pandemic. This reveals that there was a consistent framing around the need to safeguard low-paid workers within the economy, and that low-paid workers were essential workers. Union umbrella organizations or their leaders directly disseminated very few personal stories of workers, but did so strategically. This is more in line with the expectation of recent research on union digital campaigning that messaging is mainly a broadcast approach of union-centered adversarial frames.

7.5.1 Australian Council of Trade Unions (ACTU)

During 2020–2021, the ACTU produced media releases directly on the pandemic that focused on access to sick leave for hourly employees who did not have any paid leave entitlements (known as "casual" workers in Australia and estimated to be nearly a third of the workforce). For example, on March 5, 2020, the ACTU published this release:

> There are 3.3 Million Australian workers with no access to paid leave. These are the people who face the greatest health and economic risks from the spread of the Coronavirus.
>
> Yet the Morrison government has made no reference to any measures that would support them through this crisis. These workers are in many of the industries most exposed to the health and economic effects of Coronavirus.
>
> The grim reality is that if these workers become ill they will either attend work sick, be stood down by their employer without pay or potentially be subject to self-isolation regimes, imposed by the Morrison government, again without means to pay their bills. (*Statement on Coronavirus and Proposed Stimulus* 2020)

Most pandemic-specific media releases were in March-May 2020, the peak period of lockdown in major cities in Australia that year. Throughout the rest of 2020, they focused on the national government's economic package, JobKeeper, that included a wage subsidy for those not able to work during the lockdown, and on paid pandemic leave for workers who were required to isolate and could not attend their workplaces.

From this early period, the ACTU framed their core narrative as the pandemic necessitated government payments and protections for mostly insecure, low-paid workers. They also focused on areas of high-density union membership that lost work altogether such as the airline industry that collapsed with international and state borders being largely closed. However, with the exception of Australia's second-largest city, Melbourne, most of the country was not in lockdown and the spread of Covid-19 was minimal for most of 2020. It was not until 2021 when the spread of a new wave increased and a race to access vaccinations for the Australian population started that unions intensified their campaign work on recognition for essential workers. Essential workers who they argued were predominantly insecure, low-paid, and at high risk of catching the virus.

In December 2020, ACTU national secretary Sally McManus gave a televised speech to the National Press Club. This speech outlined the consistent narrative on essential workers that the Australian union movement maintained for the second year of the pandemic. In her speech, McManus said:

In the first few weeks of the pandemic there was a reckoning as to what and who was essential to our society and our lives. It wasn't hedge fund managers or mining billionaires. It was cleaners, health care workers, transport workers, supermarket and warehouse workers.

It was the workers in our post offices, electricity and water workers keeping the lights on and the water flowing. It was manufacturing workers producing essentials or re-purposing workplaces to make masks and personal protective equipment. It was the public sector workers—the public health officials, scientists, contact tracers. All these people were essential and we must NEVER forget what they did. (*Sally McManus, National Press Club, Wednesday 2nd December 2020*)

McManus's speech explicitly compared Australia and the United States, asserting that Australian unions had been able to influence the national government to provide support for workers and safety for the population in a way that the United States had not, and she used personal stories from nurses on the frontline of the pandemic.

In 2021, the ACTU continued to campaign for protections for low-paid and insecure workers, including continuing government payments. They published a series of YouTube videos under the title "Working Life" that comprised eight individual worker stories (four men and four women), including electricians, aged-care workers, cleaners, fast food workers, and nurses (Australian Unions 2022). The videos were a response to pandemic-related changes to national industrial legislation, known as the IR Omnibus Bill, that would dilute access to job security for significant numbers of workers. In these videos workers told their individual stories of insecure work, several through being interviewed by the ACTU national president, Michele O'Neill.

Other core issues in early 2021 were on extending JobKeeper, increasing the minimum wage for low-paid workers, and ensuring essential workers had access to vaccines. Note that the most populous Australian cities of Sydney, Melbourne, and Canberra went into an extended lockdown again in the second half of 2021. Many of the ACTU media releases referred especially to essential workers at risk. For example:

> The failure of this program puts frontline and other essential workers at risk. The fact that nearly 6 weeks after Scott Morrison got his vaccination we still have thousands of high-risk frontline workers unable to be vaccinated presents a risk to us all.
>
> The Morrison Government's inability to manage this program is putting the lives and livelihoods of Australians at risk unnecessarily. All around the world there are examples of Governments moving faster and more efficiently.
>
> The UK Government has received criticism domestically for a bumpy rollout but is currently delivering more vaccines every two days than we have all year. (*Failed Vaccine Rollout Leaves Frontline Workers Exposed* 2021)

Other media releases in the second half of 2021 focused on the care workforce, mainly aged-care and disability care workers, highlighting both their precarious work status and need to access vaccines earlier. In late 2021, the Australian economy reopened and most public health restrictions were removed as the 80 percent vaccination threshold for the population had been reached. However, this also coincided with a new wave of the Omicron variant of Covid-19. The ACTU released a report in late November 2021 advocating for workers' rights to safe workplaces, job security, and government income support. Personal stories from three workers were detailed (a disability care worker, a freelance photographer, and a radiographer) to emphasize the breadth of risk within workplaces from ongoing pandemic circumstances (*Support for Workers Critical to Keeping Reopening Workplaces Safe* 2021).

7.5.2 American Federation of Labor and Congress of Industrial Organizations (AFL-CIO)

The AFL-CIO drew attention to the workplace safety of American essential and frontline workers from March 2020, and at this point it particularly focused on healthcare workers such as nurses. It was also openly critical of guidelines issues by the Centers for Disease Control and Prevention (CDC) and throughout 2020 lobbied for a national workplace safety Covid-19 standard, including accurate data collection, and national level government legislation to provide a better safety net and access to healthcare for low-paid workers (that ultimately was blocked in the U.S. Senate). By mid-2020 the U.S. union movement was mobilized in support of Biden's presidential bid as a key route to enacting reforms for essential and low-paid workers. For example, a key speech on Labor Day in September 2020 was less focused on the plight of essential workers and instead centered on the poor response to the pandemic by President Donald Trump. In this speech, then AFL-CIO president Richard Trumka argued:

> Donald Trump inherited a pandemic playbook from his predecessor and tossed it in the trash. He abandoned a workplace infectious disease standard that would have protected our front-line heroes from Covid-19. And even after the virus hit, he refused to issue a national workplace safety standard, leaving millions vulnerable to infection and in too many cases, death. What have we learned from all of this? We've learned that working people cannot afford Donald Trump. (Trumka 2020)

The AFL-CIO's storytelling approach was also seen in their creation and dissemination of videos via YouTube. They produced a series of twenty-one direct to camera worker story videos throughout the pandemic, predominantly on individual experiences and linked to the implementation of the American Rescue Plan. They encapsulate the point of view of essential workers from a wide range of industries including teachers, journalists, fast food and retail workers, childcare workers, and sheet metal workers. Most of the stories were from women and/or people of color (AFL-CIO, n.d.). There is significant variation in the popularity of the videos with only three of them watched more than 10,000 times, and these were from professional workers (rather than low-paid workers): a teacher, a social worker, and a journalist. It is also worth noting here that these popular videos were from three women of color telling their pandemic stories.

    As America reopened its economy and adapted to a new government in 2021, the AFL-CIO mainly focused on legislative change of the American Rescue Plan and the "Build Back Better" campaign that highlighted fair pay, a higher minimum wage, and access to paid leave for low-paid workers. For example, on Labor Day in September 2021 Liz Shuler, the new president of AFL-CIO,[3] made a speech that clearly linked postpandemic recovery for essential workers with national level policy change. Specifically, she said:

> Covid-19, the climate crisis and technology have radically changed our lives and work. We are not going back to how it was before. I hear from working people all across the country: We won't risk our lives in this pandemic for an unreliable, low-wage Job. Our system of care is broken and it should be seen as critical infrastructure. And we shouldn't have to work two or three jobs to make it—one job should be enough.
>
> And it's the labor movement that will lead the transformation. We are innovating and fighting for what will be the next weekend. And with the game-changing leadership of the Biden-Harris administration, we will build back better with unions. To win an America where every working person has the right to a good, sustainable, union job. And with it, access to an expansive, new American middle class. (Shuler 2021b)

Yet by late 2021 unions had not successfully reframed the debate about supply lines and worker shortages postpandemic, or universally achieved the raise in the minimum wage that they aimed for. For example, Liz Shuler made a speech at National Press Club on October 13, 2021, trying to reframe the way postpandemic work for essential workers was being understood. Here, she argued that

> The headlines reporting a shortage of workers are missing the point. The pandemic laid bare the inequities of our system, and as we try to get beyond Covid, working people are refusing to return to crappy jobs with low pay. Essential workers are tired of being thanked one moment and treated as expendable the next.
>
> The real headline isn't that there's a shortage of people willing to return to work. The real scarcity story is the shortage of safe, good-paying, sustainable jobs. And the good news is that workers feel a new sense of power and leverage and aren't willing to settle anymore. And the solution, once again, can be found in the labor movement. (Shuler 2021a)

7.6 Conclusion

Communicative unionism as a strategy, based on stories of unity and collective action during the pandemic, helped unions in both Australia and the United States to successfully use personal storytelling to change how we think about essential work. In particular, storytelling tended to be used *with* workers and via the affordances of Facebook or YouTube sharing, more than in union speeches or media releases. This context-driven example reveals much about the role of unions in a crisis context as well as their ongoing advocacy role on behalf of marginalized, low-paid workers. The union campaigning strategies reviewed here built on existing practices of using storytelling for campaign work by unions and other civil society actors. In particular, the high-profile Fight for $15 campaign that preceded the pandemic and focused on low-paid workers and the need for mass access to minimum wage across the United States was used by incoming president Biden and the labor movement to focus attention on continuing inequities within the labor market. In Australia, the ACTU had a long-term campaign on insecure work and the casualization of the workforce, which had led to entrenched inequities and unequal access to sick leave, meaning that its campaign on paid pandemic leave for low-paid workers was highly resonant.

A key insight is that unions used different communications platforms (Facebook, YouTube, media releases) for different messaging around storytelling, but that their long-term campaign to increase wages for low-paid workers was core throughout the whole pandemic. Reframing frontline workers as "essential workers" helped to make visible the problems of low-paid, insecure, and now "at risk" work. This multiplatform communicative strategy also recognized that different platforms have different audiences and targets such as government and general public attitudinal change versus creating a shared sense of worker identity and urgency. Within this framework, social media and in particular Facebook were used not only to disseminate personal stories that sought to recast low-paid workers but also as fundamental channels for story collection. Posts encouraging story submissions were relatively frequent and generated considerable levels of engagement, showing both that unions are committed to crowdsourced storytelling and that their followers—both members and non—are interested in participating in it.

By expanding storytelling about essential workers beyond frontline healthcare workers, to include other frontline service workers such as those working in grocery stores, retail, and other forms of goods' delivery, unions successfully focused on inequality and risk during the pandemic. They used stories to bring to the foreground core longer-term materialist issues such as safety at work, job security, low pay, access to paid sick leave and/or compensation or hazard pay for when workers caught Covid-19, as well as priority access to vaccinations for essential workers. The shared or collective narrative that was created here was not one of union members; instead it was one of brave or "hero" at-risk workers facing the universal threat of Covid-19. By focusing on the personal aspects of stories, instead of class or union membership, unions maximized their potential to cut across political divides and exploit the heightened attention associated with crisis.

As President Biden pointed out at a White House briefing in September 2021:

> One of the good things that's come out of this godawful crisis regarding Covid is ordinary people who never thought about the technician at the drugstore, never thought about the grocery store worker, never thought about what that firefighter has to do when they go in. They don't ask, "Do you have Covid or not?" Never thought about the people who keep this country up and running before.
>
> . . . When unions win, workers across the board win. That's a fact. Families win, community wins, America wins. We grow. And despite this, workers have been getting cut out of the deal for too long a time. (Biden 2021)

CHAPTER 8

Power, Storytelling, and Advocacy for Social Change Futures

Storytelling is an increasingly important part of the strategic repertoire of advocacy organizations. In this book, we showed how advocacy organizations that campaign for progressive social change in both the United States and Australia have invested substantial resources in personal storytelling and story tech systems in recent years. While some—particularly in Australia—have stuck to a more campaign-specific approach and sometimes continued to delegate storytelling to external agencies and consultants, many others have sought to bring these functions in-house by allocating parts of their budgets to support technology-powered storytelling as an integral and ongoing part of their campaign operations for the long term.

Stories appear throughout different campaign materials and are disseminated through a range of channels—both established and emerging—to persuade key publics via a causal and personalized sequencing of events, rather than by making traditional appeals to logic and evidence. Digital technologies have contributed in fundamental ways to this expansion of personal storytelling in advocacy communication by reducing costs and enabling the collection, archiving, and dissemination of a larger-than-ever number of stories from a wide range of storytellers through online crowdsourcing. These techniques create new opportunities to influence key debates in the current media and political environment. However, they also generate an unresolved tension between their potential to democratize advocacy storytelling and their practical application, which must balance participation with strategic objectives. This has implications for power distribution and raises important questions for advocacy organizations and the groups they aim to represent.

Several key themes emerged through this book that highlighted how the intersection of technologies, people, power, culture, and values determines contemporary storytelling practices in advocacy organizations in the United States and Australia. In this final chapter, we outline these key themes and point out the connections that, in practice, make them deeply intertwined. While researching this book, it became clear that it is shortsighted to talk of a core "model" of advocacy storytelling in the digital age. Organizations constantly adapt, review, borrow, and learn from each other, as well as from other storytelling specialists and stakeholders across advocacy sectors and countries. That said, a key finding from our analysis is that personal stories are an increasingly integral component of advocacy campaigns, transcend political changes, and are here to stay. In addition, story tech systems and their uses have profound implications for the relationships that determine the distribution of power and agency among the actors involved in these processes (Han et al. 2021). Considering this, it is appropriate to draw insights on the different contexts and actors that influence contemporary advocacy storytelling. This helps us provide a framework for *interpreting* the significance of these changes in the short and long term, map their implications for power distribution, identify benefits and drawbacks, and propose empowering and ethical options for organizations that invest in storytelling techniques.

8.1 Technologies

8.1.1 Hidden Story Tech

When we contemplate core technologies that support digital storytelling, cameras and other recording equipment intuitively come to mind. Clearly, these are consequential tools that have ushered in important changes in how personal stories are produced, how advocacy organizations approach them, and what it is possible to do with them. As noted in the introduction chapter, the impact of recording technologies is widely documented in the extant literature on digital storytelling. In contrast, our book has for the first time brought into the spotlight another set of storytelling technologies that usually remain hidden from public view. These include the following:

- Online submission forms used to collect personal story ideas and information about aspiring storytellers;
- Database and Constituent Relationship Management (CRM) software packages used to store, catalogue, and organize story archives, as well as run reports to evaluate the use of personal stories; and

- Search algorithms and artificial intelligence (AI) tools used to surface and prioritize promising storylines from collections that would be inoperable without these technologies due to their large size.

Technologies like these, which collectively we called "story tech" and discussed in detail in chapters 3 and 4, may seem less centrally important to successful storytelling, compared to production equipment such as digital cameras and microphones. Further, this may have shielded new story tech from deeper scrutiny until now. Yet, as we have shown, they have a profound influence on story-based social change advocacy and, in turn, on public representations of issues and groups.

Our analysis demonstrated that today's advocacy storytelling involves five temporal phases, including (1) story collection; (2) story selection; (3) story development, editing, and curation; (4) story dissemination; and (5) story evaluation. Progressive advocates generally see the first four phases as essential. The fifth one—evaluation—helps organizations to boost campaign effectiveness, learn from past experiences, and plan. Some advocacy organizations choose to forgo evaluation for a variety of reasons, including but not limited to time and money. Research to date has focused on story development, which is arguably the most visible phase. In contrast, we critically analyzed the other four steps in this storytelling process that are typically "unseen" and often remain unclear. This went beyond assessing current practices against models of "ethical" story development that have become popular in professional storytelling circles—for example, documentary filmmaking. Instead, it interrogated the technological processes that determine *how* stories are collected and organized, *which* stories are actually "visible" to organizations in databases, and which are identified as potentially "successful" and *prioritized* for development and distribution to key publics. Hidden story tech shapes all of these processes, making it influential in a way that is fundamentally different to production equipment.

The introduction of story tech marks a new era for advocacy storytelling in which these processes are regulated and significantly influenced by technological design and digital architecture. Story tech brings in new rules for storytelling processes that are modeled after the rules of cyberspace. As the constitutionalist and Internet scholar Lawrence Lessig (2006) once wrote, "in real space, we recognize how laws regulate, [. . .] in cyberspace we must understand how a different 'code' regulates—how the software and hardware [. . .] that make cyberspace what it is also regulate cyberspace as it is" (9–10). Clearly, Lessig said, technological "architecture is a kind of law: it determines what people can and cannot do" (152) on the Internet. Story tech provides the architecture of today's advocacy storytelling and determines what can and cannot be done with it. This raises important questions about what these structures look or should look like, what factors drive their development and evolution, who or what controls all of this, and what opportunities and challenges it provides for organizations, storytellers, and their communities. In answering these questions, a first important factor that emerged from our analysis was a growing melding of participatory and "big data" cultures in advocacy organizations. These provide the rationale for many important technological and strategic choices that are supporting the transformation of personal stories into "data."

8.1.2 Crowdsourcing, Datafication, and Automation

A key driver for the expansion of personal storytelling in grassroots advocacy has been a perceived need to respond to new trends in information consumption and evaluation. The decline in trust in traditional media and information sources, and rising competition for online audience attention, have convinced grassroots organizers that people favor emotional appeals over evidence-based arguments and are more likely to listen to other "ordinary people" than any other voices. In the United States, this need crystallized for progressive advocates after the 2016 presidential election upset, resulting in a major communication watershed for many organizations. In Australia, similar beliefs are increasingly widespread, although this switch cannot be traced back to a single specific moment (Giridharadas 2022).

This media logic explains, at least partly, progressive advocacy organizations' renewed focus on storytelling and determination to embed it permanently and prominently in their campaigns. Yet it does not illuminate why certain storytelling processes have been favored over others. Storytelling itself is not new for advocacy organizations and there are multiple ways to do it. In the past, organizations tended to collect stories from volunteers and other "core" constituents. For some time, one way to innovate was to turn over storytelling tasks to external consultants. A few organizations even experimented with turning over their social media feeds to their constituents but reversed that decision quite quickly for fears of losing control over their core message. Now, the key storytelling process for many organizations is centered on crowdsourcing story ideas online to generate very large archives that include tens or even hundreds of thousands of entries. Here, stories are essentially treated like data that can be searched or even "mined" to identify and prioritize promising storylines. This has marked a digitalization and datafication turn in advocacy storytelling that has ushered in the era of political story "on demand."

Advocacy organizations have invested in crowdsourced approaches for three main reasons. First, they sought to fulfil and simultaneously capitalize on growing expectations among supporters that they could contribute to the work of advocacy organizations in ways that better align with their own lived experiences. These assumptions resonate with the key tenets of participatory culture (Jenkins 2006), "entrepreneurial" political participation (Bimber et al. 2012), and connective action (Bennett and Segerberg 2013) theories. Second, there is a widespread belief among organizers that large crowdsourced collections can generate more effective stories. The larger a collection, the better the stories that can be found in it. This represents an extension of the increasingly dominant public discourse that celebrates "big data" approaches to solving complex problems. Third, organizers are also influenced by technology companies and startups that have developed products that claim to make crowdsourced storytelling accessible to every organization by providing "one-stop shop" solutions for collecting, storing, organizing, and sometimes even editing, publishing, and disseminating personal stories. This line of business is both a product and simultaneously a driver of datafied approaches to advocacy storytelling.

It is unsurprising that organizations that have usually favored evidence-based approaches to policy and strategic communication have also embraced the idea that "big data" and technology can make storytelling more systematic and effective. At the same time, this fosters fundamental changes in the way that personal stories are treated and in the very nature of advocacy campaigns. Datafication offers the possibility to scale up an organization's campaigning and expand the scope of their members' participation; but data-driven processes also introduce new mechanisms for the filtering and selection of specific types of stories, which are opaque to the storytellers themselves. This is perhaps most evident in the story bank systems discussed in chapter 3 that use CRM software to collect, sort, and suggest stories on an ongoing basis, and both support and require the constant growth of story archives. Although story banks have somewhat of a mixed reputation and not every organization has invested in them, there is a clear trend toward "bigger" story collections across advocacy campaigning in the United States and Australia. As such, key elements of story banking are regularly adopted and adapted by organizations with different histories, size, membership, and working across a range of social issues, from gun control to abortion, in both countries.

Although story choices are not entirely automated, search and ranking algorithms, which make extremely large collections "usable," are restricting the choices that are available to organization leaders. This makes large digital story collections inherently hierarchical. Here, the problem is not necessarily with story hierarchies themselves, which are functional to organizations being able to use these collections, but rather with what determines them. Crucially, our research discovered that hierarchies in large story collections tend to be determined by external inputs including the need to satisfy current media dynamics (e.g., the attention economy and primacy of visual content) and the frequent need to address external publics, instead of internal inputs such as constituent grievances and diversity of storytellers. Search and ranking algorithms that learn from previous choices can further exacerbate these problems by fueling a vicious circle. Some organizations have also started to experiment with AI to automatically review, catalogue, and recommend textual and, more recently, even video story submissions. As we discussed in chapter 3, technology companies and startups that develop CRM and story management systems have identified this as a promising area for business growth. As such, they tend to present AI as a useful solution to several storytelling challenges or even a necessity given that—they claim—participation and user-generated content are only going to increase in the future.

While tools such as search, filtering algorithms, and AI seem destined to become increasingly central to advocacy storytelling going forward, their ultimate impact is not predetermined. Rather, it is closely tied to who programs them and what criteria they privilege. If these tools are linked to digital engagement metrics with the intention of boosting content that mirrors what was deemed "successful" in previous campaigns, there is a risk of perpetuating "more of the same" and for the preferences of external publics to be overrepresented in story selection in new campaigns. Writing about social movements, Milan (2013) described activist movements that build and rebuild technology to support their own objectives as "stealing the fire" from technology companies. Whether or not datafied storytelling can follow the same path depends on the people involved, their roles, and how power is distributed and redistributed among them through these processes.

8.2 People and Power

Story crowdsourcing promises a redistribution of power among the various stakeholders involved. That, however, is also constrained in some fundamental ways by story tech and the new datafied nature of story selection, dissemination, and evaluation that was outlined above. Who holds power in storytelling processes was a central question examined throughout this book. We demonstrated that new power relations are possible, but also closely tied to technology, strategy, and underlying cultural values in organizations.

8.2.1 New Storytellers and Inclusive Story Collection

Crowdsourced storytelling undoubtedly provides opportunities for the promotion of new and previously marginalized voices and the potential to shape organized advocacy. In this book, we outlined multiple instances when this happened across a range of issues and organizations in both the United States and Australia. For example, in chapter 4 we heard from multiply marginalized individuals such as black and immigrant trans people who had been rejected or feared being "found out" and discriminated against by their own families and communities, but felt they could more safely share their stories and advocate online. By advocating through personalized action frames and simultaneously hearing from others with similar experiences, they felt empowered and gained a sense of belonging that had eluded them thus far.

Similarly, in chapter 5 we discussed how participation in crowdsourced storytelling offered people affected by both societal and internalized stigma, such as the families of disabled children, a different and more critical lens to interpret their own experiences and subsequently be mobilized. Another important example are essential workers who are usually outside the mainstream of economic discourse and in historically low-paid and insecure work, as discussed in chapter 7, who had opportunities to bring their stories to the fore during the Covid-19 pandemic. This parallels the "logic of collection" that characterized hashtag activism such as #MeToo, #ShoutYourAbortion, and #IfIDieInASchoolShooting, which was based on "a bottom-up process in which 'the collective' is forged by 'collecting the personal'" (Gerbaudo 2022, 12), and signals a blurring of the mobilization repertoires between organized advocacy and digital native movements.

These successes, however, relied on achieving a delicate balance between designing participatory story tech systems and fully addressing the implications of crowdsourced stories for marginalized people. Most organizations seem to be aware of this but only a few have been able to balance this tension intentionally and effectively. This takes time and requires organizations to be invested in the technological design process and to involve storytellers themselves in it. In turn, this also clashes with "off the shelf" online story collection tools sold by startups and other technology companies, which usually are customizable only up to a point and often for an additional fee.

For these reasons, these select cases will hopefully serve as useful examples to other organizations considering introducing crowdsourced storytelling or developing their own story bank system. There are three main dimensions to the development of inclusive story crowdsourcing processes, including (re) conceptualizing risk, designing technological infrastructure, and boosting motivation to use it.

The starting point in inclusive story crowdsourcing processes is developing and implementing a solid understanding of risk. Clearly, there are very real risks involved in sharing a personal story online as part of an advocacy campaign on a controversial issue. These range from being attacked and harassed on social media by trolls and other nefarious actors, to being "exposed" in ways that can inadvertently but very painfully compromise personal relationships. The release forms and permission documents associated with crowdsourced storytelling we reviewed regularly emphasized a notion of risk that prioritized potential problems for the organization, with very little consideration—if any—for the risks taken by storytellers. This approach is often driven by legal teams. Communication and campaign staff expressed concern and frustration over this, and sometimes worked to safeguard personal information such as in the Center for American Progress's story bank, which was designed to ringfence stories from most Salesforce users within the organization. Yet the outward perception is that organizations prioritize themselves over potential storytellers when it comes to risk.

Individuals with the most compelling stories may be disinclined to share them with organizations that appear to be unconcerned about their safety. This raises ethical and strategic questions because it not only reduces the number of stories in a collection but also makes it less diverse given that those who are most marginalized are also those most at-risk. To address this issue, risk should be reconceptualized starting from better situational awareness of the circumstances of potential storytellers. Our research showed that online context collapse—the convergence of multiple networks associated with different parts of personal life and identity—is a top concern among aspiring storytellers who are multiply marginalized.

Second, to fully understand and unpack risk, and design story tech that addresses that adequately, storyteller involvement is essential. This was immediately evident in one of the first story tech tools we analyzed: collection forms. At first glance these forms may seem inconsequential but in practice they have a huge influence on who submits a story and the kinds of stories collected. These are not simple choices for organizations. Story collection forms often request more personal information to make story databases richer and more useful, but this can also drive concerned storytellers away. Here, organizations that work with some of the most at-risk populations are leading the way in developing innovative approaches with some smart and effective solutions. For example, the Polaris Project described in chapter 4, which works with survivors of human trafficking, has instituted a "two step" system to collect personal information for its story bank as a way of increasing trust in the process.

A third and final step that increases the inclusivity of these systems is boosting the motivation for potential storytellers to share about their lives and continue to be engaged. Storytellers greatly appreciate it when organizations "close the loop" by providing them with information about story-based campaigns and their outcomes, even when their stories end up not being published, or a campaign is unsuccessful. This mirrors a pattern already seen in other crowdsourced actions such as online petitions (Vromen et al. 2022). A few organizations stood out, for example Planned Parenthood, who had dedicated point persons to prepare storytellers for what may happen once their story was shared, and to follow up with them afterwards. These were exceptions rather than standard practice. Most organizations have overlooked this step, which supports an impression that story submissions are simply falling into a "void" a lot of the time. This is demoralizing to storytellers and will negatively affect the sustainability of story banks and other crowdsourced story advocacy initiatives.

Crowdsourced advocacy storytelling can be inclusive, but it requires intentionality, time, and openness to complexity. This is both an ethical concern and a strategic one, as a carefully constructed and more inclusive story bank system is also a higher quality and more useful story bank. This also aligns with the "big data" mantra on which crowdsourced storytelling is founded because the more inclusive a process, the bigger the number of potential contributors. The best practice approaches outlined here may not be scalable or generalizable to every organization or group of people but show that considering storyteller concerns while building successful story banks is possible. This is because organizations are in control of strategic and technological choices that can make a difference in this "speaking up" phase of storytelling. In contrast, "being heard" depends in many ways on external factors that are often outside the control of advocacy organizations. This, once more, raises the issue of power relationships in today's advocacy storytelling for social change.

8.2.2 Audiences: Constituencies, Decision-Makers, and Publics

The audiences that organizations target with personal stories play a central role in evaluating the effectiveness of storytelling campaigns. The audiences described in this book fall into three intersecting categories. *Constituencies* include people who might identify with the storytellers directly through shared experiences, grievances, or values. For example, essential workers seeing the trade union stories recounted in chapter 7. They also are likely to correspond with potential members and active supporters of the advocacy campaigns in question, which can lead to membership growth and fundraising capabilities. In contrast, *decision-makers* often fall outside of an advocacy campaign's natural constituency. They frequently occupy formal institutional positions within government and offer a very different kind of audience with an *initially* more strategic than affective outlook. Little Lobbyists in chapter 5 repeatedly addressed and made emotional appeals to this audience with its use of personal stories. Finally, we identified the *mass public* as a third kind of audience with its own dynamics of (in)attentiveness and responsiveness, as described in chapter 6 in Australia's national vote on marriage equality.

We did not find a neat distinction in our research between campaigns focusing on one of these kinds of audience exclusively. In practice the defining feature of crowdsourced storytelling is its usefulness to address multiple and different kinds of audiences simultaneously. This draws a contrast with traditional advocacy group approaches to using storytelling, where the stories told in meetings of volunteers to motivate action, or told within a group with a shared grievance, might be very different to stories subsequently pitched to journalists to frame public debate. Instead, the tendency in our case studies was to mine large databases for stories that can simultaneously mobilize core constituencies and persuade external allies, with all the tensions that created, as we described through the metaphor of the "double-edged sword" in chapter 6.

As stories tend to be crowdsourced from a broader range of storytellers than in the past, their production at mass scale can be responsive to grassroots concerns and shifts in public opinion. Yet our analysis also showed that the pervasive need to address external audiences often leads organizations to publish and disseminate more median or mainstream experiences at the expense of comprehensive representation and/or including the voices of more marginalized communities and individuals. Technology facilitates this through A/B testing and other digital metrics, which contribute to story selection. Circumstances and political opportunity often play a key role in determining which approach organizations follow, and these dynamics eschew a definite "rule of thumb." In our different campaign case studies we offer examples to illustrate these variations and new tensions.

One tension that remains unresolved (with perhaps the exception of the Australian Marriage Equality campaign, which sought to reach voters directly) is that digital innovation in story collection, selection, and development is not matched by innovation in story dissemination, which tends to follow a traditional path. Campaigns that publish hundreds or thousands of stories "in bulk" on a website or other platform can be visually striking (see the examples in chapter 4), but they are also the exception when it comes to story dissemination. More often, crowdsourced stories are used in policymaker briefs, testimony, internal communications (e.g., for community building), and media relations work. Some of these uses of crowdsourced stories—especially attempts to influence traditional media narratives—clash with the latest trends in social media driven information consumption and declining trust levels in elite information sources. This suggests that some advocacy organizations are missing the point: in interviews with us, they talked about wanting to ensure that people hear from "their neighbors" but then pursued dissemination channels that are increasingly distrusted by the general public. This demonstrates that having story content is only the first step in this process and acts as a reminder that we need to better understand the "being heard" or impact phase of storytelling.

8.2.3 Organizers and Story Tech Experts

The growing role of technology in advocacy storytelling in the United States and Australia has affected both internal organizational structure and external relationships with outside experts and technology vendors. This has important implications for power distribution in story-centered advocacy campaigns. One key trend that emerged early in our research was that advocacy organizations have now brought digitally driven storytelling in-house because they increasingly consider it core to grassroots campaigns that will continue in the long term. Many organizations have set up a central location responsible for crowdsourced storytelling. Some have done this by adding to the portfolio of responsibilities of existing staff members in communications and campaigning teams, while others have hired new specialists and established entirely new units. In the most sophisticated structures, storytelling managers often have a background in journalism or previously held a similar role in election campaign organizations, while those with entry-level responsibilities such as reviewing story submissions tend to be recent graduates of communication or political science programs. This has also reshaped the relationship between advocacy organizations and outside storytelling specialists, as well as other communication consultants. Previously, these figures were tasked with coordinating "one-off" campaigns. Now that storytelling is crowdsourced and ongoing, they are more likely to provide training and support to in-house organizers.

This type of centralization and institutionalization is strategically justifiable and does not necessarily clash with the participatory nature of crowdsourced storytelling. Having someone who is located inside the organization, has links to the community or communities it seeks to represent, and is more attuned to their concerns, as opposed to external communication consultants, is a positive step toward making advocacy storytelling more inclusive and accountable to its key constituents. In practice, however, complex technology use also leads to organizers sharing responsibilities with other specialists who are typically more removed from the communities that advocacy organizations represent. First, there are legal teams within advocacy organizations. Legal considerations weigh heavily on information release practices and other processes related to digital information storing, sharing, editing, and copyright. The approach taken is generally one that tries to maximize the benefits of digital storytelling by extending an organization's ability to use user-generated content in as many ways and for as long as possible, while simultaneously minimizing risk. At times, this has led to strained relationships between storytelling and legal teams, with the latter setting the overarching policy and the former taking a cautious and nuanced approach so as not to deter potential storytellers.

Another group involved in these processes and with which organizers have a complicated relationship are technology developers. As story collection, archiving, and retrieval systems grow more complex, it is typical for advocacy organizations to look for ready to purchase "one-stop shop" software solutions. This translates into a growing line of business for existing technology companies such as CRM software providers and emerging startups. This also means that for decision-making processes about technological architecture, organizers are being displaced by outside experts who usually have no direct knowledge of the groups and communities that advocacy organizations represent, and operate within a commercial culture rather than one based on social change advocacy. The resolution of this tension depends on who technology experts are, and through which structure—if any—they collaborate with advocacy organizations and the underlying communities in designing technology products.

For example, database design involves many decisions that, if taken without meaningful input from community members, can make the contextualization of risk and application of situational awareness to story collection efforts impossible. Although the usual caveats against overgeneralizing apply, the "off the shelf" approach is prevalent at this point among storytelling advocacy organizations. There are counter examples of how to do this in ways that more evenly distribute power between communities, organizers, and technology experts, with tech experts serving as specialized advisors to community actors rather than "decision-makers." One example from chapter 3 was the development of the Center for American Progress's "Story Bank" app. This was coordinated by a technology specialist embedded within the organization and simultaneously versed in both coding and community concerns. This model is dependent on several factors, not least organization size and resources. If, however, larger organizations can lead the development of community-centered story collection tools that also benefit smaller organizations and can be shared with them in affordable ways, it may represent a viable way toward a more equitable type of crowdsourced advocacy storytelling.

8.3 Culture and Values

The datafication and growth in story tech for advocacy storytelling is also not happening in a vacuum. Rather it is embedded and interacts with specific sociopolitical contexts and cultural systems that shape the need for the use of personal stories in campaigns. This creates new opportunities for advocacy organizations to strengthen their stated values and support their mission, but other times it also generates unresolved dilemmas around representation and inclusion.

8.3.1 Diversity and Representation, in Theory

One persistent thread tying together the experience of campaigners across issues and both countries was the difficulty in achieving the desired diversity among storytellers. Specifically, campaigners were aware (and sometimes also frustrated with) the limitations of technology-driven approaches to generate diverse and representative sets of stories. It was striking how similar these concerns were, such as the acknowledgment of the overrepresentation of white storytellers in the Australian disability rights and marriage equality campaigns. Looking back at these concerns, there are three kinds of barriers that continue to impede campaigners' goals of increasing diversity, which we label as *social, technological,* and *strategic.*

Social barriers refer to well-known structural barriers to participation in politics generally, which disproportionately affect marginalized people. For example, if we accept that non-English language speakers are less likely to participate in politics generally, then they may be more likely to refrain from telling their own stories as part of that participation. These social barriers mostly exert their force before campaigns even take place, and can help to explain why some groups appear not to take part in storytelling campaigns.

Social structures of (non-)participation are also an incomplete explanation for campaign outcomes, and can even be a convenient explanation for campaigners to direct attention away from factors within their control, such as the *technological* barriers to diversity. By this, we mean the way that the deliberate design of technological systems enables or privileges some forms of participation more than others. For example, we describe in chapter 4 how story hierarchies in collection systems, which tend to prioritize visual content, are more likely to exclude diverse and intersectional storytellers. In chapter 3, we discussed how story tech that tags and sorts databases algorithmically can automate decisions that have implications for the diversity of storytellers, especially if algorithms are "learning" the features of high-quality stories based on the biased responses of diffuse public audiences.

Closely related to these technological barriers to diversity are *strategic* barriers related to the choices campaigners face about how tightly and strategically to cater to audience preferences. In general, the larger and more diffuse the public being addressed, the more representations will shift to align with mainstream preferences. Sometimes this does not pose a direct challenge to diversity. For example, in chapter 5 we described how disability rights campaigners adopted frames resonant in their respective national contexts, focusing on freedom frames in the United States and fairness frames in Australia. However, in chapter 6 we showed how the Australian Marriage Equality campaign narrowed its representation of the queer community to exclude trans Australians and queer parents, as a direct response to the perceived lower support in the broader community. In this last case, social marginalization was causally related to a subsequent lack of diversity in crowdsourced and datafied storytelling.

As a final note on questions of diversity, we have highlighted the use of story tech that provides a "one-stop shop" platform for campaigners to collect, curate, and select stories for advocacy. There is clearly a strong appeal in tech that promises to reduce the technical expertise campaigners need to operate them, all while automating more of the work involved. Yet, in our case studies, the interventions that increased diversity in storytelling campaigns came from humans, not technology: campaigners thinking critically and reflexively, making active choices to reach out to particular groups or contradict audience preferences. If too much faith is put in the capacity of AI to automate large storytelling campaigns, there is a risk of removing the human element that is most sensitive to normative concerns based on diversity and fairness.

8.3.2 Identity-Based and Material Grievances

A second question on context is whether the nature of the issues or grievances at stake affects the value of crowdsourced storytelling. Despite some of the limitations outlined above, the collection and use of personal stories is well suited to equality and identity-centered rights and groups (e.g., disability, marriage equality), but what about campaigns that revolve around material and economic rights claims and grievances? In chapter 7 we focused on how labor unions collected and shared stories of low-paid workers and their experiences during the Covid-19 pandemic to illustrate the success of this campaign and the expansion of rights and recognition of essential workers. In both the United States and Australia, unions built on their existing campaigns to increase job security and pay for some of the most marginalized workers employed in the service economy, such as in retail, supermarkets, supply/distribution, and care work. Yet, while there was widespread shift in a recognition of the importance of these frontline workers in maintaining the economy and society during pandemic related lockdowns, accessing rights to better pay (highlighted in the Fight for $15 campaigns for a federally mandated minimum wage in the United States) and/or to secure work (highlighted by campaigns on increasing precarity of the Australia workforce) fell short.

The creation and dissemination of personal stories of frontline workers as "heroes" moved beyond economic grievance claims of union members and created empathy among the wider public and political elites. To some extent, using stories in this way dispensed with the language of class conflict, and the effects of ongoing cleavages in society during the pandemic were left unquestioned. Providing thanks to workers who risked their lives during the pandemic, both in healthcare and frontline service work, did not ultimately challenge structural inequality or corporate power in any way. Nevertheless, there has also been more recent government change in both Australia and the United States that has provided more political opportunities for labor movements as both President Biden and Prime Minister Albanese have deep historical links with unions. In Australia in late 2022, a policy-focused Jobs Summit echoed the corporatist discussions between business, unions, and the government that were held in early 2020, and Australia is on a pathway to fostering genuine industrial change in favor of low-paid workers. While it is clearly not possible to draw causal inferences between personal stories and these political developments, stories certainly contributed to the narrative and framing of these issues. From this angle, removing the class element to focus instead on the value and humanity of essential workers is a rare but important example of value-based proactive advocacy storytelling that shows a possible way forward for this tactic to counter ideological polarization and reach bipartisan publics.

8.3.3 Political and Media Contexts

Through our research in the United States and Australia, we identified context-related drivers and influences behind the shifts in storytelling. The evolution and emergence of storytelling advocacy is constrained and enabled by both existing cultures of advocacy and opportunities for influence within national-level political structures, as well as digital media systems. Our analysis identified that there has been a long-term narrative shift in campaigning. Barriers to entry have been lowered by crowdsourced technology use, leading to scale and institutionalization within mainstream organizations. Furthermore, funding from large foundations and philanthropic organizations, the increasing commercial value of storytelling to tech companies, and the emergence of public relations consultants as story "gurus" have all increased the marketability and appeal of using storytelling at large scale.

While many examples of crowdsourced storytelling emerged in both countries, the diffusion of this technique is advancing in different ways in each one of them. The United States has experienced a sudden explosion of storytelling—particularly story banking—initiatives in the wake of Trump's shock election victory in 2016. In Australia, instead, story tech adoption has been more incremental through training and knowledge sharing, particularly from U.S. experts. Here, occasional peaks occurred only when campaigners sought to capitalize on political opportunities related to specific issues. Australian campaigners see a lot of value in crowdsourcing personal stories, but at specific moments rather than as an everyday routine like their U.S. counterparts do. That said, one common denominator for crowdsourced storytelling diffusion in both countries was the work of "champion" organizations, such as the Center for American Progress and Australian Progress, which have played an important role in encouraging others to embrace crowdsourced storytelling. That story programs have continued under the

Democratic Biden administration in the United States also suggests that this approach to social change advocacy transcends political changes, and will continue to be important for the foreseeable future.

Within this framework, another factor underpinning our analysis is how political opportunity and policy debates enabled or constrained the large-scale use of storytelling. For example, throughout the book we highlighted when changing political opportunities created new spaces for advocacy organizations to scale up their existing strategies. This was clear in the case of marriage equality debates within Australia, which culminated in the marriage equality national survey, introduced by the conservative Liberal-National government at the time. As both the Australian and U.S. federal governments changed from more conservative to more labor friendly, progressive governments, this also enabled spaces for union storytelling about essential workers during the pandemic. We have also provided traces of evidence of how the pandemic itself accelerated the use of digital crowdsourced storytelling by advocacy organizations.

Discursive opportunity structures and changing social values were also important for enabling many of the successful storytelling campaigns discussed throughout. Yet, as we have noted, relying on both traditional media and increasingly problematic corporate, social media platforms to amplify and disseminate stories is also fundamental to the crowdsourced model of storytelling. Organizations need to go where there is an audience, and this audience still tends to be on platforms, such as Facebook and Instagram, and to a lesser extent Twitter. That said, all these platforms have been battling seemingly intractable disinformation and freedom of speech controversies for nearly a decade. Authenticity and trust are fundamental factors for crowdsourcing storytelling, but these will be increasingly harder to maintain in the face of platform decline and mismanagement.

8.4 Conclusion

In closing, where do our findings leave advocacy storytelling and digital politics? Predictions of what comes next in digital politics never age well. Instead of getting lost in the labyrinth of dead ends, we focus on the thread that binds our research for this book and should be closely watched to identify and understand future changes in advocacy storytelling. That is: power and agency. Overall, power and agency emerged as the single most useful key to interpret the rise of story tech and the significance of the trend toward institutionalized and crowdsourced storytelling in advocacy campaigns. Who—and increasingly what—has power to exert agency over these processes is the question that determines both the implications and future direction of digital advocacy campaigns. The answer to this sits squarely at the intersection of technology, people, strategy, and culture.

In this space, opportunities for empowerment are relational, negotiated between different actors, and ultimately dependent on three different tensions: between participation (for storytellers) and usability of story collections (for organizations); between strategy (boosted by technology) and legitimacy (needed by organizations); and between attention (determined by audiences and media systems) and representation (for groups and communities). With regard to the first tension, this book has shown that today storytellers tend to have more power and agency than before. However, their agency is also constrained by technological architecture and those behind it, which aim to make story collections as easy as possible to use for organizations. With regard to the second tension, organizers' power and agency are enhanced by having more "narrative ammunition" at their disposal but are also increasingly shared with technology specialists—including external vendors—in ways that may fuel legitimacy concerns among grassroots constituents. Finally, with regard to the third tension, crowdsourced stories boost the power and agency of advocacy organizations in political spaces because they enable them to better align their campaigns with changing audience preferences. Yet, at the same time, their agency is also constrained by the mechanisms of the attention economy in hybrid media systems, which can significantly impact the representation of groups and communities in story-based advocacy.

Taken together, these changes usher in a new phase of digital advocacy. In the first phase, which started in the late 2000s, advocacy organizations sought to capitalize on the explosion of participatory culture to activate and strategically mobilize supporters, including politically inexperienced, younger, and less motivated people. In the second phase, which took off in the 2010s, organizations began to rely increasingly on digital analytics and engagement metrics to guide their strategic decision-making. In the current phase, the interaction among organizations, constituents, technologies, and the companies that develop them is being reshaped again. With the advent of political stories "on demand," technology has intervened directly in how people and their issues are represented in advocacy communication. There is a substantive difference between running A/B tests to select the most effective version of a call to action versus using an algorithm to automatically restrict or even determine the selection of personal stories for an advocacy campaign. Autonomous technologies such as algorithms and AI are adding a new form of power and agency to these processes. At this point, whether this technological agency supplements, changes, or chips away at human agency remains an open question, but one that will be central to future understandings of effective and powerful advocacy storytelling for social change.

Appendix

This appendix provides a detailed overview of the data sources that informed this book. All of these were collected and analyzed originally for this project.

Interviews (Chapters 2, 3, 4, 5, 6)

We carried out nearly fifty in-depth semistructured interviews with three sets of key stakeholders: (1) storytelling specialists and organizers from major advocacy organizations, as well as advocacy-oriented communication agencies; (2) technology specialists ("story tech" experts) from large corporations and startups focused on advocacy communication and organizing; and (3) storytellers and aspiring storytellers from multiply marginalized backgrounds.

Here below is a detailed list (in alphabetical order by country) of the organizations for which our interviewees worked, as well as key information about the storytellers and aspiring storytellers we interviewed. All the interviews were completed at various points between 2018 and 2022.

I. Campaigners, Organizers, and Storytelling Specialists (Chapters 2, 3, 4, 5, 6)

Most storytelling specialists, organizers, consultants, and technology experts were recruited directly on the basis of direct knowledge, story banks' mapping on LinkedIn (see chapter 3 for details), and the analysis of story submission interfaces (see below for details). A handful of additional interviewees in these categories were referrals from those we recruited directly (snowballing).

Table A.1. Interviews with storytelling specialists

Organization	Country	Focus/type	Story bank?	Nr of interviews
AARP	U.S.	Multi-issue	Yes	1
American Federation of State, County and Municipal Employees (AFSCME) Union	U.S.	Worker's rights	Yes	1
Center for American Progress	U.S.	Multi-issue	Yes	1
Defenders of Wildlife	U.S.	Environment	Yes	1
Earthjustice	U.S.	Environment	Yes	1
Everytown for Gun Safety	U.S.	Gun control	Yes	2
Families USA	U.S.	Health	Yes	1
First Person Politics	U.S.	Agency/ consultant	n/a	1
Little Lobbyists	U.S.	Disability/ children	Yes	1
Parents Together	U.S.	Youth/children	Yes	1
Public Citizen	U.S.	Consumer rights	Yes	1
Ramp Your Voice	U.S.	Agency/ consultant	n/a	1
Resource Media	U.S.	Agency/ consultant	n/a	1
Rooted in Rights	U.S.	Agency/ consultant	n/a	1
Stones' Phones	U.S.	Agency/ consultant	n/a	1
The G Word Campaign	U.S.	Gender equity	Yes	1
World Food Program USA	U.S.	Food security/ refugees	Yes	1
Australian Marriage Equality	Australia	LGBTIQ	Yes	4
Australian Progress	Australia	Multi-issue	No	1
Essential Media	Australia	Agency/ consultant	n/a	1
Brotherhood of St. Lawrence	Australia	Poverty	No	1
Cancer Council	Australia	Health	Yes	1
Every Australian Counts	Australia	Disability	Yes	3
Grassroots and Co.	Australia	Agency/ consultant	n/a	1
Principle Co.	Australia	Agency/ consultant	n/a	1
Sydney Alliance	Australia	Multi-issue	No	1

2. Technology Experts (Chapter 3)

"Story tech" experts were recruited directly from the following organizations.

Table A.2. Interviews with technology experts

Company	Country	Type	Focus
Salesforce (headquarters)	U.S.	Fortune 500 company	Customer Relationship Manager (CRM) software
Salesforce (embedded within advocacy organization)	U.S.	Fortune 500 company	Customer Relationship Manager (CRM) software
Gather Voices	U.S.	Startup company	Automated video collection and management software
The Mighty	U.S.	Private company	Social media and story-sharing portal focused on health

3. Multiply Marginalized Storytellers and Aspiring Storytellers (Chapter 4)

Storytellers and aspiring storytellers were recruited mostly through notices on social media groups and communities focused on a range of different issues and concerns that affect marginalized groups and individuals (see chapter 4 for more details). A small number of storytellers and aspiring storytellers was also recruited with the help of advocacy organizations interviewed for this book.

Story Banking Manuals and Training Materials (Chapter 3)

As part of our exploration of "story tech," (chapter 3), we identified and reviewed the following story banking manuals and related training materials.

Story Banking Organizations and Submission Interfaces (Chapters 3, 4)

To map the diffusion of story banking in the United States we checked the websites and social media channels of America's top national progressive advocacy organizations as aggregated by sites such as Charity Navigator and START (Study, Think, Act, Respond Together) for evidence of story banking. We complemented this strategy by looking for advocacy professionals with experience of story banking in LinkedIn, as was discussed in chapter 3. This enabled us to identify seventy-nine story banking organizations (as of December 31, 2021) that collectively supported ninety-six story submission interfaces as detailed below.

Table A.3. Interviews with marginalized storytellers

Storyteller ID	U.S. Location	Self-identified as	Shared story?	Issue focus
A	Northeast	Cis-woman, black, 30–39	Shared	Women's rights
B	Midwest	Cis-woman, white, 40–49, chronically ill, rural resident	Considering	Healthcare
C	Northeast	Trans-man, native Hawaiian/Pacific Islander, 18–29	Shared	LGBTIQ rights
D	Northeast	Cis-woman, white, 30–39, rural resident	Shared	Women's rights
E	West Coast	Cis-man, black, 30–39, refugee	Shared	Immigration/ refugees' rights
F	West Coast	Trans-man, black, 18–29, immigrant	Shared	LGBTIQ rights
G	Midwest	Cis-woman, white, 40–49, disabled	Shared	Disability rights
H	Midwest	Cis-woman, Asian, 18–29, immigrant	Decided not to	LGBTIQ rights
I	South	Cis-woman, black, 40–49, single mother, disabled	Decided not to	Homelessness
J	Northeast	Cis-man, white, 18–29	Considering	Immigration/ refugees' rights
K	Northeast	Cis-woman, black, 18–29	Decide not to	Racial justice
L	South	Cis-woman, white, 30–39	Shared	Labor

Table A.4. Story banking manuals

Organization	Location	Title	Year first published	Notes
Families USA	Washington, D.C.	What's your story? How to create a successful story banking program	2015	Healthcare advocacy organization; pioneer of advocacy story banking in the U.S.; 18 pp. manual.
Center for | American Progress	Washington, D.C.	Storybank—basic package and installation setup	2019	Companion to the Salesforce StoryBank app; 24 pp. manual.
Community Catalyst	Boston	Our voices have power: A storybanking guide	2017	Healthcare organization; 31 pp. manual.
Center for Social Impact Communication (Georgetown University)/Meyer Foundation	Washington, D.C.	Designing a user-friendly story bank	2016	Part of "Stories worth telling" training series for nonprofits
Nonprofit MarCommunity	Toronto, Canada	How to develop a storybank system for your nonprofit	2016	Popular nonprofit sector online publication
Spitfire Strategies	Washington, D.C.	Story banking tip sheet	n.d.	Advocacy and policy-focused PR consultancy
The Arc	Washington, D.C.	Tools for building power through personal stories	2017	Intellectual disabilities advocacy organization; 19 pp. manual

Table A.5. Story submission interfaces

Story banking organization	Focus	Nr of crowdsourcing interfaces
American Civil Liberties Union (ACLU)	Civil rights	13
National Association for the Advancement of Colored People (NAACP)	Civil rights	1
Center for Responsible Lending (CRL)	Consumer rights	1
Privacy Rights Clearinghouse (PRC)	Consumer rights	1
Public Citizen	Consumer rights	1
Innocence Project	Criminal justice	1
Nation Inside	Criminal justice	1
National Coalition to Abolish the Death Penalty (NCADP)	Criminal justice	1
Tennessee Justice Center	Criminal justice	1
National Disability Rights Network (NDRN)	Disability	1
National MS Society	Disability	1
Paralyzed Veterans of America	Disability	1
The Arc	Disability	2
Little Lobbyists	Disability	1
Clean Water Action (CWA)	Environment	2
Defenders of Wildlife	Environment	1
Green for All (Dream Corps)	Environment	1
League of Conservation Voters	Environment	1
Earthjustice	Environment	1
FOOD for Lane County	Food security	1
American Association of University Women (AAUW)	Gender equity/women's rights	1
National Women's Law Center (NWLC)	Gender equity/women's rights	4
Planned Parenthood	Gender equity/women's rights	1
Women Employed	Gender equity/women's rights	1
Everytown for Gun Safety	Gun control	1
MomsRising	Gun control	1
AIDS Foundation of Chicago	Health and patient advocacy	1
American Lung Association	Health and patient advocacy	1
American Red Cross	Health and patient advocacy	1
Asian & Pacific Islander American Health Forum (APIAHF)	Health and patient advocacy	2
Association of Asian Pacific Community Health Organizations	Health and patient advocacy	1
Bloodworks Northwest	Health and patient advocacy	1

Table A.5—Continued

Story banking organization	Focus	Nr of crowdsourcing interfaces
Cancer Support Community	Health and patient advocacy	1
Colorado Consumer Health Initiative	Health and patient advocacy	1
Doctors for America	Health and patient advocacy	1
Drug Policy Alliance	Health and patient advocacy	1
Families USA	Health and patient advocacy	1
Health Access California	Health and patient advocacy	2
Healthcare Voter Campaign	Health and patient advocacy	1
Healthcare-NOW!	Health and patient advocacy	1
National Association of County and City Health Officials (NACCHO)	Health and patient advocacy	1
National Committee to Preserve Social Security and Medicare (NCPSSM)	Health and patient advocacy	1
National Organization for Rare Disorders	Health and patient advocacy	1
National Parkinsons Foundation	Health and patient advocacy	1
Patients for Affordable Drugs	Health and patient advocacy	1
Physicians for a National Health Program (PNHP)	Health and patient advocacy	1
Providence Institute for Human Caring	Health and patient advocacy	1
Pulmonary Fibrosis Foundation	Health and patient advocacy	1
Susan G Komen	Health and patient advocacy	1
Truth Initiative	Health and patient advocacy	1
Utah Support Advocates for Recovery Awareness (USARA)	Health and patient advocacy	1
National Fair Housing Alliance (NFHA)	Housing	1
League of United Latin American Citizens (LULAC)	Immigration/human rights	2

Table A.5—Continued

Story banking organization	Focus	Nr of crowdsourcing interfaces
Polaris	Immigration/human rights	1
Gay & Lesbian Alliance Against Defamation (GLAAD)	LGBTIQ	1
Human Rights Campaign (HRC)	LGBTIQ	1
Lambda Legal Defense and Education Fund	LGBTIQ	1
Operation Homefront	Military families	1
AARP	Multi-issue	1
Center for American Progress	Multi-issue	2
Center for Popular Democracy (CPD)	Multi-issue	1
Community Change	Multi-issue	1
People for the American Way (PFAW)	Multi-issue	1
TakeAction Minnesota	Multi-issue	1
U.S. Public Interest Research Group (USPIRG)	Multi-issue	1
Advocates for Youth	Youth/children	1
DC Arts and Humanities Education Collaborative	Youth/children	2
Children's Defense Fund	Youth/children	2
Children's Scholarship Foundation	Youth/children	1
National Head Start Association (NHSA)	Youth/children	1
Parents Together	Youth/children	1
AFCSME Union	Workers' rights	1
Family Values @ Work	Workers' rights	1

Story Content Dataset (Chapters 5, 6, 7)

We analyzed more than 1,100 social media posts published by U.S. and Australian advocacy organizations working on disability rights, marriage equality, and workers' rights. Different organizations prioritized different platforms—including Facebook, Instagram, and YouTube—for story distribution, depending on the media used and their target audiences. Facebook and Instagram posts were captured with Crowdtangle, a public insights tool from Meta. Given this is complex content, each post was coded manually and roughly 15 percent of each collection was coded by multiple coders to strengthen the development of the coding frames and ensure their reliability. Coding frames are described briefly in each chapter and full copies are available upon request. It is useful to note here that, in determining whether a social media post included a personal story, we applied fairly stringent criteria. Stories needed to include narrated information about one or more characters and have a beginning, a middle, and an end (this could be implied rather than explicit). Posts without stories generally sought to document important moments in the campaigns. In particular, we analyzed:

- 297 Instagram posts published by Little Lobbyists between October 2017 and October 2019, 177 of which included one or more personal stories (chapter 5);
- 12 YouTube videos published by Every Australian Counts in 2013, a including one personal story (chapter 5);
- 245 Instagram posts published by Australian Marriage Equality between January 2017 and November 2017, 50 of which included one or more personal stories (chapter 6); and
- 587 Facebook posts published by 63 U.S. and Australian unions between March 2020 and March 2022, 263 of which from 57 unions included one or more personal stories.

Notes

Chapter 2

1. This was not a referendum as participation was not compulsory, as it is for voting and other referenda held in Australia. It was more akin to a national plebiscite intended to guide but not bind government decision-making.

Chapter 3

1. One important limitation is that the StoryBank app supports the submission of videos only as links to content published elsewhere (e.g., on YouTube). This greatly complicates the use of these videos from both a practical and a legal standpoint. To address this problem, other companies have created separate platforms—e.g., Gather Voices, discussed later in this chapter—that enable storytellers to film and submit videos directly from their Internet browser.

2. Incidentally, organizers generally said that social media platforms were not as important as story distribution channels, signaling that they trusted the algorithms of Facebook, Twitter, and so on to help them collect story ideas more than to disseminate them to the right audiences.

Chapter 4

1. A relatively isolated example is the National Coalition to Abolish the Death Penalty's "90 Million Strong Campaign," which used the microblogging platform Tumblr to build a visual story wall in 2016 (https://ncadp.tumblr.com); although Tumblr's popularity is limited compared to that of other social media platforms, the fact that it can be fully customized and that content can be easily shared and commented on makes it potentially more engaging and able to reach a broader range of people than purpose-built story websites.

Chapter 6

1. It is worth noting here that participating in the national postal survey was not legally mandated in the same way in which voting in elections is in Australia; this makes participation in the survey quite high.

2. A chi-square test of independence confirmed that the proportion of posts containing storytelling did differ significantly between the precampaign and campaign periods. X2 (1, N = 245) = 5.6, p > .05.

Chapter 7

1. Images generated using https://www.wordclouds.com/

2. For example, "After she saved her baby daughter's life, Maryam Chudnoff felt she didn't have much of a choice but to pursue a healthcare career. Now a registered nurse at UNM Southeast Heights Family Practice Clinic in Albuquerque, New Mexico, she has found other ways of making her community better. 'I can't imagine not doing things that benefit others,' she says. Watch Chudnoff tell her own story."— AFSCME (US), 12/1/2021.

3. Richard Trumka died suddenly in August 2021 and AFL-CIO secretary Liz Shuler took his place in the senior role of president.

References

Adams-Santos, D. (2020). "Something a bit more personal": Digital storytelling and intimacy among queer Black women. *Sexualities, 23*(8), 1434–56. https://doi.org/10.1177/1363460720902720

AFL-CIO (Director). (n.d.). *Worker Stories—YouTube*. Retrieved December 13, 2022, from https://www.youtube.com/playlist?list=PLSIUF-toHGIUC0LLJJhE92RblPD7svm7F

Alcoff, L. (1991). "The problem of speaking for others." *Cultural Critique, 20*, 5. https://doi.org/10.2307/1354221

Aldoory, L., and Grunig, J. E. (2012). "The rise and fall of hotissue publics: Relationships that develop from media coverage of events and crises." *International Journal of Strategic Communication, 6*(1), 93–108. https://doi.org/10.1080/1553118X.2011.634866

Alexander, J. C. (2006). *The civil sphere*. Oxford, UK: Oxford University Press.

American Rescue Plan. (n.d.). Retrieved December 9, 2022, from https://www.whitehouse.gov/american-rescue-plan/

Andrews, E. E., Forber-Pratt, A. J., Mona, L. R., Lund, E. M., Pilarski, C. R., and Balter, R. (2019). "#SaytheWord: A disability culture commentary on the erasure of 'disability.'" *Rehabilitation Psychology, 64*(2), 111–18. https://doi.org/10.1037/rep0000258

The Arc. (2017). *Tools for building power through personal stories*. Washington, DC: The Arc.

Arnstein, S. R. (1969). "A ladder of citizen participation." *Journal of the American Planning Association, 85*(1), 24–34. https://doi.org/10.1080/01944363.2018.1559388

Atske, S., and Perrin, A. (2021). "Home broadband adoption, computer ownership vary by race, ethnicity in the U.S." *Pew Research Center*. https://www.pewresearch.org/fact-tank/2021/07/16/home-broadband-adoption-computer-ownership-vary-by-race-ethnicity-in-the-u-s/

Australian Broadcasting Corporation. (May 6, 2013). "Labor fails to make gains despite NDIS support: Newspoll." https://www.abc.net.au/news/2013-05-06/labor-fails-to-make-gains-despite-ndis-support-newspoll/4673322

Australian Unions (Director). (2022). *Working Life—YouTube.* https://www.youtube
.com/playlist?list=PLOSAYbdpKYdyg_HD55k2nuAYAox9-ukSi

Bagenstos, S. R. (2009). *Law and the contradictions of the disability rights movement.*
New Haven, CT: Yale University Press.

Baldwin-Philippi, J. (2019). "Data campaigning: Between empirics and assumptions."
Internet Policy Review, 8(4). https://doi.org/10.14763/2019.4.1437

Barnett, J., and Hammond, S. (1999). "Representing disability in charity promo-
tions." *Journal of Community & Applied Social Psychology, 9*(4), 309–14. https://
doi.org/10.1002/(SICI)1099–1298(199907/08)9:4<309::AID-CASP515>3.0.C
O;2-7

Behrmann, S., and Santucci, J. (October 28, 2020). "Here's a timeline of President
Donald Trump's and Dr. Anthony Fauci's relationship." *USA TODAY.* https://
www.usatoday.com/story/news/politics/2020/10/28/president-donald-trump-ant
hony-fauci-timeline-relationship-coronavirus-pandemic/3718797001/

Belenky, M. F., Clinchy, B. M., Goldberger, N. R., and Tarule, J. M. (eds.). (1986).
Women's ways of knowing: The development of self, voice, and mind. New York, NY:
Basic Books.

Bennett, W. L., and Segerberg, A. (2013). *The logic of lonnective action: Digital media
and the personalization of contentious politics.* Cambridge, UK: Cambridge University Press.

Berinsky, A. J. (2017). "Rumors and health care reform: Experiments in political
misinformation." *British Journal of Political Science, 47*(2), 241–62. https://doi
.org/10.1017/S0007123415000186

Bernstein, M., and Naples, N. A. (2015). "Altared states: Legal structuring and relationship recognition in the United States, Canada, and Australia." *American Sociological Review, 80*(6), 1226–49. https://doi.org/10.1177/0003122415613414

"'Beyond reckless': Unions call for urgent talks with Scott Morrison over isolation
rules." (2022). *SBS News.* https://www.sbs.com.au/news/article/beyond-reckless
-unions-call-for-urgent-talks-with-scott-morrison-over-isolation-rules/flaqq75vt

Biden, J. (September 8, 2021). "Remarks by President Biden in honor of labor
unions." https://www.whitehouse.gov/briefing-room/speeches-remarks/2021/09
/08/remarks-by-president-biden-in-honor-of-labor-unions/

Billard, T. J. (2021). "Movement–Media relations in the hybrid media system: A case
study from the U.S. transgender rights movement." *International Journal of Press/
Politics, 26*(2), 341–61. https://doi.org/10.1177/1940161220968525

Bimber, B. A., Flanagin, A. J., and Stohl, C. (2012). *Collective action in organizations:
Interaction and engagement in an era of technological change.* Cambridge, UK: Cambridge University Press.

Birkland, T. A. (2020). *An introduction to the policy process: Theories, concepts, and models of public policy making* (5th ed.). New York, NY: Routledge.

Blair, K. (2021). "Empty gestures: Performative utterances and allyship." *Journal of
Dramatic Theory and Criticism, 35*(2), 53–73. https://doi.org/10.1353/dtc.2021
.0005

Bonacini, C. (2015). *What's your story? How to create a successful story banking program.*
Families USA.

Borum Chattoo, C. (2020). *Story movements: How documentaries empower people and inspire social change.* Oxford, UK: Oxford University Press.

Bozdağ, Ç., and Kannengießer, S. (2021). "Digital storytelling." In M. Baker, B. Blaagaard, H. Jones, and L. Pérez González (eds.), *The Routledge encyclopedia of citizen media.* New York, NY: Routledge.

Brooks, R. (2020). "Essential workers fed up with Trump's Coronavirus response have spent months organizing for election day." *BuzzFeed News.* https://www .buzzfeednews.com/article/ryancbrooks/coronavirus-essential-workers-2020-elect ion-trump

Bruner, J. (1986). *Actual minds, possible worlds.* Cambridge, MA: Harvard University Press.

Bueno, C. (2016). *The attention economy: Labour, time and power in cognitive capitalism.* London: Rowman & Littlefield.

Campagnolo, G., Williams, R., Alex, B., Acerbi, A., and Chapple, D. (2017). *Sensitizing social data science: Combining empirical social research with computational approaches to influencer detection.* https://www.research.ed.ac.uk/en/publications /sensitizing-social-data-science-combining-empirical-social-resear

Casey, L. J., Wootton, B. M., and McAloon, J. (2020). "Mental health, minority stress, and the Australian Marriage Law postal survey: A longitudinal study." *American Journal of Orthopsychiatry, 90*(5), 546–56. https://doi.org/10.1037/ort0000455

Center for American Progress. (2019). *Storybank—basic package and installation setup.*

Center for Social Impact Communication and Meyer Foundation. (2016). *Designing a user-friendly story bank.*

Chadwick, A. (2011). "Web 2.0: New challenges for the study of e-democracy in an era of informational exuberance." In S. Coleman and P. M. Shane (eds.), *Connecting Democracy*, pp. 45–73 Cambridge, MA: MIT Press.

Chadwick, A. (2011a). "The political information cycle in a hybrid news system: The British prime minister and the 'Bullygate' Affair." *International Journal of Press/ Politics, 16*(1), 3–29. https://doi.org/10.1177/1940161210384730

Chadwick, A. (2011b). "Britain's first live televised party leaders' debate: From the news cycle to the political information cycle." *Parliamentary Affairs, 64*(1), 24–44. https://doi.org/10.1093/pa/gsq045

Chadwick, A. (2017). *The hybrid media system: Politics and power* (2nd ed.). Oxford, UK: Oxford University Press.

Charlton-Dailey, R. (April 16, 2020). "Sharing disability experiences online can be risky. It's time for that to end." *Rooted in Rights.* https://rootedinrights.org/shari ng-disability-experiences-online-can-be-risky-its-time-for-that-to-end/

Clibborn, S. (2020). "Australian industrial relations in 2019: The year wage theft went mainstream." *Journal of Industrial Relations, 62*(3), 331–40. https://doi.org/10.11 77/0022185620913889

Community Catalyst. (2017). *Our voices have power: A storybanking guide.*

Cooper, D. (2004). *Challenging diversity: Rethinking equality and the value of difference.* Cambridge, UK: Cambridge University Press.

Cooper, G. (2015). "Unlocking the gate? How NGOs mediate the voices of the marginalised in a social media context." In E. Thorsen, D. Jackson, H. Savigny, and J.

Alexander (eds.), *Media, margins and civic agency* (pp. 29–42). Basingstoke, UK: Palgrave Macmillan.

Costanza-Chock, S. (2020). *Design justice: Community-led practices to build the worlds we need.* Cambridge, MA: MIT Press.

Crawley, S. L., and Broad, K. L. (2004). "Be yourself": Mobilizing sexual formula stories through personal storytelling." *Journal of Contemporary Ethnography, 33*(1), 39–71.

Crogan, P., and Kinsley, S. (2012). "Paying attention: Toward a critique of the attention economy." *Culture Machine,* 13. https://culturemachine.net/wp-content/uploads/2019/01/463-1025-1-PB.pdf

Davidson, B. (2017). "Storytelling and evidence-based policy: Lessons from the grey literature." *Palgrave Communications, 3*(1), 17093. https://doi.org/10.1057/palco mms.2017.93

Davis, J. (2002). "Narrative and social movements: The power of stories." In J. Davis (ed.), *Stories of Change: Narratives and Social Movements* (pp. 3–30). Albany: State University of New York Press.

Dawson, P. (2020). "Hashtag narrative: Emergent storytelling and affective publics in the digital age." *International Journal of Cultural Studies, 23*(6), 968–83. https://doi.org/10.1177/1367877920921417

Debenedetti, G. (2016). *Center for American progress focuses on anti-Trump efforts— POLITICO.* https://www.politico.com/story/2016/12/center-american-progress -tanden-trump-232667

Delgado, R. (1989). "Storytelling for oppositionists and others: A plea for narrative." *Michigan Law Review, 87*(8), 2411. https://doi.org/10.2307/1289308

Dencik, L. (2021). "Authenticity." In M. Baker, B. Blaagaard, H. Jones, and L. Pérez González (eds.), *The Routledge Encyclopedia of Citizen Media.* New York, NY: Routledge.

Dencik, L., and Wilkin, P. (2020). "Digital activism and the political culture of trade unionism." *Information, Communication & Society, 23*(12), 1728–37. https://doi .org/10.1080/1369118X.2019.1631371

Dennis, J. (2019). *Beyond slacktivism: Political participation on social media.* Basingstoke, UK: Palgrave Macmillan. https://doi.org/10.1007/978-3-030-00844-4

Doan, A., Candal, C. C., and Sylvester, S. (2018). "'We are the visible proof': Legitimizing abortion regret misinformation through activists' experiential knowledge: ABORTION REGRET MISINFORMATION." *Law & Policy, 40*(1), 33–56. https://doi.org/10.1111/lapo.12094

Doddington, K., Jones, R. S. P., and Miller, B. Y. (1994). "Are attitudes to people with learning disabilities negatively influenced by charity advertising? An experimental analysis." *Disability & Society, 9*(2), 207–22. https://doi.org/10.1080/09687599 466780221

Dommett, K., Kefford, G., and Power, S. (2021). "The digital ecosystem: The new politics of party organization in parliamentary democracies." *Party Politics, 27*(5), 847–57. https://doi.org/10.1177/1354068820907667

Dreher, T. (2010). "Speaking up or being heard? Community media interventions and the politics of listening." *Media, Culture & Society, 32*(1), 85–103. https://doi.org /10.1177/0163443709350099

Dulio, D. A., and Towner, T. L. (2010). "The permanent campaign." In *Routledge Handbook of Political Management*. New York, NY: Routledge.

Dunn, A. (2020). "Who is deemed an 'essential' worker under Australia's COVID-19 rules?" *SBS News*. https://www.sbs.com.au/news/article/who-is-deemed-an-essent ial-worker-under-australias-covid-19-rules/cmspk8oes

Dush, L. (2017). "Nonprofit collections of digital personal experience narratives: An exploratory study." *Journal of Business and Technical Communication*, *31*(2), 188–221. https://doi.org/10.1177/1050651916682287

Eades, Q., and Vivienne, S. (eds.). (2018). *Going postal: More than "Yes" or "No": one year on: Writings from the marriage equality survey*. Melbourne, VIC: Brow Books.

Eaton, M. (2010). "Manufacturing community in an online activist organization: The rhetoric of MoveOn.org's e-mails." *Information, Communication & Society*, *13*(2), 174–92. https://doi.org/10.1080/13691180902890125

Ecker, S., Riggle, E. D.b., Rostosky, S. S., and Byrnes, J. M. (2019). "Impact of the Australian marriage equality postal survey and debate on psychological distress among lesbian, gay, bisexual, transgender, intersex and queer/questioning people and allies." *Australian Journal of Psychology*, *71*(3), 285–95. https://doi.org/10.11 11/ajpy.12245

Ellis, K., Kent, M., Hollier, S., Burns, S., and Goggin, G. (2018). "Reimagining Australia via disability and media: Representation, access and digital integration." *Coolabah*, *24* and *25*, Article 24 and 25. https://doi.org/10.1344/co201824&2 594–111

Entman, R. M. (2015). *Framing and party competition: How Democrats enabled the GOP's move to the uncompromising right*. Washington, DC: The Brookings Institution.

Failed vaccine rollout leaves frontline workers exposed. (2021). https://www.actu.org.au /actu-media/media-releases/2021/failed-vaccine-rollout-leaves-frontline-workers -exposed

Fernandes, S. (2017). *Curated stories: The uses and misuses of storytelling*. Oxford, UK: Oxford University Press.

Fisher, W. R. (1987). *Human communication as narration: Toward a philosophy of reason, value, and action*. Columbia: University of South Carolina Press.

Frangi, L., Zhang, T., and Hebdon, R. (2020). "Tweeting and retweeting for fight for $15: Unions as dinosaur opinion leaders?" *British Journal of Industrial Relations*, *58*(2), 301–35. https://doi.org/10.1111/bjir.12482

franzke, a. s., Bechmann, A., Zimmer, M., Ess, C. M., and Association of Internet Researchers. (2020). *Internet research: Ethical guidelines 3.0*. https://aoir.org/rep orts/ethics3.pdf

Ganz, M. (2011). "Public narrative, collective action, and power." In S. Obudgemi and T. Lee (eds.), *Accountability through public opinion: From inertia to public action* (pp. 273–89). Washington, DC: The World Bank.

Ganz, M. (2013). "Public narrative: Self & us & now" (blog). http://marshallganz.us mblogs.com/files/2012/08/Public-Narrative-Worksheet-Fall-2013-.pdf

Gavin, M. (2022). "Unions and collective bargaining in Australia in 2021." *Journal of Industrial Relations*, *64*(3), 362–79. https://doi.org/10.1177/0022185622110 0381

Gerbaudo, P. (2022). "From individual affectedness to collective identity: Personal testimony campaigns on social media and the logic of collection." *New Media & Society*, https://doi.org/10.1177/14614448221128523.

Gibson, R., Römmele, A., and Williamson, A. (2014). "Chasing the digital wave: International perspectives on the growth of online campaigning." *Journal of Information Technology & Politics*, *11*(2), 123–29. https://doi.org/10.1080/1933 1681.2014.903064

Girardin, L. (2016). "How to develop a storybank system for your nonprofit." *Nonprofit MarCommunity*. https://nonprofitmarcommunity.com/storybank-system/

Giridharadas, A. (2022). *The persuaders: At the front lines of the fight for hearts, minds, and democracy*. New York, NY: Penguin Random House. https://www.penguinran domhouse.com/books/669716/the-persuaders-by-anand-giridharadas/

Gollust, S. E., Baum, L. M., Niederdeppe, J., Barry, C. L., and Fowler, E. F. (2017). "Local television news coverage of the Affordable Care Act: Emphasizing politics over consumer information." *American Journal of Public Health*, *107*(5), 687–93. https://doi.org/10.2105/AJPH.2017.303659

Gooch, A. (2018). "Ripping yarn: Experiments on storytelling by partisan elites." *Political Communication*, *35*(2), 220–38. https://doi.org/10.1080/10584609.20 17.1336502

Goodnough, A., and Hoffman, J. (December 5, 2020). "Who should get the coronavirus vaccine first?" *New York Times*. https://www.nytimes.com/2020/12/05/he alth/covid-vaccine-first.html

Greenwich, A. (2018). *Yes, yes, yes: Australia's journey to marriage equality*. Sydney, NSW: NewSouth.

Hadley, B. (2016). "Cheats, charity cases and inspirations: Disrupting the circulation of disability-based memes online." *Disability & Society*, *31*(5), 676–92. https://doi .org/10.1080/09687599.2016.1199378

Haidt, J. (ed.). (2013). *The righteous mind: Why good people are divided by politics and religion*. New York, NY: Vintage Books.

Hall, N. (2022). *Transnational advocacy in the digital era: Think global, act local*. Oxford, UK: Oxford University Press.

Haller, B. (2000). "If they limp, they lead? News representations and the hierarchy of disability images." In Dawn Braithwaite and Teri Thompson (eds.), *Handbook of Communication and People with Disabilities*. (pp. 225–237). New York, NY: Routledge.

Haller, B., Ralph, S., and Zaks, Z. (2010). "Confronting obstacles to inclusion: How the US news media report disability." In *Confronting Obstacles to Inclusion*. New York, NY: Routledge. (pp. 9–30).

Haller, B., and Zhang, L. (2014). "Stigma or empowerment? What do disabled people say about their representation in news and entertainment media?" *Review of Disability Studies: An International Journal*, *9*(4), Article 4. https://rdsjournal.org

Han, H., McKenna, E., and Oyakawa, M. (2021). *Prisms of the people: Power & organizing in twenty-first-century america*. Chicago: University of Chicago Press.

Hartley, J., and McWilliam, K. (eds.). (2009). *Story circle: Digital storytelling around the world*. Chichester, UK: Wiley-Blackwell.

Henne, K., Shelby, R., and Harb, J. (2021). "The datafication of #MeToo: Whiteness, racial capitalism, and anti-violence technologies." *Big Data & Society*, 8(2), https://doi.org/10.1177/20539517211055898

Hennebert, M., Pasquier, V., and Lévesque, C. (2021). "What do unions do . . . with digital technologies? An affordance approach." *New Technology, Work and Employment*, 36(2), 177–200. https://doi.org/10.1111/ntwe.12187

Holtzhausen, D. (2016). "Datafication: Threat or opportunity for communication in the public sphere?" *Journal of Communication Management*, 20(1), 21–36. https://doi.org/10.1108/JCOM-12-2014-0082

Houghton, D. J., and Hodder, A. (2021). "Understanding trade union usage of social media: A case study of the Public and Commercial Services union on Facebook and Twitter." *New Technology, Work and Employment*, 36(2), 219–39. https://doi.org/10.1111/ntwe.12209

Hughes, B. (2015). "Disabled people as counterfeit citizens: The politics of resentment past and present." *Disability & Society*, 30(7), 991–1004. https://doi.org/10.1080/09687599.2015.1066664

Jackson, M. (2013). *Politics of storytelling: Variations on a theme by Hannah Arendt* (2nd ed.). Copenhagen, Museum Tusculanum Press.

Jackson, S. J., Bailey, M., and Welles, B. F. (2020). *#hashtagactivism: Networks of race and gender justice*. Cambridge, MA: MIT Press.

Jenkins, H. (2006). *Convergence culture: Where old and new media collide*. New York: New York University Press.

Jenkins, H., Ito, M., and boyd, danah. (2016). *Participatory culture in a networked era*. Cambridge, UK: Polity.

Kang, S. (2013). "Coverage of autism spectrum disorder in the US television news: An analysis of framing." *Disability & Society*, 28(2), 245–59. https://doi.org/10.1080/09687599.2012.705056

Karp, P. (November 7, 2018). "Crowning achievement or painful waste: Marriage equality campaign's complex legacy." *The Guardian*. https://www.theguardian.com/books/2018/nov/07/crowning-achievement-or-painful-irrelevance-the-dualing-legacies-of-the-marriage-equality-campaign

Karpf, D. (2012). *The MoveOn effect: The unexpected transformation of American political advocacy*. Oxford, UK: Oxford University Press.

Karpf, D. (2016). *Analytic activism: Digital listening and the new political strategy*. Oxford, UK: Oxford University Press.

Kreiss, D., and Jasinski, C. (2016). "The tech industry meets presidential politics: Explaining the Democratic Party's technological advantage in electoral campaigning, 2004–2012." *Political Communication*, 33(4), 544–62. https://doi.org/10.1080/10584609.2015.1121941

Labov, W., and Waletsky, J. (1967). Narrative analysis: Oral versions of personal experience. In J. Helm (ed.), *Essays on the Verbal and Visual Arts* (pp. 12–44). Seattle: University of Washington Press.

Lakoff, G. (2014). *The all new don't think of an elephant! Know your values and frame the debate*. White River Junction, VT: Chelsea Green Publishing.

Langer, A. I. (2011). *The personalisation of politics in the UK: Mediated leadership from Attlee to Cameron*. Manchester, UK: Manchester University Press.

Lessig, D. E. J. S. C. for E. and R. L. F. P. of L. L., and Lessig, L. (2006). *Code: And other laws of cyberspace, version 2.0*. New York, NY: Basic Books.

Lieb, D. A. (July 11, 2021). "Bonus pay for essential workers varied widely across states." *AP NEWS*. https://apnews.com/article/joe-biden-business-health-govern ment-and-politics-coronavirus-pandemic-8cbdd37a71cf34c812150b93f0e3da17

Loeb, P. (2015). "The call to action of stories: An interview with Paul Rogat Loeb (C. S. Neile, Interviewer)." [Interview]. https://muse.jhu.edu/cgi-bin/resolve_ope nurl.cgi?issn=19320280&aulast=Neile&volume=11&issue=1&spage=56

Mancini, P. (2013). "Media fragmentation, party system, and democracy." *International Journal of Press/Politics, 18*(1), 43–60. https://doi.org/10.1177/194016121 2458200

Marquez, S. (October 2, 2020). "Counteracting extractive storytelling in the American South and in global communities of color." International Documentary Association. https://www.documentary.org/blog/counteracting-extractive-storytelling-american-south-and-global-communities-color

Marsh, I. (1995). *Beyond the two party system: Political representation, economic competitiveness, and Australian politics*. Cambridge, UK: Cambridge University Press.

Matthews, G., Burris, S., Ledford, S. L., Gunderson, G., and Baker, E. L. (2017). "Crafting richer public health messages for a turbulent political environment." *Journal of Public Health Management and Practice, 23*(4), 420–23. https://doi.org /10.1097/PHH.0000000000000610

Matthews, N., and Sunderland, N. (2017). *Digital storytelling in health and social policy: Listening to marginalised voices*. New York, NY: Routledge.

Mayer-Schönberger, V., and Cukier, K. (2013). *Big data: A revolution that will transform how we live, work, and think*. Boston, MA: Houghton Mifflin Harcourt.

McAllister, I., and Snagovsky, F. (2018). "Explaining voting in the 2017 Australian same-sex marriage plebiscite." *Australian Journal of Political Science, 53*(4), 409–27. https://doi.org/10.1080/10361146.2018.1504877

McDonough, J. E. (2001). "Using and misusing anecdote in policy making." *Health Affairs, 20*(1), 207–12. https://doi.org/10.1377/hlthaff.20.1.207

McKenna, E., and Han, H. (2014). *Groundbreakers: How Obama's 2.2 million volunteers transformed campaigning in America*. Oxford, UK: Oxford University Press.

Meirick, P. C. (2013). "Motivated misperception? Party, education, partisan news, and belief in 'death panels.'" *Journalism & Mass Communication Quarterly, 90*(1), 39–57. https://doi.org/10.1177/1077699012468696

Michie, L., Balaam, M., McCarthy, J., Osadchiy, T., and Morrissey, K. (2018). "From her story, to our story: Digital storytelling as public engagement around abortion rights advocacy in Ireland." *Proceedings of the 2018 CHI Conference on Human Factors in Computing Systems*, 1–15. https://doi.org/10.1145/3173574.3173931

Milan, S. (2013). *Social movements and their technologies: Wiring social change*. Basingstoke, UK: Palgrave Macmillan.

Mintrom, M., and O'Connor, R. (2020). "The importance of policy narrative: Effective government responses to Covid-19." *Policy Design and Practice, 3*(3), 205–27. https://doi.org/10.1080/25741292.2020.1813358

Miskimmon, A., O'Loughlin, B., and Roselle, L. (2013). *Strategic narratives: Communication power and the new world order*. New York, NY: Routledge.

Murray, J., and Flyverbom, M. (2021). "Datafied corporate political activity: Updating corporate advocacy for a digital era." *Organization, 28*(4), 621–40. https://doi.org/10.1177/1350508420928516

#15 Marriage Equality. (n.d.). Retrieved November 27, 2022, from https://changemakerspodcast.org/s2-episode-5-marriage-equality/

Oliver, M. (1990). *The politics of disablement.* Basingstoke, UK: Palgrave Macmillan.

Page, R. E. (2018). *Narratives online: Shared stories in social media.* Cambridge, UK: Cambridge University Press.

Palin, M. (2017). "Gay marriage in Australia: First ad for NO campaign airs.*" news.com.au.* https://www.news.com.au/lifestyle/relationships/marriage/anti-same-sex-marriage-campaign-airs-school-told-my-son-he-could-wear-a-dress/news-story/535dcae290582136cb2445f3869ff820

Pamment, J. (2016). "Digital diplomacy as transmedia engagement: Aligning theories of participatory culture with international advocacy campaigns." *New Media & Society, 18*(9), 2046–62. https://doi.org/10.1177/1461444815577792

Panagiotopoulos, P. (2021). "Digital audiences of union organising: A social media analysis." *New Technology, Work and Employment, 36*(2), 201–18. https://doi.org/10.1111/ntwe.12184

Papacharissi, Z. (2015). *Affective publics: Sentiment, technology, and politics.* Oxford, UK: Oxford University Press.

Parsloe, S. M., and Holton, A. E. (2018). "#Boycottautismspeaks: Communicating a counternarrative through cyberactivism and connective action." *Information, Communication & Society, 21*(8), 1116–33. https://doi.org/10.1080/1369118X.2017.1301514

Pasquier, V., and Wood, A. J. (2018). "The power of social media as a labour campaigning tool: Lessons from OUR Walmart and the Fight for 15." *Etui.* https://www.etui.org/publications/policy-briefs/european-economic-employment-and-social-policy/the-power-of-social-media-as-a-labour-campaigning-tool-lessons-from-our-walmart-and-the-fight-for-15

Però, D., and Downey, J. (2022). "Advancing workers' rights in the gig economy through discursive power: The communicative strategies of Indie unions." *Work, Employment and Society, 38*(1)" 140–60. https://doi.org/10.1177/09500170221103160

Perrin, A., and Atske, S. (2021). "Americans with disabilities less likely than those without to own some digital devices." Pew Research Center. https://www.pewresearch.org/fact-tank/2021/09/10/americans-with-disabilities-less-likely-than-those-without-to-own-some-digital-devices/

Plummer, K. (1994). *Telling sexual stories: Power, change and social worlds.* London: Routledge & CRC Press.

Polletta, F. (2006). *It was like a fever: Storytelling in protest and politics.* Chicago: University of Chicago Press.

Polletta, F. (2015). "Characters in political storytelling." *Storytelling, Self, Society, 11*(1), 34–55.

Polletta, F., and Callahan, J. (2017). "Deep stories, nostalgia narratives, and fake news: Storytelling in the Trump era." *American Journal of Cultural Sociology, 5*(3), 392–408. https://doi.org/10.1057/s41290-017-0037-7

Polletta, F., Chen, P. C. B., Gardner, B. G., and Motes, A. (2011). "The sociology of storytelling." *Annual Review of Sociology*, *37*(1), 109–30. https://doi.org/10.1146/annurev-soc-081309-150106

Polletta, F., DoCarmo, T., Ward, K. M., and Callahan, J. (2021). "Personal storytelling in professionalized social movements." *Mobilization: An International Quarterly*, *26*(1), 65–86.

Polletta, F., and Lee, J. (2006). "Is telling stories good for democracy? Rhetoric in public deliberation after 9/11." *American Sociological Review*, *71*(5), 699–721. https://doi.org/10.1177/000312240607100501

Productivity Commission. (2011). *Disability care and support*. Melbourne: Productivity Commission.

"Read Scott Morrison's full statement on the new national coronavirus restrictions." (March 24, 2020). *ABC News*. https://www.abc.net.au/news/2020-03-25/scott-morrison-alll-restrictions/12087112

Rees, L., Robinson, P., and Shields, N. (2019). "Media portrayal of elite athletes with disability—A systematic review." *Disability and Rehabilitation*, *41*(4), 374–81. https://doi.org/10.1080/09638288.2017.1397775

Rhodes, R. A. W. (ed.). (2018). *Narrative policy analysis: Cases in decentred policy*. Basingstoke, UK: Palgrave Macmillan.

Ricci, D. M. (2016). *Politics without stories: The liberal predicament*. Cambridge, UK: Cambridge University Press.

Roe, E. (1994). *Narrative policy analysis: Theory and practice*. Durham: Duke University Press.

Rojas, H., and Valenzuela, S. (2019). "A call to contextualize public opinion-based research in political communication." *Political Communication*, *36*, 652–59.

Roselle, L., Miskimmon, A., and O'Loughlin, B. (2014). "Strategic narrative: A new means to understand soft power." *Media, War & Conflict*, *7*(1), 70–84. https://doi.org/10.1177/1750635213516696

Rowland, C., Stanley-Becker, I., Jacob Bogage, Bhattarai, A., and Reiley, L. (December 20, 2020). "Major U.S. companies are lobbying in a scrum for early vaccine." *Washington Post*. https://www.washingtonpost.com/business/2020/12/20/companies-unions-early-access-covid-vaccine/

S.747—117th Congress (2021–2022): Citizenship for Essential Workers Act. (2021). http://www.congress.gov/

"Sally McManus, National Press Club, Wednesday 2nd December, 2020." (2020). ACTU. https://www.actu.org.au/actu-media/speeches-and-opinion/sally-mcmanus-national-press-club-wednesday-2nd-december-2020

Scammell, M. (1998). "The wisdom of the war room: US campaigning and Americanization." *Media, Culture & Society*, *20*(2), 251–75. https://doi.org/10.1177/016344398020002006

Schmitz, H. P., Dedmon, J. M., Bruno-van Vijfeijken, T., and Mahoney, J. (2020). "Democratizing advocacy?: How digital tools shape international nongovernmental activism." *Journal of Information Technology & Politics*, *17*(2), 174–91. https://doi.org/10.1080/19331681.2019.1710643

Schradie, J. (2021). "Context, class, and community: A methodological framework for studying labor organizing and digital unionizing." *Information, Communication & Society*, *24*(5), 700–16. https://doi.org/10.1080/1369118X.2021.1874477

Sensis Social Media Report. (2018). Yellow Social Media. https://www.sensis.com.au/ab out/our-reports/sensis-social-media-report

Shergold, P., Broadbent, J., Marshall, I., and Varghese, P. (2022). *FAULT LINES: An independent review into Australia's response to COVID-19.* Paul Ramsay Foundation. https://www.paulramsayfoundation.org.au/news-resources/fault-lines-an-in dependent-review-into-australias-response-to-covid-19

Shuler, L. (2021a). "Shuler at National Press Club: Workers are refusing to settle for bad jobs." AFL-CIO. https://aflcio.org/speeches/shuler-national-press-club-worke rs-are-refusing-settle-bad-jobs

Shuler, L. (2021b). "Shuler marks Labor Day at the White House." AFL-CIO. https:// aflcio.org/speeches/shuler-marks-labor-day-white-house

Small, D. A., Loewenstein, G., and Slovic, P. (2007). "Sympathy and callousness: The impact of deliberative thought on donations to identifiable and statistical victims." *Organizational Behavior and Human Decision Processes, 102*(2), 143–53. https:// doi.org/10.1016/j.obhdp.2006.01.005

Smith-Schoenwalder, C. (2022). "How COVID-19 will shape the 2022 midterm elections." *US News & World Report.* https://www.usnews.com/news/elections/ar ticles/the-coronavirus-and-the-2022-elections

Spitfire Strategies. (n.d.). *Story banking tip sheet.*

Stanyer, J. (2013). *Intimate politics: Publicity, privacy and the personal lives of politicians in media-saturated democracies.* Cambridge, UK: Polity.

"Statement on coronavirus and proposed stimulus." (2020). https://www.actu.org.au /actu-media/media-releases/2020/statement-on-coronavirus-and-proposed-stim ulus

Stevens, A. (2011). "Telling policy stories: An ethnographic study of the use of evidence in policy-making in the UK." *Journal of Social Policy, 40*(2), 237–55. https:// doi.org/10.1017/S0047279410000723

Stone, D. (2012). *Policy paradox: The art of political decision making* (3rd ed). New York, NY: W.W. Norton & Co.

Sullivan, P. (2009). *Lift every voice: The NAACP and the making of the civil rights move-ment.* New York, NY: New Press: Distributed by Perseus Distribution.

Support for workers critical to keeping reopening workplaces safe. (2021). ACTU. https:// www.actu.org.au/actu-media/media-releases/2021/support-for-workers-critical-to -keeping-reopening-workplaces-safe

Tapia, M., Lee, T. L., and Filipovitch, M. (2017). "Supra-union and intersectional organizing: An examination of two prominent cases in the low-wage US restaurant industry." *Journal of Industrial Relations, 59*(4), 487–509. https://doi.org/10.1177 /0022185617714817

Taylor, J., and Burt, E. (2005). "Voluntary organisations as e-democratic actors: Political identity, legitimacy and accountability and the need for new research." *Policy & Politics, 33*(4), 601–16. https://doi.org/10.1332/030557305774329127

Thayne, M. (2012). "Friends like mine: The production of socialized subjectivity in the attention economy." *Culture Machine, 13.* https://culturemachine.net/wp-content/uploads/2019/01/471-1021-1-PB.pdf

Thornthwaite, L., Balnave, N., and Barnes, A. (2018). "Unions and social media: Prospects for gender inclusion." *Gender, Work & Organization, 25*(4), 401–17. https://doi.org/10.1111/gwao.12228

Thumim, N. (2012). *Self-representation and digital culture*. Basingstoke, UK: Palgrave Macmillan.

Tilly, C., and Tarrow, S. G. (2007). *Contentious politics*. Oxford, UK: Oxford University Press.

Trevisan, F. (2017a). *Disability rights advocacy online: Voice, empowerment and global connectivity*. New York, NY: Routledge.

Trevisan, F. (2017b). "Crowd-sourced advocacy: Promoting disability rights through online storytelling." *Public Relations Inquiry*, *6*(2), 191–208. https://doi.org/10.11 77/2046147X17697785

Trevisan, F. (2018). "Connective action mechanisms in a time of political turmoil: Virtual disability rights protest at Donald Trump's inauguration." *Australian Journal of Political Science*, *53*(1), 103–15. https://doi.org/10.1080/10361146.2017 .1416585

Trevisan, F. (2022). "Beyond accessibility: Exploring digital inclusivity in US progressive politics." *New Media & Society*, *24*(2), 496–513. https://doi.org/10.1177/14 614448211063187

Trevisan, F., Bello, B., Vaughan, M., and Vromen, A. (2020). "Mobilizing personal narratives: The rise of digital 'story banking' in U.S. grassroots advocacy." *Journal of Information Technology & Politics*, *17*(2), 146–60. https://doi.org/10.1080/193 31681.2019.1705221

Trumka, R. (2020). "Trumka: Union members will rebuild America." AFL-CIO. https://aflcio.org/speeches/trumka-union-members-will-rebuild-america

Uba, K., and Jansson, J. (2021). "Political campaigns on YouTube: Trade unions' mobilisation in Europe." *New Technology, Work and Employment*, *36*(2), 240–60. https://doi.org/10.1111/ntwe.12181

Vaughan, M. (2019). "Same sex marriage and its implications for Australian democracy." In Mark Evans and Michelle Grattan (eds.), *From Turnbull to Morrison: Understanding the Trust Divide* (pp. 211-24). Melbourne, VIC: Melbourne University Publishing.

Vaughn-Switzer, J. (2003). *Disabled rights: American disability policy and the fight for equality*. Washington, DC: Georgetown University Press.

Verrelli, S., White, F. A., Harvey, L. J., and Pulciani, M. R. (2019). "Minority stress, social support, and the mental health of lesbian, gay, and bisexual Australians during the Australian Marriage Law Postal Survey." *Australian Psychologist*, *54*(4), 336–46. https://doi.org/10.1111/ap.12380

Veselková, M. (2014). "Science, stories and the anti-vaccination movement." *Human Affairs*, *24*(3), 287–98. https://doi.org/10.2478/s13374-014-0227-8

Vicari, S. (2022). *Digital media and participatory cultures of health and illness*. New York, NY: Routledge.

Vicari, S., and Cappai, F. (2016). "Health activism and the logic of connective action. A case study of rare disease patient organisations." *Information, Communication & Society*, *19*(11), 1653–71. https://doi.org/10.1080/1369118X.2016.1154587

Vitak, J. (2012). "The impact of context collapse and privacy on social network site disclosures." *Journal of Broadcasting & Electronic Media*, *56*(4), 451–70. https:// doi.org/10.1080/08838151.2012.732140

Vivienne, S., and Burgess, J. (2012). "The digital storyteller's stage: Queer everyday activists negotiating privacy and publicness." *Journal of Broadcasting & Electronic Media, 56*(3), 362–77. https://doi.org/10.1080/08838151.2012.705194

Vogels, E. A. (2021). "Some digital divides persist between rural, urban and suburban America." *Pew Research Center.* https://www.pewresearch.org/fact-tank/2021/08/19/some-digital-divides-persist-between-rural-urban-and-suburban-america/

Vries-Jordan, H. G. E. de. (2021). "Marriage equality policy diffusion." In Donald P. Haider-Merkel (ed.), *The Oxford Encyclopedia of LGBT Politics and Policy.* Oxford, UK: Oxford University Press.

Vromen, A. (2015). "Campaign entrepreneurs in online collective action: GetUp! in Australia." *Social Movement Studies, 14*(2), 195–213. https://doi.org/10.1080/14742837.2014.923755

Vromen, A. (2017). *Digital citizenship and political engagement: The challenge from online campaigning and advocacy organisations.* Basingstoke, UK: Palgrave Macmillan.

Vromen, A., Halpin, D., and Vaughan, M. (2022). *Crowdsourced politics: The rise of online petitions & micro-donations.* Basingstoke, UK: Palgrave Macmillan.

Wall, M. (2015). "Citizen journalism: A retrospective on what we know, an agenda for what we don't." *Digital Journalism, 3*(6), 797–813. https://doi.org/10.1080/21670811.2014.1002513

Warhurst, J. (2007). "The Australian conservation foundation: The development of a modern environmental interest group." *Environmental Politics, 3*(1), 68–90. https://doi.org/10.1080/09644019408414125

Wellman, M. L. (2022). "Black squares for black lives? Performative allyship as credibility maintenance for social media influencers on Instagram." *Social Media + Society, 8*(1), https://doi.org/10.1177/20563051221080473

Westwood, S. (2020). "White House formally declaring teachers essential workers." CNNPolitics. https://edition.cnn.com/2020/08/20/politics/white-house-teachers-essential-workers/index.html

Wissot, L. (September 28, 2017). "Whose story?: Five doc-makers on (avoiding) extractive filmmaking." *International Documentary Association.* https://www.documentary.org/feature/whose-story-five-doc-makers-avoiding-extractive-filmmaking

Witte, G., Hauslohner, A., and Wax-Thibodeau, E. (March 13, 2021). "In the shadow of its exceptionalism, America fails to invest in the basics." *Washington Post.* https://www.washingtonpost.com/nation/interactive/2021/america-growing-disparities/?itid=ap_griffwitte

World Health Organization. (n.d.). *WHO Coronavirus (COVID-19) dashboard.* World Health Organization. Retrieved December 9, 2022, from https://covid19.who.int

Wright, S. (2016). "'Success' and online political participation: The case of Downing Street E-petitions." *Information, Communication & Society, 19*(6), 843–57. https://doi.org/10.1080/1369118X.2015.1080285

Zaharna, R. S. (2022). *Boundary spanners of humanity: Three logics of communications and public diplomacy for global collaboration.* Oxford, UK: Oxford University Press.

Zepatos, T., and Meeker, M. (eds.). (2017). *Thalia Zepatos on research and messaging in freedom to marry.* Oral History Center.

Index